T0279032

A Separate Star

Copyright © 2023 Red Braid Alliance for Decolonial Socialism

ARP Books (Arbeiter Ring Publishing)
205-70 Arthur Street
Winnipeg, Manitoba
Treaty 1 Territory and Historic Métis Nation Homeland Canada R3B 1G7
arpbooks.org

Cover design by Bret Parenteau
Interior layout by Relish New Brand Experience
Printed and bound in Canada by Imprimerie Gauvin on certified FSC ® paper

ARP Books acknowledges the generous support of the Manitoba Arts Council and the Canada Council
for the Arts for our publishing program. We acknowledge the financial support of the Government of
Canada and the Province of Manitoba through the Book Publishing Tax Credit and the Book Publisher
Marketing Assistance Program of Manitoba Culture, Heritage, and Tourism.

LIBRARY AND ARCHIVES CANADA CATALOGUING IN PUBLICATION

Title: A separate star : politics and strategy for anti-capitalist, anti-colonial, and anti-imperialist
    struggle / Red Braid.
Names: Red Braid Alliance for Decolonial Socialism, author.
Identifiers: Canadiana (print) 20230481795 | Canadiana (ebook) 20230481906 | ISBN 9781927886540
    (softcover) | ISBN 9781927886557 (ebook)
Subjects: LCSH: Protest movements. | LCSH: Anti-imperialist movements. | LCSH: Social movements.
    | LCSH: Political participation. | LCSH: Decolonization. | LCSH: Socialism. | LCSH: Red Braid
    Alliance for Decolonial Socialism. | LCSH: Indigenous peoples—British Columbia—Politics
    and government.
Classification: LCC HM883 .S47 2023 | DDC 303.48/4—dc23

# A Separate Star

Politics and Strategy for
Anti-Capitalist, Anti-Colonial,
and Anti-Imperialist Struggle

Red Braid Alliance for Decolonial Socialism

ARP Books | Winnipeg

## Dedication and acknowledgements

We dedicate this book to our fallen comrades: those we knew and loved and who are too numerous to name, and those whose footsteps we follow even though we never met. And we dedicate this book to the generations of revolutionary fighters to come, who we hope will wield lessons from the failures and successes of our project as weapons in the struggle to overthrow the rule of capitalism, imperialism, and colonialism.

We acknowledge the contributions of all members of Red Braid and Alliance Against Displacement, as well as the low-income tenants and the members of street kin communities we have had the honour of thinking and struggling alongside.

# Contents

# Introduction
## A decade of building Red Braid

Red Braid

Our revolutionary project, which we relaunched in February 2020 as Red Braid Alliance for Decolonial Socialism, did not drop ready-made from the sky, nor was it inherited from an available revolutionary socialist tendency like those developed during the long twentieth century. In hindsight, we can say that Red Braid's precursor, Alliance Against Displacement (AAD), was an organisational vehicle that moved an ideologically heterogenous group of organisers from the local activist scene of the Downtown Eastside of Vancouver (DTES) to unify around revolutionary anti-colonial, anti-capitalist, and anti-imperialist ideas and commitments. Red Braid's emergence was hard fought, worked out together in one community struggle after another, analysed and interpreted into living theory in meeting spaces together, and in the editorial spaces of *The Volcano* newspaper.

*A Separate Star* is in part a record of the first eighteen months of that difficult emergence. The bulk of the book was finalized in the summer of 2021, with one significant addition completed that fall. Red Braid voted to dissolve in early 2022, meaning that this book is both a culmination of years of struggle, as well as the organization's final articulation of its political vision.

This introduction lays out the development of the ideas recorded in this book through the history of Red Braid as an organisation. We then

review two central ways that Red Braid applied this history to our organising practices—one, we focused on developing a "social base" strategy with
"subaltern" communities, and two, we rejected any single socialist tendency.
Instead, we committed to learning from all revolutionary traditions and
experiences available to us as a means of building a new tendency. This
introduction defines the historical and political landscape that the six sections of *A Separate Star* are written upon.

The first version of this book was self-published with the launch of Red
Braid, with the goal of more completely explaining the ideas in our basis of
unity. Then the COVID-19 pandemic struck and our plans to launch and
promote that little book were foiled. When ARP Books invited us to update
and republish it a year later, we jumped at the chance. But as we worked on
this new draft, the book developed in a new direction, with more time for
research and the opportunity to more completely work out ideas we had
been discussing in group meetings and education classes. Our thinking, in
this book and in the streets, has been a necessary part of our collective action,
both in deciding what to do and in assessing the effects of those actions.
*A Separate Star* carries those ideas on. Red Braid was a useful instrument for
subaltern peoples struggles, and we hope that the lessons and ideas in this
book continue to be useful to those struggles and the histories they create,
as we struggle on without surrender.

## From Social Housing Coalition to Alliance Against Displacement

The initial form of the group that would eventually become Red Braid was
the Social Housing Coalition, which formed in the fall of 2012 to campaign
to defend British Columbia's social housing program, which had built and
operated thousands of units of non-market, low-income, accessible rental
housing since being established in the 1960s. Social housing, as a system
and relic of social democratic, Keynesian ideology, was being eliminated
through a bi-partisan austerity attack waged up to and during the 2013 provincial election. Our campaign failed. Despite dozens of disruptive actions
at campaign events, educational "stands for housing" on street corners, and
significant demonstrations, we did not manage to pressure any candidate
to utter the words "social housing." After the election, presented with the

clear need for regular militant action for "social housing now" against the re-elected BC Liberal government, this group decided to continue organising together under the name Social Housing Alliance—a campaign group still, but in a more durable form than an ad hoc coalition. The "Alliance" part we kept through all the evolving names of our group.

After the campaign activity of the election period, we kept meeting through a pretty difficult period. There were months where only two or three of us showed up to weekly meetings, and it felt unclear what we should do. Nevertheless, we kept meeting, determined to find a way out of the fog at the dawn of a new organisational initiative.

In late 2014, at an all-day meeting in East Vancouver, we decided to abandon social housing as the organising pole of our group, and to name "displacement" as the experience that the different classes and groups we imagined as our social base hold in common. We brainstormed a new set of agreements, and we decided to rename ourselves Alliance Against Displacement (AAD).

Maria Wallstam wrote an article on this point in our organisational development:

> In the words of AAD's founding vision statement, which one collective member, Herb, cheekily named the *Fiery File*, "We are challenged to develop—out of this historical position where the chances of immediate change seem remote, and out of dedication to the immediate needs and lives of our families and communities—a long-term vision for radical change." In this spirit, the *Fiery File* set out four points:
>
> 1.  Shift our basic point of unity from pro-social housing to anti-displacement (and change our name to Alliance Against Displacement)
> 2.  Focus on rooting down into communities, deepening connections and politicising our collective experiences of displacement
> 3.  Begin a multi-level education series to strengthen and deepen our collective analysis and understanding

4. Fight oppressive power relations inside and out with transformative justice work including accountability process
   structures

This move seems obvious and inevitable now. But at the time it was difficult. It strained the relationships in the little group we had. Some people
in the Downtown Eastside wing of our group were becoming increasingly
oriented towards electoral politics, which stemmed from their practised
progressive-reform politics, and which dovetailed with an electoral turn
growing amongst social democrats in the US. Opposition to this electoral
strategy had the rest of us take on the hard work of hammering out a new
political orientation.

## Turning away from social democracy and towards a revolutionary political tendency

AAD developed politically between 2015 and 2020 through organising
work that followed the theories we charted in the *Fiery File*. We defined
ourselves against the progressive reformism of the social democratic left,
which is organised around the municipal party Coalition of Progressive
Electors (COPE) and left–New Democratic Party (NDP) circles that dominate progressive politics in Vancouver. Red Braid was premised on a break
from social democracy, to coalesce around what we in the title of this book
called a "separate star," meaning a separate centre of gravity, radically apart
from the Canadian settler colonial, capitalist state, including its progressive
reformer manifestations. To manoeuvre around COPE-NDP hegemony
in Vancouver, we retreated out of the centre of Vancouver into the working-class suburbs—a geographic retreat that won us the space we needed
to develop our thinking and make a distinct political claim.

We identified the objective political need for this orientation because,
despite the gentrification of Vancouver since the 1990s and the corresponding shift towards a more multiracial working class in the suburbs, active
public cultures and collective political legacies of working-class resistance
(let alone *revolutionary* politics) were hard to find in these communities.
Everywhere we looked in Vancouver's suburbs and smaller centres around

BC we saw working-class communities under attack by real estate corporations, cops, social workers, and bosses. And for the most part they lacked organisations that could give their resistance political form and language, and through which they could coordinate collective struggles.

The same was true in Vancouver itself, though with the difference that, in the city, advocacy, social service, and legal reform groups made claims to representation of low-income communities. Our problem was not only that we were unable—with our own political vision and practices incompletely developed—to contest that reformist machinery; we also found it difficult to *think* outside of the immediate, pragmatic, and professional sorts of reform politics that held court as opposition currents against overt right-wing and corporate agendas. So we also named our subjective need to take some distance from the political influence of Vancouver's social democracy, to work out what we meant by anti-capitalism and anti-colonialism and build an organisation that facilitates the self-activity of who we call "subaltern" people.

Only in the last third of the decade did we start to define ourselves on our own terms. It's one thing to disagree with social democrats and progressive reformers, and it's quite another to develop and hold a collective and independent revolutionary vision and build the institutions needed to enact it. Once we started taking on this work of developing an independent revolutionary vision, situating ourselves not only against social democracy but alongside revolutionary traditions, we found disagreements amongst our own core group. This is a natural, inevitable, and even healthy process, but it is also fraught, stressful, and full of dangers.

## Our campaigns and political gains of the 20-teens

Alliance Against Displacement had a number of significant achievements in campaigns after 2015. We developed a militant anti-eviction campaign in Burnaby that can claim a large part of the responsibility for the overthrow of the city's sixteen-year-long Mayoral dynasty of Derek Corrigan, and wrenched significant reforms from city hall while maintaining an uncompromising anti-property, anti-capitalist perspective. We organised nearly a dozen tent cities in as many communities. Out of these largely spontaneous, organic survival struggles of predominantly low-income working-class and

Indigenous people, we developed a political vision that transcended immediate conditions and reached towards powerful unities, making revolutionary politics practically relevant to oppressed people who otherwise received only false promises and platitudes from politicians and other reformers. We carved out space for a revolutionary trans women's politics, and a group of trans women leaders found a home in our core membership. We challenged the police control over public safety and governance discourses in Surrey. We organised low-income and unhoused Indigenous people's leadership in street movements in support of land defenders. And we developed a regular organisational practice of education and discussion. The political fruit of these combined efforts are visible here in the documents that comprise this book.

But our biggest achievement was the development of our basis of unity. This new basis of unity—and the launching of Red Braid Alliance for Decolonial Socialism, not coincidentally coming at the beginning of the new decade—was the pronouncement of our hard-won revolutionary theories of strategic unity between Indigenous decolonial and working-class socialist struggles, "white abolitionist multiplicity," materialist and Indigenous trans feminism, and organising social bases amongst the subaltern.

Our achievements in the realm of political theory were inseparable from our campaign work. Our political agreements and program were both *products* and *productive* of our campaign work.

## A subaltern social base

Socialists in Canada and the USA, regardless of their specific political tendencies, tend to be plagued by their isolation from a social base. For all its intelligence and criticality, the left is still mostly isolated from the worries, thoughts, and dreams of working-class and Indigenous peoples. That was not so for us. While we struggled to integrate our subaltern social base into our membership structures, Red Braid was not isolated from our people.

In an internal education class series on "the organisation question," we read about the League of Revolutionary Black Workers in Detroit in the 1970s. When the leadership of the League moved to develop a US-wide congress, they did so at the cost of attention to their social base in the factory organisations. In this move, there was some disdain for the social base, which some of their leaders deemed too crude and uneducated, and some leaders even tried to purge the uneducated social base with a mandatory education series. The move away from the organisation's energetic unity with its social base resulted in a split and the breakdown of both the factory committees and the League's national congress.

Red Braid's social base strategy had some similarities with the broad base-building strategy of the Philly Socialists and the affiliates of the Marxist Center network. The Marxist Center, which launched in 2018 and dissolved in 2022, was a fledgling network of small revolutionary socialist groups in the US (Red Braid was the only member group from outside the US) and independent members that took on base-building as a central point of strategic unity. The similarity between what Marxist Center understood about base-building and our own approach is that both depend on a socialist organisation developing direct, material contact with working-class communities through active participation in struggle. The principle behind this politics is that a revolutionary group must be useful to oppressed people in their everyday struggles.

But base-building groups tend to downplay political education, discussion, and debate, sometimes swerving towards the opportunism of shallow or rhetorical political agreements in order not to risk pulling too hard at superficial unities. Red Braid's social base strategy was political first and last. We said, as a point of pride, that "all we have to offer people is our political analysis and vision." Ad hoc tenant unions and resident meetings and leadership councils in tent cities were part of Red Braid's organisational structure. We fought to put forward revolutionary political ideas and strategies as the best guide to action in those struggles, and we took the spaces of political struggle amongst unhoused and tenant leaders as our most important theatres of socialist politics.

Our social base was the location of the dialectical unity between our campaign work and our thought. It can be frustrating to grapple with the undeveloped politics of subaltern communities at this point in history, but we must be careful not to mistake any frustration experienced by revolutionary intellectuals amongst us for a failure of our project. The tense dialectic between subaltern survival and revolutionary vision was exactly what made Red Braid's social base relationships precious, and no matter what we decided to pursue in terms of relations with other groups and activists, we did not sacrifice this unity.

## For a new revolutionary tendency

We started the 2020s with a new organisation: a new name, basis of unity, organisational strategy, and a broader mandate, more reflective of how we had come to think of ourselves and the goals of our organising and political work. As is reiterated in different ways throughout the chapters of this book, our strategy was to develop anti-colonial, anti-capitalist, and anti-imperialist politics by organising in struggles with subaltern communities in ways that made revolutionary politics immediately relevant to peoples' survival. We were convinced that only through embedding decolonial socialist organisations in the living struggles of unfolding history could we develop a vision of the world we desire—based on consensual, reciprocal relations with other communities and our non-human kin—and the strategies we needed in order to walk together in that better world.

Red Braid was a "decolonial socialist" organisation because we believed that socialism without Indigenous sovereignty is not socialism at all, particularly in a settler colonial nation state. Sovereign Indigenous nations will always be under attack within a capitalist nation state. The laws of capitalist production demand the endless and always expanding theft and destruction of lands through the commodification of forests, mountains, rivers, and oceans, as well as their human and non-human inhabitants. It may be possible for settler colonial governments in the US and Canada to make agreements to continue land theft by making deals with Indigenous band councils and corporate partners, but capitalism will only allow Indigenous nations to choose resource extraction—never to refuse it. Decolonial socialism demands the end of capitalism by overthrowing the totality of the capitalist, settler colonial nation state through a social revolution, falling Canada like you fall a tree—from the bottom.

Decolonial socialism is necessarily multiple. Red Braid never pretended to be *the* revolutionary party. We imagined ourselves to be a contributor to struggles that must cooperate and collaborate with other revolutionary forces. Indigenous nations have sovereign political and organisational forms and Red Braid's decolonial socialism should be measured by how we supported the sovereignty of Indigenous nations in practice.

We also strove to support, challenge, and cooperate with other revolutionary socialist groups, regardless of whether they identified as Trotskyist, Maoist, Marxist Leninist, autonomist, or anarchist. Red Braid did not adhere to a particular twentieth century socialist tendency because we aimed, instead, to learn from all revolutionary traditions, experiences, and legacies. That does not mean we uncritically embraced all socialists. Critique is clarifying, and good critique is the best form of support revolutionaries can give each other. We saw more value in approaching the vast history of revolutionary struggle with openness and curiosity, seeking out tensions and moments of striving for freedom, than in fealty to a particular tendency.

We hoped that a new political tendency based on current realities of class struggle would emerge from our struggles and from those subaltern communities that have been locked out of the comfortable seat of imperial, civil society power. Throughout Red Braid's different organisational forms and projects, we continuously turned away from the cynical and sometimes seductive offerings of bourgeois, settler colonial civil society, toward making revolution at the peripheries. That's where we found our community.

## Outline of the book

A Separate Star is made up of six thematic sections, each of which formed a foundational part of Red Braid's politics and organisational strategy. Some of the chapters in A Separate Star were originally self-published, under the same title, in 2020. But most of the content is newer, the result of our members thinking-through, amending, and revisiting the vision projected at our moment of launch after a year and a half of implementing those ideas in practice.

The first two sections set out the fundamental touchstones of the book: class and settler colonialism, or put another way, the working class and Indigenous nations. Section 1, "Class struggle," begins by defining capitalism and class to assert that the world's working class remains the central protagonist of socialist revolution. While a middle class defined by its socially regulatory role dominates progressive politics in major cities in Canada and the US, this section argues that middle-class leaderships cannot represent the interests of oppressed people; that task falls to historically disorganised ranks of the subaltern themselves. The question of who constitutes this subaltern, within Canada and the US as well as globally, and what organisational forms we need to build subaltern power, rounds out the section.

While the working class has suffered radical disorganisation since the dawn of neoliberalism, beginning with the state and corporate assault on organised labour in the 1970s, Indigenous nations, and particularly low-income Indigenous people, have been disorganised by settler colonial nation states for hundreds of years. Section 2, "Decolonisation," explains Red Braid's combined anti-colonial and decolonial strategies, which centre the self-activity of low-income Indigenous people through the internal and external deployment of "sovereignty as method." The chapters in this section critically review Red Braid's experiments with forming an Indigenous Leadership Council, first as an autonomous group within Red Braid that functioned something like a caucus, and then as a sovereign, parallel group within a mixed group that united in action. Indigenous members of Red Braid reflect on the challenges of sharing a group with a majority non-Native membership, while also facing—as low-income Indigenous people living in the city—the challenges of being recognised and accepted in land-defence struggles. These struggles tend to privilege front lines that face down pipeline contractors through the hereditary leadership structures of Indigenous nations, not the front lines of the unhoused and impoverished Indigenous people who formed the social base of Red Braid.

The following sections of the book read these fundamental, objectively determined groups of classes and nations against the social relationships that they form, and through which their members come to know themselves. Section 3 grapples with gender power, which we refer to as a "thread" that runs through all theatres of power, whether reproductive relations that capitalism depends on for the anti-human vitality of its social factory, the genocidal project of colonialism's attack on Indigenous family relations as an inseparable part of disorganising nations to steal their lands, or the drawing of white supremacist world hierarchies around the bourgeois-European family and its essentialist gender roles. Based on Red Braid's call for an "adversarial" form of social reproduction that, through collective organisational forms and collective struggle nurtures kinship relations *against* capitalist production and colonial domination, chapters in this section review socialist experiments in combatting or accommodating patriarchy, and turn a critical eye to an emergent "queer normativity" as a dead end for today's feminist movements.

Sections 4 and 5 think through the struggles against white supremacy and imperialism as interconnected forms of power expressed within the heart of empire, at its borderlands, and through its wars, trade syndicates, and global logic. Section 4 develops earlier Red Braid articles about what we called "white abolitionist multiplicity," our response to the tendency to implicitly centre white people, even in the name of white abolition, as a pathway to ending white supremacy. Our thinking calls for a subaltern struggle against race and racism as alternative to, on the one hand, the socialist legacy of thinking about race as superstructural and therefore subordinated to class, rather than a living, social form of class relations; and on the other, liberal anti-racism, which has become little more than a radical, street-demo articulation of multiculturalism. The call we're making for a working-class, subaltern anti-racism is not for a more privileged place in empire to be occupied by a racialized minority, but for a socialism that explodes white supremacist empire.

So how does this working-class, internationalist anti-racism deal with the increasing influence of China and other inter-imperialist competition at this particular moment of the setting of the imperial American sun? Section 5 looks back to the way socialists debated inter-imperialist contest a hundred years ago at the outset of the first inter-imperialist war, and calls for a renewal of the slogan of "revolutionary defeatism," the principle that a revolutionary's first enemy is their own ruling power. But that does not mean we should portray the enemy of our enemy as our friend. This section explores how decolonial socialists can look at those nation states under attack by Canada and the US using the example of China, which is the target of a long diplomatic and increasing cold war by a global bloc of powers that define the US-centred liberal world order. The study of China in this section is especially important for us because Listen Chen charts immediate, pressing work for anti-imperialists against the Canada-US contest with China, and also models a method for considering the development and degeneration of revolutionary processes in other nation states from within the belly of these particular beasts.

The last section, which compiles Red Braid's organisational documents, serves as an appendix, sharing the basis of unity, political strategy, and democratic protocols that Red Braid developed through our struggles. All Red Braid group documents were living in the sense that they each arose to meet a need in our organisation or in our struggles, and we would constantly evaluate and change them based on changes in situations that confronted us. They were the highest expression of our collective agreements.

## Enduring relevance of Red Braid's experiences and ideas

A Separate Star is a Red Braid book in that it is the outcome of our years of dedicated, collective intellectual and practical work. Some chapters are credited as collectively authored, either by Red Braid as a whole, or by the Red Braid Indigenous Leadership Council. Some of these chapters have been drafted and redrafted through collective processes in meetings, and others have been drafted by one or two members and adopted as group statements in meetings. In some cases, like with this introduction, the chapter is individually written but represents well-established understandings in the organisation. Individually credited chapters build off collective experiences and established group positions but push beyond the limits of agreements and analyses that have been tested and proven as understood by Red Braid as an entire organisation. We decided that these provocations, inquiries, and experiments in analysis and thought are, both, part of our collective process that we want to share beyond the membership of Red Braid, and the responsibility of individual writers; thus, the paradox of having individually credited chapters in a collectively written book.

This book is a snapshot of Red Braid's politics, organising practices, and understandings of who we were, captured at a particularly difficult moment. The 2020s promise to be a decade defined by active struggle, a challenge that is exemplified by the intense struggles that Red Braid fought through during our difficult year and a half of active organisational life. In the average week during those years, we held a member meeting and education class for all members, and campaign meetings and actions in half a dozen different places, under half a dozen different slogans. We organised tent cities, squats, occupations, demonstrations, an unlicensed drug consumption site, a regular street community drop-in, anti-eviction stand-offs, consciousness-raising meetings, talking circles, published a print newspaper and an online newsletter, and worked with coalitions of socialist groups, often with two or three actions on a single day. The incredible density and richness of these experiences show in the content of these pages.

Red Braid's dissolution is evidence that the politics and strategies that informed and developed through those struggles outgrew the organisational form that first approached them. The legacy of our struggles lives on and is best represented by *A Separate Star*. We hope the ideas in this book are generative and useful to others who are also committed to struggles against capitalism, colonialism, white supremacy, cisheteropatriarchy, and imperialism. Active struggle in the world as it existed yesterday has made us who we are today, and struggles to come tomorrow will change us along with the rest of the world. *A Separate Star* seeks to inventory our inheritances, good and bad, so we can be the self-conscious revolutionary actors that our better tomorrow demands.

*A Separate Star* Section 1

# Class struggle

# Introduction
## Class struggle

To make an argument for social revolution led from below by the subaltern rather than political reform led from above by politicians, this section defends two orthodox Marxist positions that have fallen out of fashion in radical anti-capitalist circles today. First, we argue that the working class is the revolutionary subject within the regular circuit of capitalist production. And secondly, following from this premise, we argue that that the most significant contribution that revolutionary socialists can make during this period is to rebuild independent working-class political instruments—organisations and social and cultural institutions that are autonomous from the sprawling and intelligent apparatus of bourgeois power.

The four main chapters in this section are by Ivan Drury, and together they develop the section's overall argument. The first chapter, "In Defence of Class Struggle Socialism," presents a sketch of global capitalist production from the perspective of the working class in Canada. Taking on the prevailing attitude in the social movement and democratic socialist left that the working class and working-class struggle is antiquated, this chapter argues that the fundamentals of commodity production, namely the rule of the "law of value," have not changed since Marx wrote his analysis of capitalism over 150 years ago. Production has been dramatically reorganised, and the class makeup of working populations in the imperial core—including Canada—have changed significantly, but the production of values and of useful things remains dependent on workers and on the capitalist exploitation of the working class.

The remaining chapters develop this premise with historical specificity, explaining how class processes shape the lives of people who live under the rule of capitalist production, including how we fight against that rule. The second chapter of this section, "The Subaltern," proposes a method to fight against capitalism from within the belly of the imperialist beast. Amongst a long list of ills, imperialism tends to produce a privileged subgroup of workers within empire, which revolutionary socialists have referred to as an "aristocracy of labour," who receive higher than global-average wages and access to private property ownership and nuclear families. Strategies to work against this "right wing" of the working class have gone so far as to reject the capacity of workers in the US and Canada to fight for socialism. This chapter proposes instead that socialists build social bases in subaltern groups, including in the working class, in order to fight against the influence of the aristocracy of labour and, increasingly, the middle class.

The middle class is the subject of the third chapter in this section. A term much used and abused, this chapter offers a definition of the middle class that focuses on its role in managing and administering capitalist rule. Considering the middle class as those workers who manage finance (in banks, investment, and on the factory floor) and society (in various realms of social regulation, ranging from health care and education to policing), the middle class has swelled since the 1970s to become the slight majority of the working population in Canada. Importantly, for anti-capitalist and anti-colonial revolutionaries, the social-management middle class has, since the decline of the radical left and the working-class labour movement, taken prominent positions in social movements, even appropriating radical demands from the streets into their state projects of legal and policy reform.

The fourth chapter in this section, "Revolutionary Organisation," presents an organisational strategy to deal with the problem that, since the 1970s, the organization of this expanding middle class has been founded on the disorganising of the subaltern. The road ahead, this chapter argues, is to rebuild the autonomous organisations of and for the subaltern working class and poor Indigenous people. This organisational form, deeply rooted in the social bases of subaltern groups and making revolutionary politics relevant to their survival struggles, moves in the direction of a party where unity arises from the combined autonomy of multiple class fractions.

The final chapter in this section, by Isabel Krupp, is a case study that demonstrates the method of applying practical revolutionary solutions to social problems. The climate justice movement tends to rely on governments as the actors capable of taking action to stop and reverse climate change. Krupp criticises this lobbyist approach as stuck in a middle-class politics of advocating for reform by and through the state. She cites inspiring examples of worker self-organising as an urgent alternative to protesting and awaiting government action while the world burns.

Overall, this section of *A Separate Star* makes the case that revolution is not a far-off goal; revolution must be imagined, put into words and action, and carried out in the service of and through the demands of everyday life. The subaltern working class remains a social group that is specially situated, both in terms of access to the levers of production and in terms of revolutionary consciousness, to offer leadership through this process. The role of a socialist organisation is, therefore, to offer that emergent leadership political support and infrastructure by recognising the coming socialist world in the survival struggles of the subaltern every day, reporting on those observations to make them understood, and reorganising together to make their revolutionary potential sustained and real.

# In defence of class struggle socialism

Ivan Drury

In place of class unities sharing clear objectives, social movements since the Great Recession of 2007 have been composed of murky declassed assemblages of "people," "multitudes," and "popular groups" expressing vague slogans like "we are the 99%." Even amongst anti-capitalists there has been a significant, uncritical concession to the power of these often powerful, often inspiring, and often middle class–dominated social movements. The political rationale for this cross-class movement strategy, which Scottish Marxist writer Neil Davidson calls a "merger of movements," is elaborated in Erik Olin Wright's book, *How to Be an Anticapitalist in the Twenty-First Century*. Wright, an important scholar of class formation in the US, argues that because class has become diffuse rather than binary, "class interests" are no longer a sufficient bind to socialist coalition; instead, a unity around "moral values" can undergird a gradual "erosion" of capitalism "though the sustained action of the state." The working class, it seems, is over.

In this chapter I argue that such post-working-class views are mistaken because they are based on a distorted definition of class, a misunderstanding about the reorganisation of global capital since the 1970s, and ultimately, the displacement of the centre of social movements from the working class onto a swelled and insurgent middle class. I maintain that

class remains indispensable to understanding and attacking the development and entrenching of hegemonic power and oppression in every part of
our world today. Class *analysis* helps us understand social oppression, domination, and violence against our communities. And class *strategies* help us
fight back, revealing, defending, and building the new socialist world, hidden,
latent, within its rotting capitalist husk.

Two parallel myths have been built up about what "class" is: the liberal
mainstream misdefinition treats class as an affliction (the declining middle
class, the frustrated working class), while the alternative view floating in the
ether is a caricature of socialist thought that insists class is purely economic,
something that lives like a caged bird in the seat of the economy, imagined as
a white, male, industrial workplace. The problem shared by these two myths
is that they both treat class as a local problem. The liberal treats class as a
problem local to an individual, shaped by the fortune of your circumstances.
The socialist caricature has the advantage of seeing class as a relationship, but
a specific workplace relationship, suggesting the formality of an industrial
marriage between a proletariat and a bourgeois. These liberal and socialist
myths about class might be descriptions of how people experience class, but
they do not help us understand the operation of class power in our world.
The more we blinker our thinking about class by individual circumstance
and local situation, the less we understand it.

I see class through two fundamentals: first, class puts people into a *global*
context, and second, class is a *process* that forces our individual lives into
social motion. The most basic class division that animates that global process is between the working class and capitalist class. The working class is
the class of people who are forced under threat of poverty, homelessness,
and early death to sell their labour power in exchange for wages. The capitalist, meanwhile, is the class that buys that labour power. The capitalist
owns the means of production: the lands and raw materials stolen from
Indigenous nations that are the basic material of production; the factories,
warehouses, and strip malls where commodities are made, distributed, and
sold; the machinery and technology that workers use to speed up and perfect the actual making of things; and the labour power bought, in units of
time or task, from workers. This binary class relationship—working class

versus capitalist class—is the driving force behind the *regular circuit of production*, which is constantly moving and constantly growing as capitalists run these wheels alongside and in competition with each other.

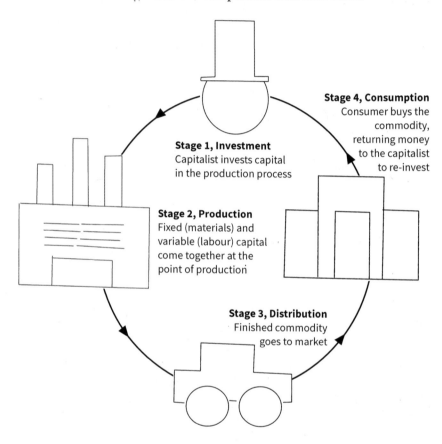

**Stage 1, Investment**
Capitalist invests capital
in the production process

**Stage 2, Production**
Fixed (materials) and
variable (labour) capital
come together at the
point of production

**Stage 3, Distribution**
Finished commodity
goes to market

**Stage 4, Consumption**
Consumer buys the
commodity,
returning money
to the capitalist
to re-invest

*Regular circuit of capitalist production*

This regular circuit goes something like *investment-production-distribution-consumption*, and then repeats. The capitalist invests capital into production, creating the stage for workers to make a commodity using the materials in a factory. The commodity is then distributed to the marketplace, where a consumer buys and uses it, returning money to the capitalist, who reinvests that money as capital back into production again.

But this deceptively simple employee-employer binary disguises a more complex class process that runs behind the scenes, in what I think of as the *expanded* circuit of production. The diagram of the regular circuit makes big assumptions that the capitalist naturally has and owns fixed capital (raw materials, property, machinery and technology, the factory and railway and warehouse and store), and that the worker has this labour power ready, day after day, to sell and expend in the workplace. Class is much more expansive than the story told by the regular circuit of production.

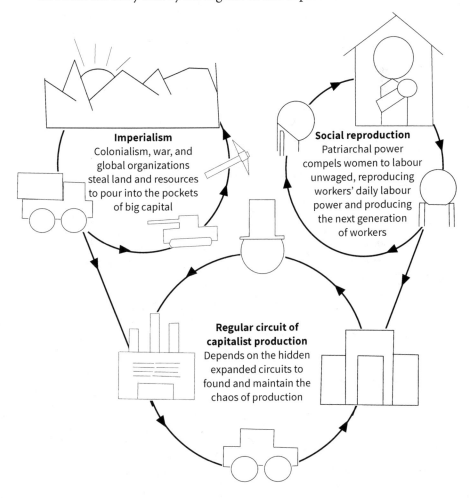

**Imperialism**
Colonialism, war, and global organizations steal land and resources to pour into the pockets of big capital

**Social reproduction**
Patriarchal power compels women to labour unwaged, reproducing workers' daily labour power and producing the next generation of workers

**Regular circuit of capitalist production**
Depends on the hidden expanded circuits to found and maintain the chaos of production

*Expanded circuit of capitalist production*

In fact, class under capitalism makes use of all social forms of power that correspond with it in the total factory of society: capitalism uses colonial and imperialist states and societies to steal lands and resources from Indigenous peoples; capitalism uses white supremacist race power to lower and even eliminate wages and develop a global labour market to the benefit of investors and corporations; capitalism uses patriarchal gender power to reproduce and sustain the energies of workers and to reproduce future generations. The expanded circuit of production includes the land theft that capitalists depend on to begin and sustain production and the gendered sphere of social reproduction that capitalists, in turn, depend on to keep workers in their workplace day after day.

The regular and expanded circuits of capitalist production have to be considered together in order to get a full understanding of how class is operating in the world at a particular time and in a particular place. Class indicates your position within both the regular and the expanded circuits of capitalist production. So, while "working class" explains my role within the regular circuit of production—as living, variable capital and a font of surplus value for the capitalist—my roles in the expanded circuit—as settler in a colonial system, citizen in an imperialist nation state, white in a white supremacist system, and cis man in a patriarchal system—are meaningful, modifying, class information. In this chapter, I focus on describing class divisions in the regular circuit of production with an emphasis on stratification within the overall labouring population, between the working class, the middle class, and the petite bourgeoisie. I complicate the quantitative description of class in following chapters, where I analyse the influence of these regular class divisions on our social lives and, most importantly for this analysis, on the politics of social movements against colonialism and capitalism that take place in interaction between the regular and expanded circuits, in what the Italian autonomists called the total "factory of society."

This chapter begins with a discussion of prominent myths that mar our understanding of class processes today. It then focuses on critiquing the classical Marxist framework of "productive" and "unproductive" labour that thinkers often lean on to argue that working-class struggle is a thing of the past. Following that, I review data about the organisation of jobs in the different fields of Canada's labour markets, with a focus on the meaning of the seeming rebound of the petit bourgeois independent owner and oper- ator. Ultimately, this chapter shows that the working class, and especially the *subaltern* working class, has become a minority amongst workers in Canada, which has seen a massive growth of middle class and, to a lesser degree, petit bourgeois workers since the 1970s. But, as I argue in the concluding section of this chapter, this minority must still contribute leadership to any revolu- tionary overthrow of the settler colonial capitalist system.

## Class struggle and the myth of deindustrialisation

Some sceptics say that the working class has been so disorganised through the post-post-war restructuring of global capitalist production that it no longer exists, at least in the industrial form it once did. These doubts stem from the undeniable fact that the longstanding, predominant form of global capitalist production, where the machinery of production itself is housed by and in imperialist countries, has been revolutionised by the development of industrial capacity in the Global South and the advent of highly efficient technology and global transportation networks. But while location, dis- tribution, and organisation of capitalist production has changed, the *law of value*—the rule that the price of a commodity reflects the amount of human labour power required to produce it, which binds commodity pro- duction to the exploited activity of the working class—has not. To defend the basic premise of class struggle socialism, I'm going to sum up some of Marx's laws of capitalist production that stem from his fundamental law of value in order to show that these laws endure despite important changes in technology and the organisation of production.

For about 200 years, from Marx's time until the end of the twentieth cen- tury, capitalist production was organised by and within a home, imperialist nation state. For the US, the golden age of this classical model of nation- al-industrial production was during the years following the Second World War, after the industrial capacity of European producers had been smashed by the bombs of war and before the development of industrial manufac- turing in Asia. During this national-capitalist heyday, governments used Keynesian consumer welfare state policies to regulate and subsidise the necessary cost of living for workers in order to reduce the cost of labour for employers, giving them a competitive advantage against manufacturers in other countries and enabling workers to buy and consume the products of their own alienated labour. This postwar period ended once Europe rebuilt and with the rise of the manufacturing capacities of Japan, India, and China—where capitalists were not saddled with the relatively powerful labour unions, labour and environmental regulations, and tax rates in the US and Canada won by workers during and immediately after the Second World War. To adapt and deal with growing competition, which arrived along with the first major recession since the war, capital in the US, as well as in Canada, the UK, and western Europe, sought what geographer David Harvey calls a "spatial fix"—carrying out imperialist wars and occupations with one hand, and with the other, ensuring neocolonial economic and legal hegemony by international trade and diplomatic organisations led by the US and its bloc.

Thinkers within and around the "communization" tendency, associated with the journals *Théorie Communiste* in France and *Endnotes* in the UK and US, point to the post-1970s capitalist spatial fix of globally reorganising production as the "deindustrialisation" of the economies in the US, Canada, UK, and Europe. In the words of Italian autonomist Antonio Negri, this means that "productive labour" (commodity production) has been subsumed by "immaterial labour" (the production of culture and information) and the "general intellect" (the accumulated knowledge of society captured in technology).[1] In the late nineteenth century, craft unions that relied on artisan trades workers and apprenticeship programs were replaced by industrial unions that relied on the coordinated strike activity of thousands of workers packed into plants working shoulder to shoulder. In the same way,

1    Antonio Negri, "The Labour of the Multitude and the Fabric of Biopolitics," *Meditations* 23, 2 (Spring 2008). See also, Riccardo Bellofiore and Massimiliano Tomba, "The 'Fragment on Machines' and the Grundrisse: The Workerist Reading in Question," in *Beyond Marx: Theorising the Global Labour Relations of the Twenty-First Century*, ed. Marcel van der Linden and Karl Heinz Roth (Leiden and Boston: Brill Press, 2014); Maurizio Lazzarato, "Immaterial Labour," in *Radical Thought in Italy: A Potential Politics*, ed. Paolo Virno and Michael Hardt (Minneapolis: University of Minnesota Press, 2006).

communizationists say that today's highly automated factory and the importance of financial speculation to the major cities of the world means that organised unions (and their general social form, revolutionary political parties), have been hit by an extinction level event, but don't know it. In place of working-class organisation and action, communizationists say the "multitude" and "popular groups" raise socialism "imminently" out of the shadows of everyday social life, as a spontaneous part of their historical existence.

This is wrong for two reasons. Firstly, it is wrong because *deindustrialisation* is a misnomer. Major sites of industrial production have spread to new countries and cities, but the old imperial workhouses of the world are still manufacturing commodities, which are *values* in the capitalist system. And secondly, it is wrong because *productive labour* is employed all throughout the circuit of capitalist production, not only inside the gates of a factory. It is incorrect to say that a peripheral location of a factory means that value-production is remote to a financial centre. Values are not created start-to-finish inside a factory; productive labour is employed all along the total circuit of capitalist production, from the theft of land wealth from Indigenous peoples to production itself, distribution, and consumption.

While employment in manufacturing in the US and Canada has shrunk, it is not only because some of those jobs have been moved to China and Mexico. More than any other single cause, the culprit for job losses in manufacturing is automation, speed-up, and "just in time" production techniques. In a 2018 article in *Catalyst*, Kim Moody shows that US manufacturing output has not declined overall since the early '80s; despite all rhetoric to the contrary, it has actually increased by 131 percent from 1982 to 2007 at an increasing rate of five percent a year. The US and UK are no longer the dominant workhouses of the world, but the imperial core is still home to the production of values, with a higher efficiency than before. So while fewer people in the US and Canada work in manufacturing now than before the 1980s—because of increased technological efficiency, meaning higher rates of exploitation—the production of values in industrial manufacturing is still a site of class struggle and potential working-class power in the West.

Unions have not kept ahead of these shifts, partly because capital's adaptations towards higher rates of exploitation have been paired with a race and gender demographic shift in the ranks of the employed working class. Moody explains that between 1990 and 2010, while the manufacturing sector shrunk by 4.6 million jobs due to another wave of mechanisation, the service economy in the United States grew by 14.2 million jobs. Moody explains that 57% of these jobs were in the fields of commercialised social reproduction—health care and food services—where workers are more likely to be racialized than white. Meanwhile, between 1981 and 2020, the number of Black, Latinx, and Asian workers in production and transportation industries went up from 15% to 40%. In construction there was a similar increase in racialized workers, from 15% to 37%. All in all, Moody estimates, members of Black, Latinx, and Asian communities make up 35% of the employed working class, 22% of the middle class, and 11% of the capitalist class in the US. At the same time and overlapping with increases in racialized demographic shifts, women's labour market participation doubled between 1979 and 2012, from 600 hours per year to 1,560 for women with children and 925 hours per year to 1,664 for all women.[2] What this all means is that the working class has not faded or become a thing of the past; it has become less racialized white and less gendered male—corresponding with a reduction in unionisation rates that have traditionally been highest in industries dominated by white, male workforces.

Unionisation rates have historically been lower in those social service, agricultural, and commodity distribution industries that have also been feminized and racialized Black, Latinx, and Asian. In Canada, union density peaked in 1984, when 41.8% of the workforce were members of unions. Union rate differences by gender and industry were significant. Forty-six percent of male workers and only 36.6% of women workers were members of unions, a difference partly explained by the difference of 45% of full-time workers and only 23% of part-time workers who were union members. In Canada in 1986, 31.8% of women workers and only 6.2% of men workers had part time jobs.[3] Only 2.8% of agricultural workers, who were more likely to be workers of colour, and 12.1% of sales workers and 16% of retail workers,

2   See Kim Moody, "The New Terrain of Class Conflict in the United States," *Catalyst Magazine* 1, 2 (Summer 2017).
3   Rachel A. Rosenfeld and Gunn Elisabeth Birkelund, "Women's Part-Time Work: A Cross-National Comparison," *European Sociological Review* 11, 2 (1995): 111–34.

who were more likely to be women, were union members.[4] In 2020, the percentage of all workers in Canada who were members of a union had fallen by one third to 31%, about the rate of unionisation for women workers in 1984. Maybe just as important is that in 2020, women workers swapped positions with men and became the gender group more likely to be part of a union, with a higher (33.7%) unionisation rate than men (29.1%).[5] The gendered shift in the tendency to unionisation followed the shift in workforces from production-dense to services-dense industries.

The haemorrhaging of union density suffered in Canada was common in imperialist countries that underwent such a shift in labour market emphasis from production to services, including the US, France, Japan, Germany, Sweden, Italy, Finland, the UK, and Australia. Canada's union losses were on the mild side of this cohort, especially in comparison to the US, partly because of the robust public sector in Canada where unions were disempowered but not often decertified.[6] In 2020, the industries with the highest unionisation rates were in the public sector, which had an overall unionisation rate of 77.6%, while the private sector's unionisation rate was only 15.8%.[7] The highest unionisation rates in the public sector were in the feminized industries of health care (64.8%), education (82.1%), and social services (57.7%). Industries with workforces that tend to be made up of racialized people of colour or gendered male had the lowest rates of unionisation, including retail and wholesale sales and services (17.4%) and agriculture and natural resource extraction (13.5%).[8] The traditionally union-dense manufacturing industry did not drop below the overall average of about 30%

4   Craig Riddell, "Unionisation in Canada and the United States: A Tale of Two Countries," in *Small Differences that Matter: Labour Markets and Income Maintenance in Canada and the United States*, ed. David Card and Richard B. Freeman (Chicago: University of Chicago Press, 1993); Mitchell Thompson, "A Brief History of Canadian Labour Woes," *Canadian Dimension*, February 10, 2017.

5   Statistics Canada, Table 14-10-0129-01, Union status by geography, https://doi.org/10.25318/1410012901-eng.

6   Jim Stanford, "Holding the Line: Canadian Union Power in International Perspective," *The Law of Work*, February 28, 2020.

7   Statistics Canada, Table 14-10-0132-01, Union status by industry, https://doi.org/10.25318/1410013201-eng.

8   Statistics Canada, Table 14-10-0319-01, Union status by occupation, inactive (x 1,000), https://doi.org/10.25318/1410031901-eng.

unionisation, but because manufacturing suffered a significant decline in the number of workers employed, the number of union members lost from its ranks accounts for a significant decline in male unionists. So while unions are now stronger in feminized, public-sector industries, it is not because of unions pivoting to these workplaces, but because of job losses and the overall weakening of unions, with the exception of public-sector, middle-class jobs. Unions have not managed to follow the transfer of masses of workers from union-strong, white and male-majority *industrial* workplaces to the *service industry* job sites of working-class women and people of colour, which has led to a decline in union density overall, particularly for the working class.

## Productive and unproductive labour

Changes in the composition and industry-location of unions have followed historic changes in the sorts of jobs that people have done since the 1970s, from the shrinking manufacturing sector to the blossoming consumer and personal services sectors. In Canada, jobs in industrial production declined from thirty-five percent of the total workforce in 1976 to twenty-one percent in 2020, with the major job losses occurring in the decade between 1986 and 1996 when 10,000 industrial jobs were lost. Between 1976 and 2020, Canada's manufacturing industries gained only 60,000 jobs—a growth rate that meant losses in comparison to population and labour-market growth generally. Working-class consumer and personal services jobs (including retail and transportation) remained basically steady at twenty-eight percent of the workforce, but that meant adding 1.5 million of these jobs over these critical forty-four years. So while I think it is important for our understanding of the landscape of class struggle that manufacturing production is still happening in Canada, we also have to address the meaning of the shift of such a significant proportion of the working-class workforce from industries directly associated with production to those in the chain of circulation—a problem that socialists often think about as the shift of workers in the imperialist West from employment in *productive* to *unproductive* labour.

The kind of work someone does matters to socialist strategy because workers have different kinds of power in relation to capitalism depending on where they work in the overall factory of capitalist society. Productive labour, Marx says, is "the wage-labour which creates more value than it costs," meaning it is employed as part of the capitalist production of commodities, which prioritizes the creation of *abstract* values (including profits) over and above the socially *useful* value of the thing being made. From the perspective of socialist strategy, a productive worker is the producer of things that society needs and whose labour the capitalist steals to warp into values and glean profits. The productive worker has the power, latent in their everyday work, to produce only and entirely for the good of people and the planet rather than for the boss's profits. That imminent fact is the basic strategic advantage of the working class against capitalism.

Unproductive labour is different. From the standpoint of the capitalist, unproductive labour is an "expenditure" rather than an investment. In his review of industrial capitalism in the throes of automation, Italian Marxist Mario Tronti says that "the productive worker produces a commodity for the buyer of her labour power, while the unproductive labourer produces a mere use-value for this buyer." With unproductive labour, then, "labour does not transform into capital, for it does not create a profit for the capitalist; [unproductive] labour is a simple expense."[9] This does not mean that unproductive workers are outside of capitalist production; being "unproductive" to capitalist surplus value is not the same as being socially unnecessary. So unproductive workers can still leverage influence in capitalist society through protest and through strike actions that complement productive workers, but from the standpoint of worker's strategy, it means they are not in a position of *seizing production*; ultimately, they are disempowered of class agency.

But where does productive labour end and unproductive labour begin? Even Marx is ambivalent about this. He is clear that he sees productive workers as more than those masculine tropes who throw a hammer against hot iron to forge steel; productive workers are all those employed in any stage of the production of any commodity. All those who work all along the line of commodity production—from the point where land wealth is torn from the earth, through factory production, all the way to market—are mobilised

9   Mario Tronti, "Productive Labour," in *Workers and Capital* (New York: Verso Books, 2019), 161.

to produce more value for the capitalist than they receive in wages, and are instrumental to the circuit of capitalist production. In the production of a table, the logger who cuts down a tree, the logging truck driver who hauls it, the mill worker who hews the log into lumber, the joiner who fits leg to table top, the sander and painter who finishes the wood, the shipper who arranges transportation and moves it out of the factory, the train switcher who steers the cargo across continent, the short-haul trucker who moves it out of the rail yard, the warehouse receiver who jacks and stores the crate, the delivery driver who moves it to the retail store, the stock worker who unloads and uncrates it, the retail sales worker who convinces a consumer to buy it, and the cashier who processes the sale are all productive workers.

Looked at this way, the binary of productive and unproductive labour is not actually a very helpful way to understand how value is produced under the capitalist mode of production. Marx's description of productive labour includes jobs that occur down the supply chain and even in the cultural and social exchanges necessary for capitalist reproduction. In *Theories of Surplus Value*, he uses the following example:

> An actor...or even a clown, is a productive labourer if they work in service of a capitalist to whom they return more labour than they receive... in the form of wages; while a jobbing tailor who comes to the capitalist's home and patches his trousers for him, producing a mere use-value for him, is an unproduct- ive labourer...The former's labour is exchanged with capital, the latter's with revenue. The former's labour produces a sur- plus-value; in the latter's, revenue is consumed. [10]

When service work is part of the production of a commodity, includ- ing its total movement from genesis to consumption, and when service labour is a point of investment in the creation of value and surplus value, the consumer of the labour power is a capitalist, and the worker is engaged in productive labour. When service work is done for an individual purchaser, as an expense rather than an investment, the consumer is not acting as a

10   Karl Marx, *Theories of Surplus Value*, vol. 1 of 3 (Moscow: Progress Publishers, 1975), 157.

capitalist, and it is unproductive labour. A textbook example of unproductive labour is the employment arrangement in the 2019 movie *Parasite*, where the wealthy Park family hires members of the working-class Kim family to perform a number of services. The Kims make incomes from their work as chauffeur and housekeeper, and tutor and art therapist for the Park children, and they are exploited because they receive market rates, remaining in a subordinate position to their employers. But the fact that they are exploited does not mean they are producing surplus value. Their labour is unproductive because the Parks purchase the Kim family's labour for the uses it provides, not for a return on an investment.

But the story of the Kim family's exploitation is, in today's capitalist world, a bit fantastical. While nineteenth century European aristocrats relied on unproductive labour, hiring servants to keep their estate gardens and scrub their personal linens, autonomist Marxist theorist Harry Cleaver says that the development of personal services sectors has rendered this worker, paid out of "revenue" rather than invested-in by a capitalist, an anachronism. "Where the landed gentry employed extensive kitchen staffs, housemaids, launderers and gardeners," he explains, "increasingly such work is done by caterers, restaurants, laundry, cleaning and landscaping services, all employing waged workers generating surplus-value."[11] The kind of personal services once restricted to aristocrats have, through a global, racial, gendered division of labour and the creation of personal services companies, been made available far more broadly to middle-income consumers. Geographer David Ley argues that the expansion of personal services companies is linked to the growth of the financial- and public-sector middle class since the 1970s because "the urbane middle class place a premium on customised goods and services which are labour-intensive."[12] Taking the Vancouver Yellow Pages as a sample for tracking business listings, Ley says that between 1975 and 1995, the number of restaurants and house cleaning businesses in the city almost doubled, home security firms increased fivefold, and nanny services,

11  Harry Cleaver, 33 *Lessons on Capital: Reading Marx Politically* (London: Pluto Press, 2019).

12  David Ley, *The New Middle Class and the Remaking of the Central City* (Oxford and New York: Oxford University Press, 1996).

which only appeared as a distinct listing in the 1980s, grew from zero to fifteen agencies. A Yellow Pages search in December 2021 returned thirty-six results for nanny services, 130 results for childcare, and sixty two for house cleaning in the city of Vancouver—though growth in the personal services industry since Ley's book was published in 1996 is surely much more substantial than these numbers show because the Yellow Pages is no longer the gold standard for business listings.

All this suggests that productive versus unproductive is no longer a helpful way to think about the relationship of particular forms of labour to capitalist production. In his *Lessons on the Grundrisse*, Antonio Negri says that productive and reproductive labour are so mixed that they become impossible to differentiate, so "the Marxist definition of productive labour is a reductive definition" that relies on a socialist cultural fetish for point-of-production industrial working-class struggle—a location in production that happens to be gendered male and racialized white. Negri calls this an "axiology" that remains "even when the theoretical conditions have changed"—and calls for a rethinking of the productive versus unproductive binary in understanding how labour produces value under capitalism.[13] I think Negri's observation is correct, but the lessons he draws from this fact, that the overflowing of productive labour into all social labour means no particular labour is any longer productive, is a mistaken conclusion. Theorist George Caffentzis critiques Negri's conclusion that capitalism has innovated beyond the need for human labour power by pointing out the obvious, that "the computer requires the sweatshop, and the cyborg's existence is premised on the slave."[14] The trend mistakenly called "deindustrialisation" might more accurately be termed the decentralisation of production, into what a World Bank report of 2020 calls "global value chains." Between 1995 and 2015, the number of people employed producing commodities in these "chains," where factories in two or more countries are involved in production, grew from 296 million

---

13    Antonio Negri, *Marx Beyond Marx: Lessons on the Grundrisse* (Massachusetts: Bergin and Garvey Publishers, 1984).

14    George Caffentzis, "The End of Work or the Renaissance of Slavery? A Critique of Rifkin and Negri," in *In Letters of Blood and Fire: Work, Machines, and the Crisis of Capitalism* (Oakland: PM Press, 2013).

to 453 million, employing one in five workers globally. [15] Many millions more are employed in the distribution of these commodities—between factories located in different countries and then, in completed form, to consumer market. Surplus value is produced in every leg of that complicated global journey of production and consumption.

To make use of how the categories of productive and unproductive labour have been reorganized by global shifts in production, we can look more precisely at the degree of any particular job's productivity: is it *directly* productive, like that work employed in the point of production itself; is it *second hand* productive, like at the point of distribution, where value is added and surplus value extracted through the "change of location" necessary to be sold in a global supply chain; or is it *third hand* productive, like in childcare, teaching, health care, and unwaged housework, where values are added socially, over the long term, and where the maximisation of surplus value extraction is an *effect* of the labour, even if the labour itself is not directly productive of surplus values. [16] While there are strategic implications for how class struggle can be most powerfully coordinated between workers in these three proximities to production, the question of which productive workers are best placed to fight against capitalist domination today has more to do with the consciousness of a particular group of workers and the mobilisation of a particular sector within a given moment of capitalist production, rather than a static predetermination.

Productive and unproductive labour is all tangled together because, as Marx explains in *The Grundrisse*, production itself is a unity of production and consumption. Workers employed in *directly* productive labour may have a strategic advantage in class struggle because production itself is the "dominant moment" in the "syllogism" of production as a whole circuit, including the constituent points of distribution and consumption. [17] But that does not mean that workers employed in labour that is productive to the second or

15   See Benjamin Selwyn and Dara Leyden, "World Development Under Monopoly Capitalism," *Monthly Review* 73, 6 (November 2021).

16   Karl Marx, *Capital*, vol. 2, in *Collected Works of Marx and Engels*, vol. 36 (Electric Book: Lawrence and Wishart, 2010), 154.

17   Karl Marx, "The Grundrisse (Part 1): Economic Works, 1857–1861," in *Marx and Engels Collected Works*, vol. 28 of 51 (London: Lawrence and Wishart, 2010), 27.

third degrees are relegated only to protest. Rather than rushing to conclude that the reduction of direct manufacturing jobs means apocalypse for the working class, we should see that the number of workers employed in production itself, particularly in manufacturing, has been reduced since the 1970s and the number employed in middle-class administrative positions has increased, but the number of workers involved in productive labour, including industries of production, distribution, and consumer and personal services, has not significantly changed. And while the capacity of workers to intervene against capital through direct and organised class struggle has been hampered by decades of capitalist offensive that has gutted formerly powerful unions, these dynamics do not mean class struggle is over. This new global class situation demands coordination and cooperation between workers in different industries along the whole unified chain of commodity production, including from deep within the factory of society. Such coordination and cooperation is also compelled by the fragmentation of the working class into smaller and smaller workplace units, including the precarious workplaces-of-one that form the new, highly exploited petite bourgeoisie.

### The new petite bourgeoisie

In Canada, the biggest labour market change between 1976 and 2021 has been an overall increase in public-sector social service jobs and private-sector financial services jobs, a group that, together, I'm referring to as the *middle class*. Alongside this trend has been a more minor increase in small business ownership, largely overlapping with the financial services–working middle class, which I'm referring to as the *petite bourgeoisie*. Counted all together, the middle classes have significantly grown from 37% of Canada's workforce in 1976 to 49% of the workforce in 2020. The number of middle-class social managers in the public sector have grown during this period of government cutbacks and austerity, but the majority of this growth has been in the number of private-sector middle-class financial managers, which has nearly doubled from 8% to 15% of the workforce. This growth explains the growth of the petite bourgeoisie through this same period because most of the growth of the petite bourgeoisie has been in white collar industries.

After decades of decline, the petite bourgeoisie rebounded in Canada, though not in the same form it had previously. In 1901, 28% of workers in Canada self-identified as self-employed, with a greater number (33%) in rural industries where primary economies were paramount.[18] But by 1948, with the rise of monopoly capitalism, the self-employed declined to 14.7% of the total workforce, bottoming out at 10.9% in 1968, when the class was plagued by poor economic returns on investment and lower wages than those of the average worker.[19] The decline of the petite bourgeoisie—the self-employed class—throughout most of the twentieth century is something that Marxists would expect; one of Marx's fundamentals is that capitalism tends to eliminate independent producers and small owners. So, when this decline not only stopped but reversed in almost every Western imperialist country in the late-1970s, it came as a surprise. In Canada in 1976, the number of the self-employed rose slightly to 12% of the workforce overall, then to 15% in 1986, where it has stuck since.[20] This seems to refute Marx's maxims.

But although independent owners are part of this class, the return of the self-employed has not meant the return of the petite bourgeoisie as a class of independent owners and producers. Self-employment as a category in Canadian census statistics is not itself an indicator of a petit bourgeois class position because it includes larger employers who live off the exploitation of the labour power of others, making them more of a lower tier of the bourgeoisie rather than of the classical petite bourgeoisie. It also includes those at the other end of the petit bourgeois spectrum—those workers whose bosses force to sub-contract, marking them self-employed for tax purposes, but who bring nothing but their own labour power (and some of their own tools) to market. For all intents and purposes they remain wage labourers, and in some cases, exploited and insecure wage labourers disinherited of

18  See Chris Minns and Marian Rizov, "The Spirit of Capitalism? Ethnicity, Religion, and Self-Employment in Early 20th Century Canada," *Explorations in Economic History* 42 (2005).

19  See Leo A. Johnson, "The Development of Class in Canada in the Twentieth Century," in *Capitalism and the National Question in Canada*, ed. Gary Teeple (Toronto: University of Toronto Press, 1972).

20  Statistics Canada, Table 14-10-0027-01, Employment by class of worker, annual (x 1,000), https://doi.org/10.25318/1410002701-eng.

legal protections other wage labourers can expect.[21] The clearest example of the precarious position of this new petite bourgeoisie is the "self-employed" Uber driver, who bears the burden of bringing their own means of production (their car) to the workplace, who does not have the security or legal protections afforded by regular employment, and who is also a far cry from being an independent producer because they remain chained to the Uber app and communications platform and therefore to Uber's profit-seeking machinations. They are employees in all ways but legal.[22]

The biggest difference between the petite bourgeoisie before and after its resurrection is in how many of them work alone versus how many have employees. In 1976, 52% of self-employed people worked alone without employees; in 2020 that number had increased to a whopping 72%, mostly as part of that swelling professional group of financial services contract workers. Between 1976 and 2020, the private-sector financial services sector—which I'll refer to as the "financial management" sector (including finance, insurance, real estate, rental and leasing, professional, scientific and technical services, and business and building services)—doubled its contribution to the workforce in British Columbia from about 10% to 20% of the workforce, employing 492,000 white collar workers in 2020.[23] In Canada overall, private-sector financial services also nearly doubled from 8% to 15% of the overall workforce.[24] As Erik Olin Wright argues in his 1989 study of the "fall and rise of the petite bourgeoisie," the labour demands of what he calls these "postindustrial industries" account for a lot of the rebound of self-employed workers.[25] In the US, business, legal, engineering, professional, and medical services accounted for 55% of self-employment gains in that first decade of the petit bourgeois rebound, and the growth of financial service industries

21  See Angela Dale, "Social Class and the Self-Employed," *Sociology* 20, 3 (1986).

22  Canada Labour Congress, "Labour: protect worker rights, not gig employers," March 24, 2021.

23  Statistics Canada, Table 14-10-0023-01, Labour force characteristics by industry, annual (x 1,000), https://doi.org/10.25318/1410002301-eng.

24  Statistics Canada, Labour force characteristics by industry.

25  See Erik Olin Wright and George Steinmetz, "The Fall and Rise of the Petty Bourgeoisie: Changing Patterns of Self-Employment in the Postwar United States," *AJS* 94, 5 (March 1989).

in the world cities of Vancouver, Toronto, and Montreal during that critical decade of 1976 to 1986 suggests a similar pattern was at play in Canada. So, in financial management, the middle class is composed of an accountant who is a regular employee of a firm who works alongside an accountant that is self-employed and petit bourgeois; the employed and self-employed horizontally integrated.

Most of the petite bourgeoisie in production, distribution, and commodity services are independent contractors, a position that has some cultural cachet but not much material benefit over being a regular employee. In primary industries, including the direct land theft industries of logging, fishing, and also agriculture, 62.8% of all workers are self-employed, mostly as independent contractors who have no employees of their own, and nearly all others work for that minor petit bourgeois subgroup that employs workers. Ninety-nine percent of businesses in primary industries are classified as "small." Race and gender play a significant (but not entirely determinant) role in sorting out who is part of this large group of independent contractor petite bourgeoisie and who works for that smaller group of petit bourgeois exploiters. White men are, overall in every industry, more likely to be self-employed than racialized workers. If we discount Francophones, who have lower rates of self-employment than whites generally, then 16.8% of white workers and 13.4% of racialized workers are self-employed. Only in distribution (including warehousing, trucking, and retail shops), where 20% of workers are self-employed, do racialized workers nearly match whites in self-employment.[26] In primary industries this difference is more stark; white male workers are twice as likely as racialized workers to be self-employed.[27] But besides having some cultural cachet, which, along with their whiteness, has more meaning for their petit bourgeois class consciousness than for their material well-being, for all intents and purposes these petit bourgeois

26  See Reza Nakhaie, Xiaohua Lin, and Jian Guan, "Social Capital and the Myth of Minority Self-Employment: Evidence from Canada," *Journal of Ethnic and Migration Studies* 35, 4 (April 2009): 625–44.

27  Innovation, Science and Economic Development Canada, "Key Small Business Statistics 2020" (Ottawa: Government of Canada, 2020), https://ised-isde. canada.ca/site/sme-research-statistics/en/key-small-business-statistics/ key-small-business-statistics-2020.

contractors are wage workers whose bosses decided to contract rather than hire. While accountants and stockbrokers who contract out their labour may benefit from their specialised labour, the same is not true of independent owner-operator truck drivers, drywall hangers, child care workers, and domestic cleaners, who, through becoming "small business owners," lose job security and gain only the risk and responsibility of buying and maintaining their work equipment.

The smaller number of petit bourgeois owners that employ workers are significant beyond their numbers because they rule over the majority of the private-sector working class. Out of the private workforce (which is 75% of the workforce), 69% of workers are employed by bosses with fewer than 100 workers. As the chart below shows, in Canada in 2020, 21% of all jobs were in production (including the primary sector of resource extraction), 5% were in distribution (transportation and warehousing), and 20% were in retail and trade. Prior to the capitalist offensive that began in the 1980s, workers in these industries (exempting retail) would be more likely to work for large employers, but an effect of that capitalist offensive is that many of these working-class jobs are now commissioned through small businesses, either hiring independent contractors or organised through often short-lived businesses with a small number of employees. Petit bourgeois workers without employees live from contract-to-contract, and even the rebounded petit bourgeois small employer has an extremely precarious existence. In Canada, about 95,000 small businesses were created every year between 2001 and 2017, and about 91,000 small businesses shut down; during two of these years, more small businesses died than were born.[28] The diffusion of workers between many, various, and short-term employers eludes labour laws that demand a union's collective agreement be staked out against a common employer and union organiser strategies that favour long-term employment, demanding new organising tactics that can span specific workplaces. This means that the hill of class struggle has gotten steeper and slipperier, and it can feel like a lonelier and more precarious climb.

---

28  Innovation, Science and Economic Development Canada.

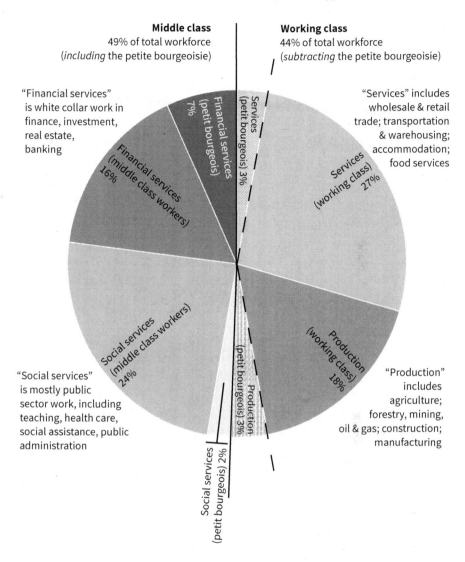

**Middle class**
49% of total workforce
(*including* the petite bourgeoisie)

**Working class**
44% of total workforce
(*subtracting* the petite bourgeoisie)

"Financial services"
is white collar work in
finance, investment,
real estate,
banking

"Services" includes
wholesale & retail
trade; transportation
& warehousing;
accommodation;
food services

Financial services
(petit bourgeois)
7%

Services
(petit bourgeois) 3%

Financial services
(middle class workers)
16%

Services
(working class)
27%

Social services
(middle class workers)
24%

Production
(working class)
18%

Production
(petit bourgeois) 3%

"Social services"
is mostly public
sector work, including
teaching, health care,
social assistance, public
administration

"Production"
includes
agriculture;
forestry, mining,
oil & gas; construction;
manufacturing

Social services
(petit bourgeois) 2%

*Workers in Canada, 2020*

These challenges do not mean the end of the working class or the end of militant class struggle. If anything, the scattering of workers out of concentrated plants where thousands of people worked alongside each other means that radical anti-capitalist class analysis and strategies that foreground class unity across job locations are more immediately relevant and applicable to the needs of the working class today. The extralegal strategies of autonomous worker self-organisation, which rely on the democratic and insurgent cooperation of subaltern people against class enemies as they appear (rather than as they are legally recognised by the labour relations board), suit such a diffuse global workplace. Revolutionary socialists have long complained that corrupt union bureaucrats and the short-term promises of legally contracted, job site–specific collective agreements get in the way of universal, socialist organising. So now that government-regulated, legal union politics falter and cannot offer the reforms to subaltern workers that they once could, the challenge of revolutionary politics potentially becomes immediately relevant. But seizing this opportunity for deep-rooted class struggle requires engaging in struggle, whether workplace or community struggles or multi-class movements of the "multitude," with the goal of identifying and amplifying working-class struggles in particular.

## From class analysis to class struggle

But if the contemporary global organisation of capitalist production has made the working class a (slight) minority in Canada, the revolutionary fragments of this class are narrower still. Not pictured in the rough class outlines above are the jobless; the illicitly, informally employed; the too young and too old; the day-workers and temporary foreign workers; the masses of Indigenous peoples locked out of labour markets by racism and settler colonialism; and those sovereigntists who refuse jobs to turn instead to non-capitalist, land-based economies of reciprocity. From a bird's eye view we can see the working class generally, but we can't see the wage disparity and social status differences between those who have long-term, secure, well-paid jobs, and those who don't make enough to pay rent in leaky apartment buildings infested with black mould, roaches, and rats. But those lines of stratification are there, demarcating the dramatically different worlds and radically different political perspectives of the aristocracy of labour and the subaltern. Since the end of the Second World War in Canada and the US, the subaltern has been reduced from being a majority that rioted against their criminalisation and oppression in the streets of Vancouver in

1912 and organised general strikes of work camp denizens during the economic depression of the 1930s, to a minority of the population overall. The disorganisation of the subaltern by capitalist offensive and their resulting powerlessness in political and social power structures is partly explained by this demographic weakness.

But being a minority does not foreclose the possibility of wielding or even seizing power from the capitalist ruling class and its circles. The Bolsheviks faced a comparable problem before the 1917 revolution in Russia, when the working class made up only about ten percent of the overall population. The great majority of Russia was peopled by peasants, who, while terribly oppressed, also harboured individualist ambitions to hold and operate lands. A great strength of the Bolsheviks, and one of their roles in the revolution, was to convince millions of peasants that they would come out on top if they threw in their lot with a worker-led socialist revolution. From a perspective of historical development, the Russian Revolution brought together a counter-hegemonic, historic bloc of classes where the working class led and the peasants were participants along with important layers of the middle-class intelligentsia against the landlords of Tsarism and the capitalist class. Subaltern people are locked in struggle for survival every day, but without a revolutionary political program and powerful organisations of its own, the subaltern cannot take a similar leading position in a counter-hegemonic bloc including disenfranchised and disillusioned members of the middle-class intelligentsia, castaways from the imperilled ship of labour's aristocracy, and dissident, racialized members of the petite bourgeoisie.

The problem with identifying and quantifying this revolutionary vanguard, as I explain in the next chapter, is that the subaltern does not occupy a static position in the capitalist relations of production. Subalternity is a historical position developed in relation to the classes that form a hegemonic bloc—it is that radically excluded group who experiences capitalist, colonial, imperial power as force wielded against them rather than as a relationship they can navigate to their relative advantage. The most reliable tell of a group's subalternity is the political program they reach for, and the strategies and tactics they use to deploy those politics.

Although I am discussing class as produced through the global system of capitalist production, most of Red Braid's experiences in class struggle were outside of workplace points of production. Seeking out the self-activity of the subaltern, we worked mostly with tenants fighting against mass eviction by city-organised demolitions of the apartments where they live, and unhoused communities in struggle against their displacement from ad hoc tent cities by police sweeps. We did not see this as a gap between our thinking and practice because we did not see the working class as people who spend their days at paid jobs. The working class includes those thrown out of the labour market, disposed of, paying the price of death on the streets because they cannot or will not sell their labour power to capitalists. A hallmark of our historical moment under the terrible rule of capitalism is that death by exposure or overdose on the streets is the dark night of the worker's long day. Ending poverty and homelessness demands an analysis of how they are produced by class and capitalism and a revolutionary strategy to topple these systems from their base.

# The subaltern

Ivan Drury

As if the prospects for decolonial socialist revolution were not already difficult enough with the working class eroded to less than half of the overall labouring population, we also have to reckon with the problem that many workers in Canada and the US not only cannot imagine a world beyond capitalism but reject the very idea. We cannot exclusively blame the power of capitalist ideology; though it has swelled to an overwhelming and disorienting common sense since the collapse of the Soviet Union, it is nevertheless not the entire problem. Yes, inside the US empire there is a highly sophisticated cultural machinery churning away with the determined persistence of a twenty-four-hour news cycle and the adaptive intelligence of millions of highly trained and free minds coordinated organically through innumerable universities and many more publications. But workers are not so easily fooled; they won't buy so mightily into an idea that does not, in some way, suit them. The truth is that many workers lean eagerly into their exploitation and alienation not because they are dupes but because they expect to get what they need out of their wage labour jobs, and to some extent, for some workers, capitalism delivers.

Putting aside the power relations that inscribe sub-class divisions within labouring classes (the regulatory power of middle-class social managers over the working class and Indigenous peoples; the financially determining and thieving power of middle-class fiscal managers; and the directly exploitative class power of the petite bourgeoisie over workers in their employ), there are differences of social influence, prestige, and security in the working class itself that we have to reckon with when identifying potentially revolutionary working class constituencies. Unlike class divisions, which structure social power relations between dominant and subordinate groups in the service of capitalist production generally, working class sub-divisions are relative, precarious, and mutable. They are, nevertheless, meaningful, and they often determine the political commitments and allegiances of the members of a subgroup within the working class.

In this chapter I'm presenting these subgroups as a binary: the aristocracy of labour and the subaltern. It is always tricky to use binary models to analyse social structures. I'm not suggesting that the working class has only two subgroups, but that these two groups represent the opposite poles of a political field—the far-right wing and far-left wing of the working class. Most workers are unseated from either pole and are pulled at by the centre of gravity of each side, which may be stronger or weaker depending on the conditions of struggle in a given time and place.

The *aristocracy of labour* is the relatively privileged subgroup of workers who receive higher wages, greater job security, and in a settler colonial context, tend to own land in the form of personal property. This relatively privileged group of workers tend to experience class through the race prism of being white in a white supremacist society, the colonial framework of being settler in a settler colonial nation state, and the gender gaze of being a man in a patriarchal system. Although these workers are exploited under the capitalist mode of production, the privileges they enjoy relative to other workers (especially relative to other workers internationally) draw them into the trap of identifying their wellbeing and security with the stability and power of the system that exploits them. As an expression of their allegiance, they advocate for government policies against other groups of workers, like border controls and cuts to social services. They have used vigilante violence against Black, Indigenous, Latinx, and Asian people.

One of the jobs of revolutionary socialists in particular, as Lenin explained a century ago in his article "Imperialism and the Split in Socialism," is to organise against those right-wing sections of the working class, invested as they are in the petty privileges bequeathed to them by imperialism, settler colonialism, white supremacy, and patriarchy, and "go down lower and deeper, to the real masses"—which I am referring to as the *subaltern*. The term subaltern was popularised in socialist lexicon by Italian communist Antonio Gramsci's *Prison Notebooks*, where from a fascist prison cell he reflected on his experiences in the revolutionary struggles waged by his Party during the First World War and in the 1920s. This period saw both powerful communist-influenced factory committees that were on the threshold of seizing Soviet-style power, and also the rise of fascism that drowned these worker's movements in blood. At our moment in history, characterised by the apocalypse of global warming climate change, the endless, constant deaths of our loved ones in communities poisoned by criminalised drug supplies, and the narcissistic spiralling decline of the US empire and its accompanying capitalist crisis, the ranks of the "lower and deeper," "real masses" are growing. If we fail to recruit those newly fallen subalterns into revolutionary socialism, then we run the risk that they could be swept up by the ready sirens of fascism, or that they'll die alone in ravines, alleyways, and decrepit, isolated apartments. Our task could not be more urgent.

In this chapter I argue for revolutionary socialists to go "lower and deeper" by orienting towards subaltern layers of the working class and other oppressed groups. A *subaltern orientation* locates the protagonist layer of the working class according to their subordinate, exploited place in the capitalist relations of production, as well as by the class consciousness they express through their organic survival activity (inside and outside workplaces) and the cooperative, autonomous forms of organisation they develop. Once we recognise that germ of class consciousness and autonomous initiative in the everyday life of a subaltern group, the role of a revolutionary organisation is to reflect back to the subaltern the positive, resistant elements of their survival strategies so they can see and grow their power. By expressing that power, the subaltern can do more than survive: it can assume its historical role as a vanguard and lead the working class as a whole away from the recuperation of bourgeois hegemony and into cooperation as a revolutionary, counter-hegemonic bloc.

This chapter starts by reviewing the Black Panther Party's focus on the working-class subgroup they called the "lumpenproletariat" in order to argue that "subalternity" is a more useful analytical framework. This is a partial review of the history of social debate about the lumpenproletariat, and an introduction to the rich debate about the aristocracy of labour from different socialist tendencies. I then move on to think through subalternity by reflecting on the dangers and difficulties that Red Braid experienced when centrally involved in subaltern struggle. Throughout this latter part of the chapter, I draw heavily from Gramsci's writing on the subaltern and hegemony, with a reading of his notes on the development of hegemonic blocs. These blocs have been formed through the leadership of capitalist classes that have successfully drawn elements of civil society into state activism to the violent exclusion of others. Dialectically, it is through exclusion that the seemingly powerless and subaltern have the possibility of exercising revolutionary power and leadership over the rest of the working class.

## Aristocracy of labour and lumpenproletariat

In his germinal writings on imperialism, one of Lenin's most central theses was that imperialism corrupts the possibilities of revolution in the imperialist core by buying off the aristocracy of labour with higher wages, access to personal property—which in settler colonial countries include houses and vacation homes—and standards of living closer to those of the bourgeoisie than the average worker of the world. Since then—including through the bloating of that aristocracy to unheard of proportions during the post–World War II US-imperialist expansion and the period of so-called labour peace— socialists have been divided on whether the aristocracy of labour critique is useful or not. Some socialists complain that writing off as counter-revolutionary the most stable and socially powerful group of workers divides and weakens the working class, sabotaging the electoral "political revolution" they promise will bring social democratic reformers to office. Revolutionary socialists disagree and have fought against the influence of the aristocracy of labour in the worker's movement by placing revolutionary protagonism on non-aristocratic layers of the class—a stratum most famously articulated by the Black Panther Party in the 1970s as the lumpenproletariat, or the lumpen.

In his 1970 article "On the Ideology of the Black Panther Party," Panther leader Eldridge Cleaver claims that the "lumpen proletarians," the criminalised underclass, were transforming "from the forgotten people at the bottom of society into the vanguard of the proletariat." Cleaver writes that the lumpen proletariat are:

> All those who have no secure relationship or vested interest in the means of production and the institutions of capitalist society. That part of the "Industrial Reserve Army" held perpetually in reserve; who have never worked and never will; who can't find a job; who are unskilled and unfit; who have been displaced by machines, automation, and cybernation, and who were never "retained or invested with new skills;" all those on Welfare or receiving State Aid.
>
> All the so-called "Criminal Element," those who live by their wits, existing off that which they rip off, who stick guns in the faces of businessmen and say "stick 'em up," or "give it up!" Those who don't even want a job, who hate to work and can't relate to punching some pig's time clock, who would rather punch a pig in the mouth and rob him than punch that same pig's time clock and work for him, those whom Huey P. Newton calls "the illegitimate capitalists." In short, all those who simply have been locked out of the economy and robbed of their rightful social heritage.

In this passage, Cleaver leaps between descriptions of the objective relations of this "lumpen" to capitalist production, and of subjective problems about how lumpens feel about their place in the world and, therefore, how they act. The conclusion he takes from this objective exclusion and subjective rebellion is that "the Working Class is the Right Wing of the Proletariat, and the Lumpenproletariat is the Left Wing."

There are two problems with Cleaver's lumpen theory. First, it is not true that experiences of oppression automatically produce a revolutionary consciousness. Our experiences produce important information that feeds our decisions, including our political commitments. But without a revolutionary framework for interpreting those experiences—and an available revolutionary channel to develop those analyses as collective power—experiences of oppression can break a person. People may turn to acts of desperation, including visiting their pain upon others. In *Black Reconstruction*, W. E. B. Du Bois analyses the reasons that poor whites in the south during slavery, who lived in absolute misery, embraced racism and rejected unity with enslaved Black people. He says that their lack of any tradition or active possibility of organising against their class enemies left poor whites with the compelling feeling that their best available option to save their children from the destiny of eating mud cakes to dull their hunger was to mobilise their whiteness and join the slave catcher police forces. Cleaver does say the Panthers offered a radical path to the lumpen, but he does not explain why this same path is closed to other sections of the Black working class, given the opportunity.

Secondly, Cleaver explains the social attributes of the lumpenproletariat, but he is not clear about what role they play in or against the capitalist mode of production. It is therefore not clear how he thinks the lumpenproletariat can wield power. This problem flows from the ambivalence of the term "lumpen" in Marxist methods of analysis. Rather than a fixed class role within capitalism, the role of the lumpen in socialist strategy has been radically different depending on the circumstances. Marx's assessment of the role of the lumpenproletariat in the Paris Commune of 1871 is far from glowing. He treated the unemployed and criminalised underclass as a "parasite" on the working class and a "scum layer of society." Hardly a vanguard in Marx's eyes. During the Commune, the criminalised, socially dislocated underclass lacked positive group consciousness, and many were recruited into right-wing vigilante groups and counter-revolutionary militias on the basis of their isolation and individualism. In the Chinese Revolution of 1949, Mao estimated the lumpen, which he referred to as the "floating class," as twenty million people, constituting six percent of the population overall. In the protracted armed struggle, those declassed and socially dislocated groups were recruited into revolutionary warfare rather than the boss's hit squads. In the Great Depression of the 1930s in the US and Canada, vast groups of unemployed workers organised collectively, including in and through organisations associated with the Communist Party, in widespread militant struggles against capitalism. They used street battle tactics, mounted mass demonstrations, occupied government buildings, walked off and sabotaged their humiliating public works assignments, and applied unhoused and transient survival strategies like riding freight trains to get around, in service of the struggle. In each case, the lumpen played a different role in revolutionary struggle because the circumstances that produced their unemployment, poverty, social dislocation, and immiseration differed.

The problem with the theory of the lumpen as vanguard of revolutionary struggle is that the lumpen is not an objective group necessary to capitalist production like the working class and capitalist class are, but Cleaver's analysis treats it as though it is. He says that there are contradictions between the working class and the lumpen class, and he also says that the lumpen is part of the working class generally. Reflecting on Cleaver's article in a speech at Boston College, Huey P. Newton said that it may seem incredible to suggest that the lumpen could be a revolutionary vanguard because it was so small a minority in the United States. But he theorised the historical dynamics surrounding and determining the reality of this social group and predicted its growth owing to developments in capitalist production:

> If revolution does not occur almost immediately, and I say almost immediately because technology is making leaps (it made a leap all the way to the moon), and if the ruling circle remains in power the proletarian working class will definitely be on the decline because they will be unemployables and therefore swell the ranks of the lumpens, who are the present unemployables... The attribute that I am interested in is the fact that soon the ruling circle will not need the workers, and if the ruling circle is in control of the means of production the working class will become unemployables or lumpens.

Since Newton gave this speech in 1970, capitalist production has been revolutionised by just such computerisation and technological development, but not exactly as he foresaw.

In *Capital* Volume One, Marx explains that poverty for the many is as much a product of capitalism as is wealth for the few. The accumulation of capital by bosses "makes an accumulation of misery a necessary condition, corresponding to the accumulation of wealth," he writes. Fundamental to the capitalist system is that capital is the social centre: its demands are task-master for the rest of social life. When the working population exceeds the requirements of the labour market, capitalism discards the surplus population into miserable poverty, until (unless) there is a market use for their labour power once again. Marx broke down this "surplus population" of his time into four categories: the "floating," transient, irregularly employed; the "latent" agricultural seasonal workers, pushed from the fields into towns in search of jobs; the "stagnant," who are extremely irregularly employed, which he calls the poor of the working class; and the "paupers" who are unable to work due to age, ability, illness, or demoralisation. Marx says that capitalism makes use of this surplus population by holding sections of it as a "reserve army of labour," available to pour back into the labour market as needed. He predicted that automation in production would produce an increase of pauperization, as "capital increases its supply of labour [in the form of machinery] more quickly than its demand for workers." What he did not anticipate was the increasing internationalisation of the labour market as imperialist governments make free trade pacts with governments of the Global South to ship the labour power of impoverished workers in Mexico, Jamaica, and the Philippines to Canada to work in unfree and fixed-term contracts in farm fields, hotels, and elder and child care, for example. Surplus populations have developed in these contexts who are not a "reserve army of labour" which can be drawn from ready labour markets globally; who are paupers who cannot work but must, regardless of their state of health or age; who are part of the working class structurally but culturally and socially cut out, condemned, shunned.

I am not arguing that Newton and Cleaver's combing out of the hier-archies and contradictions within the overall working class is wrong, but I do think that treating these sub-strata class positions as objective facts or as immutable, which they do sometimes but not always, can be misleading. One of the problems is that the concept of the lumpen ascribes a social fixity to an outcast group that, as Newton explains himself, is far more elastic than fixed: it stretches and expands out and away from the compass of hegemonic power, and it can quickly snap back into the fold. Members of a pauperized surplus population may be unhoused and working a midnight cleaning shift in a Walmart or living squeezed into a one-bedroom apartment with four others and flagging for a roadwork crew. They may be hustling drugs out of a doorway at night and delivering food for UberEats for the lunch rush and picking up their kids from school in the afternoon. And they may feel socially excluded and subaltern at one moment in this complicated day, and an entitled part of civil society at another.

Like Newton and Cleaver, we need to reckon seriously with the problem that there is, in any given historical moment, not just one working class of the world. Some sections of the class have, as Cleaver says, carved out a comfortable niche for themselves, and their outlook and aspirations can become cut off from the interests of the global proletariat and identified instead with empire, white race power, and patriarchy. Lenin explains this as an aspect of the imperialist division of the world and also a matter of class relations. In his book *Imperialism, the Highest Stage of Capitalism*, Lenin says:

> The receipt of high monopoly profits by the capitalists in one of the numerous branches of industry, in one of the numerous countries … makes it economically possible for them to bribe certain sectors of the workers and win them over to the side of the bourgeoisie of a given industry or a given nation against all the others.

And, in pointing out that if the lumpen swelled the ranks of the far-right mob in the Paris Commune, the aristocracy of labour were its "labour lieutenants," Lenin explains:

> This stratum of workers-turned-bourgeois, or the labour aristocracy, who are quite philistine in their mode of life, in the size of their earnings, and in their entire outlook, is … the principal social (not military) prop of the bourgeoisie. For they are the real agents of the bourgeoisie in the working-class movement, the labour lieutenants of the capitalist class, real vehicles of reformism and chauvinism. In the civil war between

the proletariat and the bourgeoisie they inevitably, and in no small numbers, take the side of the bourgeoisie, the "Versailles" against the "Communards."

Unless the economic roots of this phenomenon are understood and its political and social significance is appreciated, not a step can be taken toward the solution of the practical problems of the communist movement and of the impending social revolution.

But Lenin also qualifies this bleak prognostication with a warning against casting too broad a net, as some third worldist socialists have since by declaring the entirety of the working class inside imperialist countries counter revolutionary. Lenin writes, "Neither we nor anyone else can calculate precisely what portion of the proletariat is following and will follow the social chauvinists and opportunists. This will be revealed only by the struggle, it will definitely be decided only by the socialist revolution." The aristocracy of labour, whether expressed through job title and benefits, patriarchal masculinity and ownership over household and family, settler colonial property claims and entitlements, or white supremacist identity politics, is not an objective class relation that expresses the power of one section of the working class over another, but a set of privileges and petty lordship fantasies that form the real basis for the influence of colonialism, imperialism, and capitalist idolatry in the working class movement. Ultimately, as W. E. B. Du Bois argues, such privileges and fantasies can romance workers into identifying with and defending their own alienated and exploited class position. But no matter how consequential, these privileges and fantasies are historical, situational, and fleeting. They may induce white workers to side with their bosses and act as whites, not workers, betraying the ultimate interest of the class, but they amount to *privileges*, not structural power. Their fragile precarity is part of their allure and what arouses such passionate defence from their betrothed.

Lumpen is a framework that assigns structural fixity and permanence to an outcast group that we should instead understand as defined by uncertainty, precarity, and growing social dislocation. I argue that rather than lumpen, we should think of the natural constituency of socialist revolutionaries as *subaltern* groups. As a method of analysing subjective aspects of class structures, *subalternity* is active; demands testing, not assumption; and can include those layers of the class that wield producing power, as well as those who have the proclivity to fight in the streets. As a categorical group, the subaltern is open to adaptation and insists on unity—not a unity around the lowest common denominator of immediate reforms, but a unity that rejects the lies of bourgeois society, that looks to a separate, revolutionary star.

## Subaltern exclusion, subaltern power

Subalternity is objective because it is based on the position of a group within the process of capitalist production and in relation to the capitalist hegemonic bloc. And subalternity is subjective because it is the experience, including the feeling, of a member of a group within that process. This "feeling" and "experience" mean that it is the interaction between objective and subjective that produces subalternity. The subaltern are workers object-ively stationed at the periphery of wage labour, in precarious, low-wage, dangerous jobs that keep them barely making ends meet; they are those unemployed and living unhoused on the streets, dealing drugs to others in their community to get by; they are temporary foreign workers working wage-labour jobs outside of the free labour pool, bound to the employer that holds their visa over their head; they are the Indigenous land defenders refusing the pipeline Canada is trying to push through their territory and fighting to survive on land-based economies outside capitalism. The object-ive position that the subaltern have in common, across their different, often rapidly changing daily survival struggles, is that they do not have access to the benefits of being citizens of empire: they do not own their homes; they do not have vacation properties; they do not have secure jobs with a future; they cannot look forward to a good pension. The subjective part of being subaltern is that they *feel* this exclusion. *Feeling* is not a secondary aspect of history. Individuals experience exclusion through feeling and locate them-selves in a social group through feeling. Subalternity is not a fixed category or position relative to capitalist production; it is a historical problem, always in flux, in relation to the dominant, hegemonic bloc of power at the centre of capitalist society, and it is a matter of struggle.

Radical insecurity characterises so much of the working class—during different seasons for resource workers, different ages for manual labourers and restaurant servers, different family situations for women workers, as well as unpredictable shifts in employment thanks to the chaos of the labour market. To recognise that insecurity and to include workers' responses to their legitimate feelings of social exclusion, we need a more flexible way to locate revolutionary actors in the class. Gramsci says that a "complex of feelings" emerges in both oppressed and oppressor groups through our experiences within and as conduits for structures of cultural and social power. For example, he says the racist ideology of colonisers is nested in feelings of desperate hunger for land that colonialism breeds in the settler. The petite bourgeoisie turns to fascism thanks in large part to their feeling that their social entitlements have been disappointed. And workers structurally excluded, forced to participate in a system that depends on their consent but returns them a raw deal, feel a crisis of representation and turn subaltern, towards revolutionary solutions—should those solutions prove relevant to their lives.

To explain what the subaltern feel excluded from, we need to look first at Gramsci's model of hegemony—a framework he uses to think about how power is exercised by a dominant hegemonic bloc of social groups structured and processed in modern bourgeois society. Gramsci's hegemonic bloc is best imagined as overlapping as well as exclusive spheres of social groups, with a *leading* group at the core, closely circled by the *led*, who participate in the exercise of power and wield some influence through that participation, in order to rule together those excluded by the relationship between the leading and the led, the *subaltern*. Gramsci says the capitalist ruling class has become more powerful and durable in the monopoly capitalist societies of the West thanks to the historical development of the led group, which he calls "civil society." The unity of the ruling bloc, between the leading (capitalist) and led (civil society) groups is what makes the state intelligent and adaptive in a mature capitalist society. This is where there are some limits to anarchist conceptions of the state, which tend to see the state as an externality—an apparatus alien to society. It is more correct to see subaltern groups as external to the bloc of social groups whose motions, driven by the demands of capital, harmonize to tune up, run, and perfect the state, and, through this process, constitute the state as an organism.

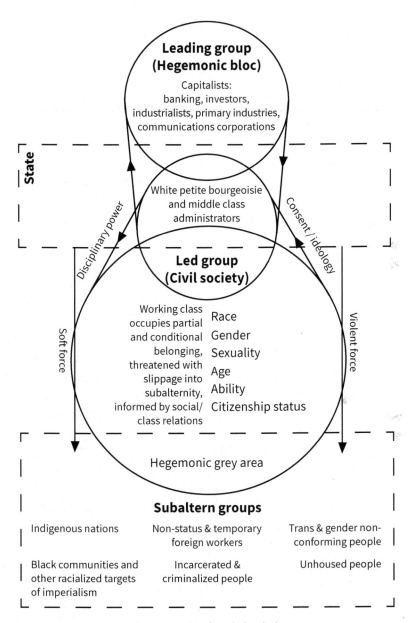

*Hegemony: Leading, led, subaltern*

Gramsci explains that the ruling group dominates by "continually enlarging its compass through the continual appropriation of new spheres of industrial-productive activity." The coming-together and operation of a historic bloc (and the exclusion of others) produces social order, cultural norms, laws and legal reforms, and government policy. The leading group and civil society may come into conflict over differences of opinion about the best ways to govern a particular crisis, but even critical discourse and protest, ultimately, produces a stable and adaptive system that secures the consent of the led and domination over the subaltern. To be excluded from civil society means being excluded from the benefits of imperialist society, which the subaltern can see being enjoyed by others, and it also means being excluded from power and influence in the formation and direction of that society. It means, as Gramsci says, being dominated by "force alone."

Revolutionary alternatives to this hegemonic power bloc, which Gramsci calls "counter hegemony," must come from outside the governing power bloc, but can include those in its grey areas, who can switch sides. However, to assume that those radically excluded from power are automatically a counter-hegemonic, revolutionary force would be naive. A person can be part of a social group that is objectively subaltern but, because of their overlapping membership in non-subaltern groups, may carry themselves into civil society by force of will. Identifying and organising the subaltern is therefore non-schematic and must consider the partial consciousness of subaltern people as well as the multiple centres of a hegemonic bloc. For example, an unemployed, low-income, unhoused white man may cover the distance between his objective, impoverished subalternity, and his feeling of entitlement to civil society-belonging by grasping tight to his whiteness and masculinity. His whiteness may be a paper shield that cannot block the violence done to him by his objective situation, but its illusory nature will not stop him from enthusiastically investing it with the expectations of what he feels he deserves.

Gender informs subalternity through patriarchal structures of capitalist and colonial hegemony, which are mirrored in the internal life of subaltern communities. Working-class women's unwaged housework labour is accumulated by capital as the reproduction of labour power and the biological reproduction of future generations of workers, but often it is the violent hand of a working-class man that disciplines women to clean and keep the home and smooth and maintain community relations. Violence against Indigenous women is a colonial technique of genocide against Indigenous nations and the settler colonial campaign of land theft, but that imperial army more often takes the living form of a white man in the family or community. The social policing of the gender binary and its gendered labour roles is expressed through violence against trans and gender non-conforming people, often carried out by a conspiracy of social exclusion exercised by a bloc of cis men and women in communities and enforced by violent men. In terms of exclusion from social power and belonging, and also in having the latent capacity to flip their victimisation into separate power, women are the subaltern of the subaltern. As we argue in the section of this book about gender power and women's revolution, subaltern women can flip the eliminatory and disciplinary violence they experience into resistant and adversarial reproduction—against capitalism and colonialism, and against patriarchal and colonial gender power as it manifests in subaltern communities.

While subalternity is determined by race, gender, and colonial violence, it is not itself a category of analysis like class, gender, or race, but a *measure*, a relational category that is legible within historical power blocs rather than a fixed subject position within these structures of power. For example, the bourgeois innovation of liberal multiculturalism has forged a new hegemonic bloc in the heart of empire. This "multicultural" bloc has not unseated whiteness from its hereditary, primary position at the core of power but has forged an interdependent nucleus of multinational and multiracial bourgeois power. This nucleus of multinational and multiracial capital has its own spreading logic. For example, while the South Asian petite bourgeoisie in Surrey, the largest suburb in Metro Vancouver, may be excluded socially and culturally from white supremacist bourgeois society as a whole, it is not a matter of partial consciousness that they are invested in Canada's civil society. They have a seat of power that is conditioned by race power, but it is a seat of power all the same. So while civil society is white, it is, through arrangement of hegemonic blocs, also Asian and even Black and Indigenous—though in more limited and incomplete ways.

Colonialism draws a harder border around the circle of hegemonic belonging, excluding the masses of Black and Indigenous people from civil society and relegating them to subalternity generally. Ghanaian anti-colonial theorist Ato Sekyi-Otu argues, in his reading of anti-colonial revolutionary Frantz Fanon's work, that across the "colonial dividing line" there is no civil society because there is no "appeal to a shared community and a common humanity." This dividing line, he says, allows "no public space ... no political relationship, only violence." A revolutionary politics does not seek admission for select members of a subaltern group to hegemonic civil society; it seeks the development of a counter-hegemonic bloc with its own distinct forms of inclusion and exclusion—particularly the violent exclusion of the capitalists and colonisers and their minions. Revolutionary subaltern politics rejects inclusion and integration as goals, and instead works to exacerbate division, clarify and stand upon difference, and articulate difference as a unity through multiplicity.

The relationality of the subaltern category makes it a reflexive rather than predictive or schematic category. Subalternity could be called "alienated being" because it is the social experience of being adrift from hegemonic society. So long as they seek readmission to the civil society that rejected them, subaltern people experience this dislocation as dehumanisation and failure. Many subaltern groups that are outside the civil society bloc because of fleeting historical circumstance may develop subaltern institutions but not assert complete autonomy from the hegemonic order. In our experience in Red Braid, this means that communities in tent cities may work together to barricade a camp and stop police from getting in to destroy their tent-homes, exercising collective subaltern power, but some may jump at the opportunity to meet with government representatives to plead for the state to recognise their humanity, appealing to the hegemonic bloc for admission into civil society. These offers for a seat at the table may come from a politician who has an earnest desire to involve affected people in their decision-making, or it may be a cynical move by city planners to create go-nowhere consultation groups, but the effect is the same because so long as the state remains an instrument of capitalist class rule, it folds these efforts into the smoothing of its own operation. The role of counter hegemonic, revolutionary organisation and politics is to relocate the subaltern subject within a separate sphere of influence, so that their alienated being can fuel the destruction of bourgeois and colonial hegemonic power, rather than its adjustment.

The opening decades of the twenty-first century are a time of tectonic shifts in global power. Gramsci characterises such moments as processes of "transformismo," when hegemonic blocs, globally and locally, are being readjusted, and the whole apparatus of civil society becomes especially attentive and alert for useful social innovation and adaptation that can be brought into use to secure the longevity and stability of bourgeois rule. By looking at the subaltern, and particularly at those groups in its grey area, we can see that hegemony is never a final, totalized social form, but rather a historical movement between social classes, including the subaltern. Within this broad social arrangement, the subaltern are particularly well positioned to strike out from hegemonic combination and create revolutionary counter hegemonies, a potential danger to hegemonic power that the capitalist state is armed to undo and oppose, using violent as well as soft force.

## The danger of the "soft force" of state power

Gramsci considers the particular character of subalternity that we are discussing here to be specific to modern capitalist society. Exclusion from civil society would not matter if bourgeois rule were not organised so powerfully through a sophisticated civil society. And it would not matter so much if a group were subaltern but did not depend upon capitalist production and its social order for survival and social belonging. Gramsci describes this state of exclusion and disorganisation as historically developed. In the *Prison Notebooks*, he writes:

> The modern state abolishes many autonomies of the subaltern classes—but certain forms of the internal life of the subaltern classes are reborn as parties, trade unions, cultural associations. The [fascist] dictatorship abolishes these forms of class autonomy as well, and it tries hard to incorporate them into the activity of the state: in other words, the centralization of the

whole life of the nation in the hands of the ruling class becomes frenetic and all-consuming.

The historical process Gramsci points to here is not a switch of centralised bourgeois power that is turned on at a certain moment with the emergence of industrial capitalism; it is a gradual, partial, and incomplete process. Historian E. P. Thompson describes the disorganisation of such previously self-actualized subaltern groups into civil society's sub-stratum in his 1967 article, "Time, Work-Discipline, and Industrial Capitalism." Thompson explains that the introduction of time as a bourgeois method of organising the day disorganised the whole living world of workers in England. Before industrial capitalism, the measurement of time had been set by the "familiar processes in the cycle of work or domestic chores," where the day was measured by sunrise and sunset and the year by planting and harvest times. Thompson observes that such "task-oriented" time tended to dissolve the difference between "work" and "life," intermingling social and productive labour. Clock-time did exist at the outset of the industrial revolution in England—time pieces mostly hung from clock towers to ring out as a symbol of a power from outside the everyday world calling parishioners to worship— but they were not synchronised between towns and depended on sundials for their approximate setting. It was mechanisation and the degree of labour synchronisation it demanded that, in turn, conjured the synchronisation of time and choreographed the whole social world of the English working class. It's not for nothing that Luddites distinguished themselves by their violent assault on timepieces as a social expression of the domination of the machine over England, or, as Marx puts it, of dead labour over the living.

What Gramsci calls the "modern state" did not put an end to class divisions; it formalised them through legal and social recognition and systems of universal order that measured and set the pulse of social and even individual existence, drowning out the natural rhythms of the cosmos with the metronome of capital. Capital's abolition of Gramsci's "many autonomies of the subaltern classes" is not the abolition of subalternity. This new, "all-consuming" power eliminates not the existence of the poor, but their autonomous self-recognition, self-confidence, and self-organisation. The abolition of the many autonomies of subaltern groups is the most important fundamental of the bourgeois state system of domination. In a country with a highly developed civil society, the most everyday form of domination is through what I will call "soft force," the offering of improvement for the everyday needs of the subaltern by deferring power to civil society groups.

But behind the exercise of soft force there is always the first and most fundamental form of the modern state's power: direct violence. This violence is typical to colonialism and imperialism, but also readily deployed against workers in times of capitalist crisis. In a 1924 newspaper article, "Democracy and Fascism," Gramsci explains that the first acts of Italian fascism in power was to destroy remaining workers' autonomies:

> The sacking of subversive workers; the exiling or assassination of workers' and peasants' "leaders"; the ban on meetings; the prohibition on staying outdoors after working hours; the obstacle thus placed in the way of any "social" activity on the part of the workers; and then the destruction of the Chambers of Labour and all other centres of organic unity of the working class and peasantry, and the terror disseminated among the masses—all this had more value than a political struggle through which the working class was stripped of the "rights" which the Constitution guarantees on paper.

Such state-organised violence is not limited to fascism in its mid-twentieth century, European garb. The most devastating aspect of Canada's *Indian Act* was its provisions—a germ of which can be found in nearly every clause—that sought to attack and destroy the sovereignties of Indigenous nations. The *Indian Act* banned the Coastal potlatch because it was a superstructure that facilitated economic and social exchange outside of capitalist production, sovereign from settler society. It banned the self-organisation and gatherings of Indigenous people in ceremony and for purposes of political expression. It outlawed even the use of Band Council monies to hire lawyers for the pursuit of legal reform in Canada's court system.

In most instances, direct violence is wrapped in the velvet glove of soft force, a necessary, absorptive bulk that gives social form to state power.

Mobilising Frantz Fanon's critique to analyse Canada's reconciliation frameworks as revised forms of colonial power, Dene scholar Glen Coulthard argues that "a colonial system of governance that does not rely entirely on the execution of force must entice Indigenous peoples to identify with the profoundly asymmetrical forms of recognition either imposed on or granted to them by the colonial-state and society." These forms of recognition are "determined by and in the interests of the oppressor" and designed to dangle before the subaltern the fantastic hope of being admitted to civil society. Coulthard's focus is on "master-sanctioned" forms of recognition as cultural, ideological, and symbolic balm that promises—and cannot but fail—to heal the "internalised ... derogatory images imposed on them by their colonial 'masters'" by killing the Indian and revealing the assimilated white child within."[1] Coulthard's critique is devastating, and it leaves the lies of reconciliation behind as a smashed and wrecked myth. But while Coulthard acknowledges that the psychological realm of struggle alone will not end colonial and capitalist domination, the material problems of settler colonial and capitalist domination over the wretched of this earth under our feet are underemphasised in his text.

Material conditions like being unhoused, hungry, malnourished, sleep deprived by the cold rain and constant danger, taking stimulants to stay awake and guard your possessions, walking until your feet rot and stink of a dying limb attached to your body and being: these are words in the concrete language of bourgeois society that forge the subjective realm of subaltern inferiority. The state's soft force technique of denying or conditioning access to the necessary means of subsistence defines the terrain of struggle over the exercise or abolition of subaltern autonomies. This everyday terrain of survival—for control over the necessary means of subsistence—is where we fight for control against the totality of state actors in subaltern community struggles.

## Subaltern autonomies at Anita Place tent city

After two years of struggle, the City of Maple Ridge broke up Anita Place tent city in the spring of 2018. It was a moment that demonstrated the assault on

1    Glen Coulthard, *Red Skin White Masks* (Minneapolis and London: University of Minnesota Press, 2014).

subaltern autonomies the modern state must regularly commit in order to maintain its centralised system of domination. Anita Place formed because unhoused people had been displaced from an earlier tent city to an ad hoc, one-room homeless shelter, which the provincial government promised would be temporary. Eighteen months later, that same government announced they were closing the shelter and returning the forty people warehoused there to the streets. Since the last tent city closed down, I had been organising on-again-off-again meetings in the community on behalf of Red Braid, and all anyone ever talked about was starting another tent city. With the shelter closure on the immediate horizon, a lot more people started showing up at meetings, which we held in the shelter sometimes, and then, after the shelter operators forbade it, at the nearby McDonald's. A couple weeks before the shelter was scheduled to close, we marched down the street, removed a section of fencing around an abandoned, city-owned lot, and set up tents.

Self-organised and politically self-conscious tent cities have two interdependent political and social meanings. Like spontaneous, organic tent cities—which tend to emerge at the point of least resistance from police forces that inadvertently steer a critical mass of unhoused people together in a certain location by attacking them everywhere else—organised tent cities have a practical, economic function for unhoused people. In a tent city of any form, unhoused people have sanctuary from the daily displacement visited upon them by the armed forces of the state should they come to rest in any other alley, doorway, park, or under any other bridge or awning in a city. All tent cities also have the economic benefit of relief from the inevitable theft and destruction of your personal possessions by municipal workers and law enforcement if you fall asleep for a moment or leave your tent or cart—carrying your medication, ashes of lost loved ones, photographs of your children, clothing, blankets, and food—to use a bathroom.

But self-organised tent cities have other benefits that come out of their more complex and contested meaning—as a political and organisational form that subaltern people can use to reorganise their "many autonomies," disincorporated from the activities of the state. In "Democracy and Fascism," Gramsci writes, "Reorganising the working class...means

in practice 'creating' a new force and causing it to intervene on the political scene: a force which today is not being taken into account, as if it no
longer existed. Organisation and politics are thus converted one into the
other." The character of tent cities, either as police-organised low-points in
the ground that gather subaltern people like water, or as forms of subaltern
autonomy, depends not on the existence of the tent city, but on who holds
power within it. The police were an obvious and occasional force that contested the autonomous power of subaltern people over Anita Place tent city.
Police attacked and dismantled peoples' barricades and tore down fences,
performed raids and arrests, rushed the passageways between tents, and
surveilled, harassed, and intimidated people in their tent homes. But the
more pernicious threat was the seductive embrace of the camp by softer,
more malleable state forces—the health care and social service workers that
offered much needed material support to the desperately poor, unhoused
people in the camp.

After the city tried and failed to win a court injunction to break up the
tent city with violent force, soft force state actors swept in with offers of
help. Suddenly this town beyond the limits of Vancouver's progressive
civil society was awash in social programs. Harm reduction vans rolled
up and handed out crates of needles and Naloxone kits. Nurses handed
out Band-Aids and occasionally did wound care for people with infected
abscesses or trench foot—though never set up an actual health care tent.
Community workers with knuckle tattoos from housing NGOs lured
people into consultation meetings where they set up peer harm reduction programs plied with seemingly bottomless government funding. Soon
they rolled in a mobile bathroom and shower trailer and gave thousands
of dollars to one shift manager in the camp, who was immediately corrupted by the unaccountable position of power and began skimming off
the top of the wages for bathroom cleaning shifts, sending the authority
and credibility of the whole operation, in the minds of residents of the
camp, down the toilet.

Red Braid organisers, including those of us who were residents of the
tent city, were attuned to the dangers of soft force to misdirect subaltern
people out of their autonomous self-organisation and into the influence of

state actors. But we found it impossible to argue against government funding. Residents of the tent city were, obviously, desperately poor. We simply
could not convince people to turn down government funding, in the form
of stipends that amounted to approximately $15 per hour, for cleaning and
maintaining the camp bathroom, for distributing health care resources like
harm reduction supplies, and for weekly clean-up of camp. But this money,
and the good-feeling and individual trust-building relationships with state
actors that it facilitated, worked into and calcified the joints of the tent city as
an autonomous organism of subaltern power. Every point of action needed
for the self-sustaining survival of the camp became influenced and then
dependent upon that state support.

   We can see the link here between the problem of material power, or practised, everyday mastery over the necessary means of subsistence, and the
self-consciousness and self-confidence of a social group capable of wielding power. On the face of it, the problem was that the soft force wielded
by state actors led residents of the tent city to relate to the reproduction of
everyday life—the regular maintenance of the camp—through an alienated
system of management. At the beginning of the tent city, when the antagonism between the residents and the whole state apparatus was clear and
felt by all, the camp leadership set out rules saying that everyone staying in
the camp had to contribute to the wellbeing of the whole camp by doing
security shifts guarding against police raids, cleaning up garbage, cooking
food, and serving on the political council. But the more state actors were
able to exercise soft force within the camp, the less residents felt that the
camp depended on their active participation, and the more they felt an
expectant resentment of the camp. It's like there were two tent cities at the
same site: one a resistant, self-organised, autonomous subaltern institution,
and the other a government camp, which some residents started to refer to
cynically as a "FEMA Camp" (after the Federal Emergency Agency in the
US). The greater the role that state actors played in operating the camp, the
more residents expected the state to operate the camp, and the more their
resentment grew that the state was providing them *only* with a mud pit to
slip through and a tent to sleep in. If the government was pouring money
into the tent city, why not fund actual housing?

From these calcifying joints of self-organisation at the points of regular maintenance and collective care grew a cancer of resentment that poisoned the culture of the tent city, disorganising the instrument of resistance and turning subaltern rage inwards. During the last few months of the tent city, higher level and more organised drug dealers, motivated by their investments in their illicit capitalist economy, played an increasingly central role in the social and political life of the subaltern society. They sent debt collectors into tents within the camp, a practice that the elected camp council had previously outlawed, and rumours spread about terrible things happening within the camp. It became more and more difficult to bring residents to meetings, and few trusted people were willing to sit on the leadership council because they were wary of the dealers who ruled from the shadows. Gangsterism, male violence, and white racial terror are forms taken when the state abolishes subaltern autonomies.

That was why the tent city ended in fire. In the last weeks of Anita Place tent city there was a plague of fires, including sensational explosions as propane tanks went up inside tents. Some of those fires were certainly lit by anti-homeless vigilantes who sensed the vulnerability of the camp and seized their opportunity to burn it down, as they had always threatened. Others were probably the result of the individual carelessness and disinterest of residents who were no longer paying attention. And some may even have been the result of overzealous enforcement actions ordered by drug dealers. In any case, these were all symptoms of the problem—that state actors had, through the petty corruptions of soft force, disorganised the precious autonomies of the subaltern.

### Conclusion: Creating subaltern institutions and building counter-hegemonic power

As a method of defining a revolutionary subject or constituency, subalternity has the advantage of recognising the significant problem of the aristocracy of labour without discounting them out of hand, as though that relative privilege was a problem of structural class power rather than a problem of corruption and of consciousness made partial by favoured status. The truth is that the great majority of workers who circle capitalist civil society inclusion do not draw much actual benefit from its corrupting promises. When the power of the subaltern grows, its revolutionary program will become more feasible and appear as an alternative to capitalist inclusion to the majority of the working class, which is otherwise drawn to the capitalist-powered flame of the aristocracy of labour. This approach allows for coalition and unity across the working class as a whole, but on the terms set by the subaltern, mobilising the most oppressed sections of the class as political leaders.

"Subaltern" is, like "state," better thought of as a verb than a noun: an activity filled with political meaning; not a static social group. But that does not mean that subaltern groups do not really exist in the real world or that their existence is not politically contested. For the state as a whole, the subaltern is a group to be disorganised and repressed, kept in limbo in hegemony's grey area, or locked up, deported, abandoned, or condemned to death. The crisis of authority that is accompanying the decline of the US empire and the rise of climate and capitalist crises has more layers of the working class slipping into subalternity, and their responses to their social dislocation and suffering are not automatically revolutionary socialist. Without revolutionary organisations that can discuss these questions with them, what Gramsci calls the "loss of prestige" they suffer could lead them into terrible, desperate politics like fascism, or, more likely, into deeper social isolation, despair, addiction, and doom.

Gramsci explains that the self-activity of the subaltern is necessarily "episodic," "fragmented," and "defensive." But these descriptions of weakness should not be mistaken for defeat. If the subaltern can develop institutions of their own—class-independent institutions built radically apart from hegemonic power including civil society—then they are no longer subaltern. The development of self-conscious politics and autonomous organisations transforms them from an excluded, outcast group into the leading group of a new, emergent hegemonic bloc, autonomous from the dominant bloc and contesting its power.

We saw the work of developing political vision and autonomous infrastructure around the defensive self-activity of the subaltern, which we call their survival struggles, as Red Braid's central reason for being.

But there are other questions left to answer here. What about those regulators who showed up to exercise soft force in the Maple Ridge tent city? If the working class as a whole is not a lost cause despite the corruption of its aristocratic layers, what are we to make of this regulatory middle class? The problem of the middle class, including its left-wing movements, is the topic of the next chapter.

# Middle-class insurrection

Ivan Drury

It is no longer innovative to propose that the 2020s will be a decade of capitalist crisis. It occupies the minds of politicians, activists, and thinkers across the political spectrum. Those in the driver's seat of the US empire know it, from the politically conservative editors of *The Economist* who distinguish themselves by their ideological marriage to the present status quo, to the militant, nationalist fanatics at the US state department. And millions of radical anti-capitalist young people have intuited the depths of the crisis, leaping boldly into the knuckle between the past and future and lighting the institutions of US hegemony aflame in the heart of the empire.

In the first half of 2020, behind a radical Black police and prison abolitionist leadership, these young fighters set symbolic and sometimes literal fire to the streets of every major city in the US. North of the border, in response to an inspired call to "Shut Down Canada" from the Wet'suwet'en nation, young militants led by Indigenous sovereigntists blockaded Canada's commodity infrastructure. Highways, railways, and ports all fell, for a wonderful moment, one by one and all together. These movements cracked the monolithic facade of capitalist and colonial society in Canada and the US and showed that the inertia of people in motion can, once started and united in a great mass, overcome any obstacle.

Those in the church of spontaneity have celebrated the movements of 2020 as proof that organisation is unnecessary at best and at worst, inevitably a mechanism of authoritarian control held over the freedom-seeking masses. This position is elaborated in an article published at the end of 2020 by the *Endnotes* collective, a group important to the "communization" tendency in socialism that sees revolutionary transformation as imminent and not a distant goal. In "Onwards Barbarians," *Endnotes* goes beyond their usual anti-organisation rhetoric and cites sociologist Asef Bayat as describing the uprisings of 2007–2020 as "non-movements…the collective action of dispersed and unorganised actors." This pessimistic and, frankly, liberal read of Indigenous land defence against Canada and of the months-long George Floyd and Breonna Taylor uprisings against the afterlives of slavery has rubbed even many communization-heads the wrong way. But it is the logical outcome of their fundamentals—that revolution is everywhere, in every spontaneous action, and therefore inevitable and also fleeting.

The radical mass movements of 2020 were, in fact, organised by well-established leaderships. They were spontaneous in the sense that mass movements are always spontaneous; they were expressions of the coming-together of innumerable historical forces that found life through the voluntary and passionate actions of millions of people. No single organisation coordinated pre-planned events or advertised or outreached to get people to come to the streets. People flooded into the streets through a spontaneous momentum that exceeded the capacity or intelligence of any organisation. But that does not mean formal organisations and political leaderships were irrelevant to the shape, direction, and destiny of these movements, even in their original explosions. The movement in response to the police killings of George Floyd in Minneapolis and Breonna Taylor in Louisville, Kentucky spread rapidly to 400 separate cities in every state in the US because it was buoyed and coordinated by institutions that are inheritors of the Black freedom struggle, ranging from police and prison abolitionist groups to Black churches. Alongside these formal organisations were also militants, who philosopher Idris Robinson refers to in a talk in Seattle, delivered in the midst of the conflagration, as the "avant-garde who spearheaded [the movement], we set it off, we initiated it."[1] Robinson's point

1    Idris Robinson, "How It Might Should Be Done," *Ill Will Editions* (August 16, 2020), https://illwill.com/how-it-might-should-be-done.

is that the spontaneous movement spread from that spark. The movement was not *led* by a particular group, but its spontaneity included organisations. And the broad political spectrum and multiple class composition of the organisations in the movement generated a politically wide ranging and multi-class movement, even in those initial days and weeks of street fighting. As Robinson says, "If you were out on the streets, you know you saw people of all different kinds. Different bodies, different shapes, different genders, manifested themselves in the streets together."

The sparks of the movement and its initial flame were multiple, organised, spontaneous, and multi-class in agenda, composition, and leadership, but once a clear leadership emerged, its middle-class character was more certain, and its outcomes more reformist. The tremendous power of the George Floyd and Breonna Taylor uprising caused, according to pollsters, a jump from forty-two percent to fifty-two percent in support for the Black Lives Matter movement in the early summer of 2020, with eighty-four percent approval from registered Democrat voters.[2] Progressive politicians, legal reformers, and policy wonks responded by leaping into the fray and seizing the opportunity to affect policy change, watering down the revolutionary agenda of abolishing police and prisons into practical, piecemeal reforms of defunding, reforming, transforming, and even renaming police.[3] In most cases, movement demands for radical transformation of white supremacist, capitalist society as a whole—levered by stripping power from that society's violent, murderous law enforcement wing—were filtered by middle-class advocates and carried by progressive politicians into milquetoast reforms like banning choke holds, funding new police oversight committees, and hiring more doctors to ride-along with cops. A year and a half later, the most ambitious of the reformist programs, including the Minneapolis Mayor's historic promise to dissolve the police department that executed George

2    Civiqs, "Black Lives Matter," accessed December 7, 2021, https://civiqs.com/ results/black_lives_matter?annotations=true&uncertainty=true&zoomIn=true; Nate Cohn and Kevin Quealy, "How Public Opinion Has Moved on Black Lives Matter," *The New York Times*, June 10, 2020.

3    Tobias Winright, "Defund the Police' Hits a Wall of Reality in Major U.S. Cities," *America Magazine*, June 23, 2021, https://www.americamagazine.org/politics-society/2021/06/23/defund-police-reform-new-york-240918.

Floyd, had collapsed. The wave of excited public opinion these reforms rode in on crashed and trickled out, and with it, the usefulness of the issue for politicians.

The middle-class actors that carried the politics of street movements into absorbable, reform-sized pieces are the non-government organisations, political parties, progressive churches, and radical lawyer groups that have been part of social movements since the development of monopoly capitalism in the West. Such middle-class organisations have often played critical roles tethering public opinion to the tides of street movements, increasing the influence of even revolutionary movements. But they are not, of themselves, revolutionary and cannot, independently, represent a revolutionary rupture with the dominant order. Lacking similarly powerful and stable autonomous organisations, subaltern people in the uprising had only the weapon of spontaneity, which outpaces any organisation in the moment (even, as we saw repeatedly, the organised police), but which has the disadvantage of lacking the cohesion and focus of a self-conscious political unity and the long-term capacity for strategic action of formal organisations.

Middle-class groups, including progressive NGOs, social service groups, and radical lawyers, are part of "the ensemble of private organisations" that Antonio Gramsci calls "civil society"—the articulating and adaptive layer of the ruling hegemonic bloc which "have the function of organising the consent" of subordinate groups within the dominant order. The prevalence of these civil society groups during and after the George Floyd and Breonna Taylor uprising, alongside the emergence of the petit bourgeois Trumpist far right, points to the centrality of the middle class in the organisation of social life in the US and Canada. And our inability to stop either one from using and abusing the historical crises of our moment says a lot about the disorganisation and pacification of the subaltern working class over the last few decades.

The great movements of 2020 were made up of different classes, but the challenges to governments that followed—the play-acted Capitol Hill siege of January 6 and the defund-the-police legislation coups mounted in dozens of city council chambers throughout the US and Canada—are of middle-class character. Middle classes have their own grievances—dissatisfactions with their treatment under an existing order—but they cannot have their own class-independent political program because middle classes, by their very nature, do not have their own material base for existence. They play an administrative role in capitalist production on behalf of capital, as the managers of finance, distribution, or social life. That means that middle-class movements are, regardless of the militancy of their rhetoric, essentially lobbyist uprisings—with the important proviso that the middle class can change sides and support a rising revolutionary class. In historic moments of revolutionary rupture, middle classes have sometimes risked themselves along with the rising class, but at other times they have fallen in line with the old power. During the powerful, initial moment of the movements of 2020, working-class, Black, Indigenous peoples' rage carried the movement over every obstacle. But since then, through the autumn and winter of the movement, the historic disorganisation of subaltern people has meant that the middle class stepped over the subaltern, taking leadership and positioning themselves to misrepresent and steer the energy of the people into the dead end of state reform projects.

Our answer to the historic crisis of subaltern disorganisation is to embrace the task of building autonomous organisations, separate and independent from NGO, legal, and reformer organisations. While demands to abolish or defund the police, for example, may garner the support of people and groups from different class backgrounds, there are fundamental differences obscured by that common slogan. Working- and middle-class currents may both agree with taking funding away from the cops, but middle-class reformers look to the state to organise the redirection of funding from the police to other regulatory institutions. Working-class and Indigenous revolutionaries, however, want to disempower the police in order to build their own independent power. The true class character of a multi-class movement that includes the leadership of insurgent middle classes cannot be determined by the class of its participant-groups alone. To assess the class meaning of middle-class dominated movements, we must ask whose power they are fighting to build.

This chapter begins by defining the middle class as a group of wage workers situated between the capitalist and working classes that administers the rule of capital over human society. Emergent since the Great Recession of 2007, the radical left wing of the middle class expresses the radical dissatisfaction of a new generation of middle-class actors born during the decline of the US empire, but, without a corresponding working class revolt to give it materially separate power base, this middle class rage cannot but point back to the recuperation of the bourgeois colonial state. Ultimately, I argue that revolutionary socialists should not entirely dismiss the middle-class insurgency, particularly not of the Black and Indigenous middle class. But to leap over the limits imposed by middle-class leaderships, which are, in the end, reformist state actors, we must centre and follow the leadership not of the middle-class intelligentsia, but of the subaltern.

## Defining the middle class

As an analytical term, "middle class" has been contaminated by the mainstream contemporary language of news broadcasters and politicians who use it as an appeal to the imagined majority of the population of the US and Canada. Members of this group may feel they are middle class because they live non-political lives, neither imperilled nor powerful, and they may feel they *deserve* such lives and resent the threat of coming misfortune that is always on the horizon. The more accurate term might be "middle income," but the discourse surrounding the populist use of middle class goes further than income to stand also for social and historical middle-ness. The members of this happy group are promised insulation from excessive excitement and danger by swaddling in the thick polyester down of good jobs, the humble intergenerational investment of home ownership, and safe streets should they find themselves on a downtown sidewalk between the bar and their car. This hegemonic use of the term middle class—which, in reality, describes the lives of almost no one—is one I reject as a worse-than-useless framework for understanding the movement of classes and groups in capitalist production.

Even in the realm of Marxist political theory, the term middle class is contested and often confused. In their 1977 article that coined the term "professional-managerial class" (PMC) as a new "true" class with an independent class character, Barbara and John Ehrenreich set out from a definition of class that drops the indispensable framing context of capitalist production. First, they cite venerable Marxist historian E. P. Thompson's definition of class: that "we cannot have two distinct classes, *each with an independent being* [emphasis added]," without understanding each's existence as constituted by their relationship with the other. Then the Ehrenreichs reframe Thompson's definition in their own words. They drop the relationship of the social group to its "independent being" and recast class as "defined by actual relations between groups of people, not formal relations between people and objects." Marx explains in *The Grundrisse* that it is in the "definite relations" between the different elements of capitalist production (production, distribution, exchange, and consumption) that class operates as animator, connecting these images into dynamic movement like individual frames wound into a reel.[4] For Marx, the actual relations between groups of people are created through the relationship between the different component parts of capitalist production—which these different groups of people (classes) represent. In order to position their PMC as an independent class like the working and capitalist class, the Ehrenreichs take capitalism out of the equation.

What is special about class as a way of understanding the world under capitalism is that classes are not groups of people doing groups-of-people things. For Marx, classes are groups-of-people that act as groups-of-capital. The relationship between the capitalist class and the working class is only a relationship between groups of people insofar as these opposing groups represent their role under capitalism. Capital is a great bodysnatcher, an alien force that excels in occupying and profoundly influencing the activities and consciousness of people according to its interests. In *Theories of Surplus Value*, Marx explains that the capitalist rules over the worker "only in so far as he *is* 'capital,' his domination is only that of materialised labour over living labour, of the labourer's product over the labourer himself."[5] Marx, in this sentence, introduces a slippage between the activities and the figures that make capital exist in the living world. The boss becomes capital when dominating the worker, and through that contact, the worker's act of working becomes

4    Marx, *Grundrisse*, 36.
5    Marx, *Theories of Surplus Value*, vol. 1, 390.

capital. The fingers of capitalist power reach into the bodily activity of the worker, so the worker *as capital* dominates the worker *as person*. Marx is attributing a super agency to capital here. Capital employs the worker as an instrument to produce surplus value, making the worker a person channelling an abstract force that possesses them.

That means that people exist in capitalist production not as people but as the people-form of stations in the circuit of production—as personifications. In his classic 1962 article "Factory and Society," Italian autonomist theorist Mario Tronti argues that the working class exists simultaneously in two worlds. World-one is a human, natural world of concrete, living labour, where the society of the collective worker exists for its own ends, through its own organic activity producing the material and relationships of life. World-two is capital's world of abstract, accumulated labour, where the thick fog of the "collective capitalist" metastasizes the energetic limbs of the worker as variable capital. As a class in the capitalist relations of production, then, we can say that the actual relations that define people in the world as members of the working class are duelling: workers produce concrete labour in the world of human beings as the condition for their personification of abstract labour in the world of capital. The actual relations that define people as members of the capitalist class are more simplistic, and I can quote Marx directly here: capitalists are those who "hold power as the personification of capital."[6]

What force in these "actual relations" does the new middle class personify? Management? Management is a *task* delegated and adapted within the social factory produced through this elaborate class choreography, a task that must be assigned, therefore relying on the authority of the assigner. In the 1979 South End Press book published to critically discuss the Ehrenreich PMC article, Erik Olin Wright argues that professional intellectuals "do not have a class identity in their own right: their class character is determined strictly by their location between classes." In his book published about the same time, he says the class position of managers is "contradictory" and that they "may be in more than one class simultaneously." Wright's analytical trick allows for the social operation of a special class group of wage

6    Marx, *Theories of Surplus Value*, vol. 1, 389.

labourers (even if salaried) whose job is to ensure the reproduction of capital, including the disciplining and regulation of other wage labourers. But "it's complicated" is not a satisfactory answer to the question of what role the new middle class plays in global capitalist production, because if we say their class location is everywhere, it does not help us understand which side they're on. And it is the tremendous influence of the middle class—including in the streets but also in the emergence of democratic socialism in parliamentary politics in the US (and to a lesser extent, in Canada)—that makes this question critical.

## The role of the middle class in the capitalist state

Some writers have sought to downplay and dismiss the significance of the growth and influence of the middle class, characterising the disappointingly minor social status and low wages suffered by young middle-class recruits as the "proletarianization" of the middle class, saying, "we're all working class now." This Jacobin-ite analysis seems to be taking "proletarianization" as a loan word from Marx's analysis of the shattering of the social and economic bases of pre-capitalist classes, filtering it through bourgeois bemoaners of the loss of postwar purchasing power by privileged, white sections of the working class, and using it to explain the feeling that young middle-class people have about their own loss of prestige.[7] A prominent new labour writer, Alex Press, has argued that the PMC is an unhelpful or even reactionary miscategorisation of workers, insisting that all people who must sell their labour for wages, including salaries, are workers.[8] But these apologists for

7   Nicki Lisa Cole, "Proletarianization Defined: Shrinking of the Middle Class," *ThoughtCo.*, last updated July 3, 2019, https://www.thoughtco.com/proletarianization-3026440; Joel Kotkin, "The US Middle Class Is Turning Proletarian," *Forbes*, February 16, 2014, https://www.forbes.com/sites/joelkotkin/2014/02/16/the-u-s-middle-class-is-turning-proletarian/?sh=358160236256.

8   Alex Press, "Forget Your Middle Class Dreams," *Jacobin Magazine*, March 29, 2019, https://jacobin.com/2019/03/middle-class-white-collar-unions-kickstarter; Alex Press, "On the Origins of the Professional-Managerial Class: An Interview with Barbara Ehrenreich," *Dissent Magazine*, October 22, 2019, https://www.dissentmagazine.org/online_articles/on-the-origins-of-the-professional-managerial-class-an-interview-with-barbara-ehrenreich.

the middle class overlook the social role these social managers play in relationship to the subaltern working class, and its subservient role in the broad administration of finance capital.

Despite his deft handling of the disorientations of the Ehrenreichs, the quirk about capitalism's managers that Wright trips over is that, as a total system of production, capitalism assigns managers to control traffic at intersections of public streets, as well as to operate the glass elevators between the floors of financial towers. As geographer David Ley argues, the middle class is not a "unitary" class; it is made up of a *free-market group* of private-sector managers, professionals, and sales workers and a *public-sector group* of social workers, teachers, health care workers. Both are upper-level service workers, with the private-sector group managing capitalist financial services directly and the public-sector group managing the society necessary for the everyday operation of those financial services. To adopt another framework set out by Mario Tronti, both subgroups of the middle class come to exist through the management of capitalist production. The free-market group manages the reproduction of capital itself, and the public-sector group manages the "socially combined worker"—Tronti's term for the working class as its lives are known and categorised by capital. Tronti sees the socially combined worker as variable capital walking around in the world, not as people doing people things. That means the "public-sector" subgroup of the middle class also manages the reproduction of capital itself, as the representative of the interests of workers *as* capital (not as people) in the social world of capitalist production.

So the capitalist class personifies capital as a whole process, the working class personifies abstract labour, and the middle class personifies *the state*— which is not actually a class at all but a structure that serves and administers the power of a ruling bloc. This brings us to another term-definition problem because there is also no end of misunderstandings about what the state is. The classic Marxist definition, in Lenin's review of Engels' thinking, is:

> The state is a product and a manifestation of the *irreconcilability* of class antagonisms. The state arises where, when, and insofar as class antagonisms objectively *cannot* be reconciled. And,

conversely, the existence of the state proves that class antagonisms are irreconcilable [emphasis in original].[9]

Lenin's image of the state haunts the imagination of radical activists a
hundred years later; it is a "power standing *above* society" that consists of
"special bodies of armed men" which serve the ruling class, an alien force
that hovers over human society, lashing out to strike down the disobedient—
an ever-present, scaly and violent force. But Lenin's state is an anachronism
belonging to a semi-feudal Tsarist Russia, not a monopoly capitalist and
bourgeois democratic world of plastic speech and identities. This is the point
made by Italian communist leader Antonio Gramsci, who referred to the
Tsarist state as "primordial and gelatinous," its preponderance shutting the
door to its formal halls of power against the influence of people outside its
gates. In the monopoly capitalist societies of the West, however, the state
not only incorporated upper stratums of citizens into its management of
class antagonisms to the benefit of the ruling class, but as imperialist nation
states continued their sophisticated social development, the gap between
civil society and state narrowed. That narrowing means the state became
less of a remote armoured ship hovering, lasers at the ready, above human
society, and more of a self-preservation action mobilised by the members
of civil society, which is ultimately an unconscious defence of the interests
of the collective capitalist. Gramsci argues that "every citizen is a [state]
functionary if he is active in social life along the lines outlined by the state
government" and "every homogeneous social element is 'state' or represents the state insofar as it adheres to its program." He insists, "The state is
organised society itself." The more organised the society, the more far reaching and intimately enacted is the state.

In the nation states of the imperialist West, the state has developed
beyond a repressive apparatus, becoming composed of a far more adaptive
set of social gaskets around hammering pistons, electric lines shot through
the walls of its whole social structure. The state in the West never surren-
dered the power to kill, but it added to its arsenal the power to protect the

9    See Vladimir Lenin, "State and Revolution," in *Selected Works of VI Lenin*, vol. 1
      (Moscow: Progress Publishers, 1977).

lives of even the poor, even when it meant restricting the power wielded by individual capitalists. In *Capital* Volume One, Marx wrote that "factory legislation ... is ... just as much the necessary product of large-scale industry as cotton yarn, self-actors and the electric telegraph." Because capital exploits the living labour power of the working class, it demands the wellbeing of the working class—exactly to the degree that this exploited class's wellbeing corresponds to the efficient and continuous function of the capitalist circuit of production and not beyond. It is not (only) because of the threat of revolution that bourgeois governments pass regulations that redistribute wealth from the rich to the poor through socially regulatory social programs, or that they pass factory legislation restricting the profits of particular capitalists by limiting the amount of coal smoke they can belch into the atmosphere or the age of children they are allowed to singe by the flames of the furnaces that burn that coal. Bourgeois democracy is capitalism's most perfect form exactly because it is composed of a reiterative and dynamic synthesis of the state and civil society, and because it is capable of disciplining even the most powerful individual actors in society in the interests of capitalist production as a whole—though, as China is proving, other governmental forms may be even more effective at shepherding capital out of crisis than multi-party bourgeois democracy is.

Gramsci's analysis casts a demystifying light upon the endlessly recuperative power of twenty-first century imperialist society, where, in Mario Tronti's words, the neoliberal expansion of "political democracy brought forward by capital possessed great weapons, and not only ideological weapons of propaganda but mechanisms for the overall operation of capitalist society."[10] While the more privileged layers of the working class—with access to land ownership and practically unlimited consumer debt—has especially been folded into the edges of this power bloc, it is the neoliberal expansion of the middle class as service operator for financial capital and variable capital that has created a state actor that can interpolate the greatest income inequality gaps the world has ever known into the dead ends of reforms

10   See Mario Tronti, "Within and Against," in *The Weapon of Organization: Mario Tronti's Political Revolution in Marxism*, ed. and trans. Andrew Anastasi (Brooklyn: Common Notions Press, 2020).

accompanied by revolutionary-sounding slogans. These slogans denounce the state while also promising "non-reformist reforms" that would perfect the state. The social-manager subgroup of the new middle class, as Greek socialist Nicos Poulantzas argues in his study of fascism, "aspires to be the arbiter of society" because of its managerial position as the ideologically articulating and coalescent layer of the state. Whether the middle-class social manager expressing their arbiter position between capital and subaltern groups is a business improvement association representative advocating for anti-panhandling laws and more police sweeps, or a social justice legal advocacy group advocating for beat cops to be replaced with front line social workers, those who touch the middle class, touch the state.

Regardless of the terminological difficulties, I think the term "middle classes" is useful, so long as we are careful to be clear about what we mean by the term; by *middle* we mean in-the-middle of the primary classes and not "middle class" as a class of its own.

## Insurgency of the new middle class

A good deal of the 1970–1990 growth in the services sector of the labour market was in the sectors that manage and regulate the poor, criminalised, elderly, and infirm sections of the working class. According to David Ley's study of the new middle class in Canada, the number of social work jobs in Canada tripled in the 1960s with the professionalization of the industry, almost tripled again in the 1970s, and added a further 30,000 positions from 1981–86, despite the deepest recession since the Great Depression and the beginning of neoliberal austerity cuts to public spending. Neoliberal attacks on the welfare state, which relegated poor people to prisons and abandoned them to death by homelessness, did not similarly hurt social workers. Theirs remained a growth industry, like munitions in wartime. Health, education, and welfare departments added over 700,000 jobs between 1971 and 1986, principally in major cities.

Politicians made big promises to the members of this growing middle class, offering them a more complete and secure inclusion in civil society, mostly in the form of rights. The rights deal, won through various legal cases in the US and through the *Charter of Rights and Freedoms* and newly amended *Immigration* and *Multiculturalism Acts* in Canada, worked to appropriate and neutralize the challenges against the overtly white supremacist, settler colonial, patriarchal social order that came from the revolutionary movements of the 1970s. As Lisa Duggan explains in her book on the cultural politics of neoliberalism, some of those involved in subaltern revolutionary struggles in the 1960s and '70s got a whiff of possibility and turned away from liberation for all peoples globally, and towards their own inclusion in civil society through the ascension of members of oppressed groups into the growing middle class. "Multiculturalism" appropriated Black Power and anti-imperialism; "women's rights" appropriated socialist and radical feminism; "gay rights" appropriated gay liberation; and later, "reconciliation" appropriated Red Power.

After four difficult decades, and in the context of the downward spiral of US empire, these deals have soured. The threat of downward mobility and incomplete citizenship faced by the middle class, and the material threat of poverty and death faced by low-income working-class and Indigenous communities, suggest that these groups could unite and fight a common enemy. But a distrust and disdain for workers movements and for the poor remains characteristic of the middle-class leadership that is quick to appropriate the energy of the poor and carry it out of the streets and into boardrooms where they can use it as a bargaining chip to better their own positions.

But we are visiting slippery terrain here. There is a short step from decrying middle-class self-interest and careerism, as well as bemoaning the multiculturalist turn to the selective inclusion of middle-class racialized and, more recently in Canada, Indigenous people, and making the analytical error of dismissing the relevance of settler colonialism, imperialism, and white supremacy in constituting, along with capitalism, the essence of Canada and the US. There has been some limited discussion about this question in the radical left, which I think can be framed as: are middle-class Black and Indigenous people subaltern? The radical left's responses to this question have fallen into about three camps.

The first and most common is to ignore the question of the social role of the Black and Indigenous middle class altogether, including their role in the George Floyd and Breonna Taylor uprising. The more orthodox Marxist left has tended to abstain from these discussions, saying little or nothing at all, instead electing to reinforce a flattened binary of the street movement as an unproblematic whole against the police. I think that silence from prominent socialist groups invests a greater meaning in the discussions that are openly happening, even if they're on the fringe of the fringe.

In response to this most widespread camp, I want to say that the class character of the movement, including of Black and Indigenous leaderships, are matters of importance for the movement as a whole, including white participants. In Vancouver, during the movement for Black lives and the Shut Down Canada mobilisations, we saw a consequence of a majority white movement deferring to an undifferentiated Black and Indigenous leadership, without interest in questions of the class interests of that leadership. Within two weeks of the beginning of the George Floyd and Breonna Taylor uprising, Black Lives Matter Vancouver released a set of demands that steered local energies towards policing reforms at Vancouver City Council, demanding "to prioritise the expansion of community-led health and safety initiatives over future financial investment into the Vancouver Police Department." This demand was taken up by progressives inside and outside civic politics and resulted in a motion put forward by progressive councillor Jean Swanson that relied heavily on the language and spirit of the Black Lives Matter petition.

The council meetings about Swanson's resolution, called "Decriminalising Poverty and Supporting Community-led Safety Initiatives," were a political event in themselves, with over 400 speakers coming out in favour of the motion and only two speakers against. The problem was that the rhetoric marshalled by speakers was not matched by the actual content of the resolution. An editorial published by the University of British Columbia Social Justice Centre called for support for Swanson's motion in order to demand "that all of our politicians take a stance against anti-Blackness and police violence by publicly supporting defunding the Vancouver Police Department in the 2021 City of Vancouver budget."[11] It argues, using language common

---

11   The University of British Columbia Social Justice Centre, "Letter: It's Time to Defund the Vancouver Police Department," *The Ubyssey* CII, III (July 28, 2020), https://issuu.com/ubyssey/docs/the_ubyssey_july_28.

to the police and prison abolitionists in the US: "By defunding, disarming and disbanding the VPD, we can begin to dismantle white supremacy, give ourselves opportunities to reimagine how we address harm and create space to build systems grounded in community safety and liberation." But Swanson's motion did not contain anything about "defunding, disarming and disbanding" the city's police department. The original motion, which was passed with some additional watering down, called for the following: the police board to "itemise the work they do that is related to mental health, homelessness, drug use, sex work, and the amount of money spent on it;" Council to "seek input" from Black Lives Matter and a number of NGOs and social service organisations; city staff to write a report with a "plan, timeline, and budget to de-prioritize policing as a response to mental health, sex work, homelessness, and substance use and to prioritise funding community-led harm reduction and safety initiatives"; and for Council to "inform the police board" that the City's priority is "community-led initiatives rather than policing." The words that defined the militant character of the street movement, "abolish," and "defund," did not appear in Swanson's motion.

The obvious problem here is that state actors, like legal reformers and progressive politicians, appropriate and neutralise radical politics. By bringing radical working class and Indigenous sovereigntist demands into legal and government policy frameworks, reformers reframe them within the limits imposed by their practical, pragmatic implementation within existing property and social relations, stripping out socially transformative politics that depend on the self-organisation and power of subaltern people against bourgeois and settler colonial institutions like city councils. A more cynical view might be that the Swanson motion, by diverting urgent demands into the narrow and specialist hallways of city staff, directed to come back later with a report, was stalling, killing the momentum of the insurrectionary moment by committee. All that seems to have been the case in Minneapolis, where a serious challenge to police power was mounted in the streets, and where the mayor and city council responded with a motion to dissolve the police department entirely, as Minneapolis Council President Lisa Bender said, "to end policing as we know it, and to recreate systems of public safety that actually keep us safe." A year later, according to the Minnesota poll,

Minneapolis voters, led by middle-class home and business owners who believed there was a "rising crime rate," voted down the motion to replace the police department.[12] The militant and transformative passions and revolutionary determination of the collective that took the streets did not survive translation into legal policy in the ledgers of city council.

But in Vancouver there was another problem. The demands formulated by Black Lives Matter Vancouver sounded similar to those that came out of the militant street movements in the US, but on closer inspection, they rely on repressive state institutions that function as unarmed branches of policing. The petition's central demand, to fund "community-led health and safety initiatives" instead of the police, is not clearly defined. The closest it gets is to list "alternatives like education, increased mental health services, housing initiatives, income security, harm reduction services, accessible rehabilitation, mutual aid, social workers, conflict resolution services, transformative justice, and other vital community-based support systems." Few clients of mental health and social workers would characterise these repressive and disciplinary state powers as "community-based support systems." The record of the operators of supportive housing projects in British Columbia, for example, is of hand-in-glove operation with police, as they surveil, punish, and strip the rights of tens of thousands of poor people stuck in these soft institutions. Without autonomous, revolutionary political organisations to identify and defend their own interests, working class, Black, and Indigenous people most preyed upon by police were spoken-for by activists and legal reform advocates who led the movement against white supremacist terror into the controlled and stifling grasp of city hall.

The problems of cross-class organisation in Black and Indigenous national struggles are not the work of non-Black and non-Indigenous radicals to fix, but working-class movements cannot adopt the posture of middle-class whites in relation to Black and Indigenous movements. In the example of the Swanson motion, middle-class white deference to supposedly classless Black

12   Will Bunch, "Black Lives Matter marches of 2020 were surprisingly white and educated. Is that why results have been so mediocre?" *Philadelphia Inquirer* (October 14, 2021), https://www.inquirer.com/columnists/attytood/george-floyd-protest-marches-2020-white-educated-20211014.html.

and Indigenous leaderships organised—through mystification—Vancouver City Council's appropriation and neutralisation of "defunding" and police abolitionist politics, thereby reproducing state forms of power that attack the autonomies of subaltern people. If revolutionary socialists were to adopt this same deferential and disinterested posture, the message they would send is that their groups and movements are white—that Black and Indigenous people, and their distinct politics, are not part of their movements.

## Two hearts of the Black and Indigenous middle classes

The other two camps in this debate are divided between those who are debating the class composition of the George Floyd and Breonna Taylor uprising. One of these, most clearly stated by the writers Shemon and Arturo on the website *Ill Will*, sharply opposes the "Black middle class" as a decisive force of counter insurgency, putting down the rebellion by seizing control over it from above and outside. The counter to this position, explained by the autonomist writer Bromma, is worth quoting at greater length because I think it is a valuable correction to a tendency to wave off all middle-class actors as an integrated part of the total imperialist society. In an interview responding to the writing of Shemon and Arturo, Bromma says:

> But demonising the entire Black middle class, which itself routinely experiences racist cop violence and other forms of oppression, and which includes many supporters of revolution, isn't helpful on any level. Shemon's argument seems to be based on a misunderstanding of the class nature of both the Black freedom struggle and its white self-declared allies.
>
> The Black/New Afrikan freedom movement is fundamentally a *national liberation movement*. The enemy of this movement is the US settler state, a prison-house of oppressed nations and nationalities. So class struggle here can't be oversimplified into a struggle between proletarians and capitalists. *That's class reductionism—trying to simplify everything down to "class against class" in a country defined by centuries of national oppression.* In fact, in this country, as in other settler states,

*the class structure is based on and shaped by a highly racialized*
*form of colonialism* [emphasis added].

Bromma is correct that Black and Indigenous peoples have not been integrated into bourgeois settler colonial power structures in any meaningful way. The oppression of Black and Indigenous communities is carried out, first and foremost, through *imperialist* power, logic, and imperative. So the class position of Black and Indigenous peoples within the global processes of capitalist production is different from those who have been proletarianized, whose social lives have been amalgamated into the productive and reproductive rhythms tapped out by capitalism's metronome. In a general sense, Black and Indigenous peoples are confronted by capitalism as an outside, invading force—a force bent on stealing land and labour, and dispatching those who stand in the way through military and police and vigilante violence.

But to correct against Shemon and Arturo, Bromma bends the stick too far in the other direction. As Malik Miah explains in *Against the Current* in January 2021, the "second class status of African Americans has remained, even with the growth of a vibrant Black middle class. The class gap between haves and have-nots has widened within the oppressed nationality, even as the wealth gap between African Americans and the dominant 'white caste' has grown."[13] Miah's point corresponds with Bromma's: that Black communities are, regardless of class, relegated to second class status in the US (and Canada). Miah says, "Class differences exist. But that's within each class group." The problem he points to is the class domination of a white supremacist capitalist class, which is also a race domination of whites over Black communities.

Miah's recognition that "class differences exist" *within* Black, and relatedly—though in a less developed and institutionalised way—Indigenous communities, means that class *struggles* also exist within nationally oppressed groups, even though the proletarianization of Black and Indigenous communities is incomplete at best. Shemon and Arturo attend to these class

13   Malik Miah, "The American Caste System," *Against the Current*, no. 210 (January/February 2021), https://againstthecurrent.org/atc210/the-american-caste-system/.

differences by saying that white radicals should attack middle-class Black leaders in the movement. In a podcast, Shemon, who is racialized but not Black, says, "White comrades should always be looking to out-organise ... to basically ruin everything that is about the Black middle class in these protests. Luckily now we all get to wear ski masks, so no one can call you out if you're a racist. If you're challenging the Black middle class in the effort to open up more space for the proletariat, my line is fuck the Black middle class." Bromma, to the contrary, says white radicals should abstain entirely from the problem of middle-class Black misleadership.

Power relations within Black and Indigenous societies are a product of imperialist intervention through the racist and colonial operations of capitalist society as a whole, and they cannot be combated by those who are integrated into capitalist society, even by oppressed working-class people within capitalism. Subaltern Black and Indigenous leaderships are the ones who must reckon with Black and Indigenous middle classes. So far this pretty much agrees with what Bromma is saying.

But Bromma is also insensitive to the actual composition of subaltern communities, and of revolutionary organisations, instead seeing Black and Indigenous communities as existing in radical isolation. We know that everyday life and struggles for survival in subaltern communities are racially mixed. While Linda Mama Bear Whitford, a member of Red Braid who was killed by the colonial health care system in 2020, focused on fighting for Indigenous sovereignty on the street, she was also clear that her multiracial street kin were who she was fighting for. There is a communion between these multiracial facts of everyday life and the possibilities for struggle that is missing from Bromma's analysis that working-class whites have no stake in Black and Indigenous leaderships.

And the experiences of the George Floyd and Breonna Taylor uprising and the Shut Down Canada movement for Wet'suwet'en sovereignty show that movements today for racial justice and against colonialism and against capitalism are multiracial as well as cross-class. The multiracial character of the movement means that white radicals and people of colour who are not Black or Indigenous are not apart from, unaffected by, nor indifferent to the class character of Black and Indigenous leaderships. To pretend indifference is, as is always the case, to side with the hegemon, which naturalises power as an aspect of wielding it.

## Reflecting on our conflicts with the Indigenous middle class

In the heat of the movements of spring 2020, most significantly during the Wet'suwet'en solidarity movement and then in struggle against the danger of state-organised executions of street kin by neglect at the beginning of the COVID-19 pandemic, Red Braid came into significant and troubling conflict with some sections of Indigenous leadership. Through an anonymous letter circulated through Signal groups and then on Instagram, Red Braid was accused of taking advantage of the movement for our own ends, of exaggerating our Indigenous membership and leadership, and of manipulating unhoused people into taking reckless or dangerous actions.

At the time, because we were still finding our feet as Red Braid, after relaunching our organisation in February 2020 with a new name and basis of unity, just weeks before the Wet'suwet'en movement took off, and because some of the critiques pointed at political problems we were still grappling with ourselves, we were not able to respond in completely self-reflexive ways. These critiques were also hard to accept on a human level. They felt unfair. And to a large degree they *were* unfair. But to dismiss the totality of these critiques because so many of them were mean, baseless, and nearly inexplicable does not help us. With the benefit of the passage of time, with so many more struggles under our belts and careful self-criticisms to consider, we have revisited these critiques by looking for the truths they contain.

The essential criticisms of Red Braid raised in the spring movements of 2020 were two: first was the criticism that our strategy of "braiding" Indigenous and working-class struggle was mistaken and premised on the political exploitation of Indigenous struggle by non-Indigenous activists. We do not dispute that this is a challenge and a danger, and one that we were attentive to. In the spring of 2020, we were still in the initial stages of working through this problem in practice. There is a deeper reflection on how we have addressed this challenge in the chapter *For Decolonial Revolution: A History of the Indigenous Leadership Council of Red Braid*. But given the character of subaltern communities in which we are so rooted, where Indigenous and non-Indigenous people support and fight alongside each other every day, we did not abandon the struggle for an insurgent universality—a unity through multiplicity.

Second, and more difficult to dismiss, was the charge that we posed our leadership as a majority non-Indigenous organisation alongside the leadership of Indigenous youth during the Wet'suwet'en movement. That was certainly not how we understood our actions at the time. We saw the Indigenous Youth for Wet'suwet'en stand up and we cheered. And because we had been cooperating with the Indigenous-led group Wet'suwet'en Solidarity Coast Salish Territories in the days prior, we did not recognise right away that anything had changed. In the fast moving and overwhelming waters of days-long blockades in the mid-winter cold, this confusion could be understandable, but it has its political roots that are not so easily dismissed.

One case cited by our critics was that non-Indigenous members of Red Braid went to demonstrations and tried to recruit Indigenous youth to come to a meeting called by Destiny, a young Indigenous Red Braid member. At the time Destiny was a full-time retail worker who could not make it to the actions herself, and she asked her comrades to talk with Indigenous youth who might be interested in working with her to organise actions. Innocent enough. But because these meetings relied on the embodied work of non-Indigenous members of Red Braid, the organisation's work of supporting Indigenous leadership internally appeared as if it were non-Indigenous socialists undermining emerging Indigenous leadership outside the group.

Red Braid's appraisal of the political character of the Indigenous leadership that was forming organically through the Wet'suwet'en solidarity movement should have been of secondary importance to the fact of that leadership's emergence. Rather than supporting that leadership in the particular form that it took, we overly focused on our own internal project of Indigenous leadership development in our group. We were right to throw ourselves into the development of Indigenous leadership in Red Braid. But to put this organisational project ahead of the organic development of Indigenous leadership in the movement where we were active meant that we were putting the interests of our group ahead of the interest of the movement. That was sectarian.

But we were not able to discuss or correct against that sectarian tendency in the aftermath of the Wet'suwet'en movement and instead were drawn quickly into another desperate struggle, against the mass death-by-neglect of our street kin once the COVID-19 pandemic began. When we started the Stewart Squat in an abandoned wing of the Strathcona school in Vancouver, we were criticised by the same people who felt we had tried to take advantage of the Wet'suwet'en movement. Some of these critics claimed that we had parachuted into the Downtown Eastside (DTES) and started a squat in an abandoned school without the support of the community. This was not true. We had worked with unhoused people in Oppenheimer Tent City at the request of Indigenous community members who called us and asked to work together and alongside longstanding DTES organisations Carnegie Community Action Project (CCAP), Our Homes Can't Wait, and Vancouver Area Network of Drug Users (VANDU). But a major reason for the suspicion was the dynamic that we had failed to recognise in the Wet'suwet'en struggle.

We had worked hard on developing a critique of the domineering role of middle-class people in Indigenous communities, but we did not remain sensitive to the double role that middle-class Indigenous and Black people play in a white supremacist, colonial society. The Indigenous and Black middle class function as social regulators, particularly over poor Indigenous and Black communities in service of imperial power. But outside of workplaces, in family and social worlds and in the heat and speed of movements in struggle, middle-class Indigenous and Black people can leave behind their middle-class role assigned by capitalist society and play a role as Indigenous or Black fighters in their nations and communities. While middle-class Indigenous and Black people may be social regulators on one hand, their total social existences are *also and always* forged in the problematics of settler colonialism and anti-Black white supremacy on the other. The question of whether Black and Indigenous middle-class people are subaltern has to be situated and active: are they an active contributor to a subaltern struggle? The answer to this question should not be one of general principle. It must be active, critical, and worked out by and for the leadership of Black and Indigenous subaltern peoples, even if and when they are part of multi-racial movements or groups.

Reflecting on our work within and alongside the mass movements of 2020, as a whole organisation, I think we trended too much towards blanket dismissal of middle-class Indigenous and, to a lesser extent, Black leaderships. This dismissal came out of our organisational allegiance to the Indigenous leaders within Red Braid, and in our subaltern social base. But, as a mixed organisation, I think we had a difficult task of both supporting the subaltern Indigenous leadership and emergent Black leadership within our group, and of not acting as though we were an entirely Indigenous organisation.

It is still the case that the problems of Black and Indigenous middle-class misleadership are the responsibility of Black and Indigenous national movements. But when Black and Indigenous national movements are expressed through multiracial street movements and class struggles, the class character of any leadership is not something the movement can be indifferent to. Building subaltern power and organisations requires clarity about the class interests and political programmes of different leaderships, which is a task that requires careful thinking, bravery, and cultures of critique and inquiry, not blanket dismissal.

The truth is that the non-Indigenous sections of our group had greater numbers and took up more active space in Red Braid than in its Indigenous Leadership Council. That means that it was not enough that non-Indigenous Red Braid members consistently and persistently supported subaltern Indigenous fighters when they were in conflict with middle-class Indigenous leaders. We also should have committed support to middle-class Indigenous leaderships outside the group when they were leading overall movements against colonialism and towards freedom and power for subaltern people.

### What to do about cross-class mass movements?

Who is representing what and when is not always clear, because subalternity, as a subjective historical factor, is often partial, insecure, and wavering. Compared to nascent subaltern centres of power, the gravitational pull of civil society is strong, often pulling even the struggles that seek to challenge its hegemony into its orbit. Drawing the progressive movements of 2020 in a revolutionary direction, away from a politics of recognition, diversity, and inclusion within Canada and US civil society, requires splitting the double character of the Black and Indigenous middle classes and reinforcing their subaltern aspects. This requires the revolutionary leadership of poor Black and Indigenous people, who have antagonistic relationships to middle-class institutions, to intervene and exercise power.

From the perspective of poor Black and Indigenous communities, it is clear that the slogan "Abolish the Police" must also mean an end to the web of anti-poor laws and bylaws that bring poor people into confrontations with cops and send them to jail. As well, it must mean a struggle against the soft power of the state, including social workers and supportive housing, which amount to police and prisons in another form. For poor Indigenous people, "Land Back" requires an end to the property regime that legally empowers landlords to throw Indigenous tenants out of their homes and into the streets to face homelessness, sometimes on their own territories.

There is no substitute for the self-activity of Black and Indigenous subaltern leadership in these internal movement struggles. While anyone committed to revolutionary struggle is responsible for analysing the class interests and political program of movement leadership, multiracial organisations need to assess our capacities to intervene based on the power we represent. Our Black and Indigenous comrades should expect and command the whole force of our organisations behind them, supporting their interventions against the Black or Indigenous middle class, but these interventions must be their independent initiative. To intervene means mattering; it means being relevant to the movement. Non-Black and non-Indigenous socialists are not relevant to sovereignty and Black freedom struggles, and they cannot substitute themselves for Black and Indigenous subaltern leaders in those struggles.

Our work as revolutionaries is to build autonomous subaltern power and to make unities with others who are determined to build this power. If a revolutionary organisation does not have the power to intervene against middle-class misleadership, we can still be involved in the movement but in another way. We can look for subaltern aspects of middle class led movements, and support those currents which struggle against colonialism, towards freedom and power for subaltern struggles: for Indigenous sovereignty and Black liberation. We can judge our involvement against the question: What kind of power are we building—subaltern power, which is the base for a revolutionary politics, or middle-class power, which is the reformist power of the state and capital?

Many voices on online forums discussing the mass movements of 2020 reject any proposals to *build organisations*. That is because the middle classes *are* organised. They have gotten organised by way of their central role in the restructuring of imperialist society since the beginning of the global neoliberal and austerity projects. Activists and community organisers are organised by their non-profits. Front-line workers are organised by their service organisations. Band council families are organised by the federal government's colonial apparatus. Academics are organised by their university departments. Any middle-class activist or commentator who makes a sour face at the mention of the word "organisation" is as organised as water in the wave that crashes down on the head of the subaltern classes, who are already struggling to stand.

In the context of a capitalist system in crisis—with a relatively well-organised middle class and a historical low in the organisation of subaltern working-class and Indigenous communities—the most decisive project of our moment is to contribute to the reorganisation of subaltern social groups independent of invasive and meddling middle-class forces. The next chapter lays out a proposal of what such organisations could look like, and how they can work together.

# Revolutionary organisation

Ivan Drury

All around us is evidence that, no matter how difficult the prospects of victory, subaltern people have not given up fighting. In addition to the tremendous street movements of 2020, in the shadow of which this book has been written, the opening decades of the twenty-first century have been characterised by heroic global struggles against imperialism and dictatorship, the emergence of the first forms of worker resistance against the so-called "gig" workplace, of public-sector workers' mass strikes, and of Indigenous-led resistance against colonial land theft and the related global warming and climate crisis. But as much as these struggles have been inspiring and hopeful, besides the Indigenous struggles that are grounded in the consistent organisational forms of nationhood and the persistent politics of sovereignty, many of these struggles have been fleeting and have not been able to develop a positive unifying vision beyond their coalescent swell of opposition to the established order. In the Arab Spring of the early 20-teens and the uprisings in Hong Kong, Myanmar, Belarus, and Haiti in the early 2020s, as in the George Floyd uprising, the clarity of opposition to the world-that-is has been muddled with uncertainty about the specifics of the better world-to-be. Antonio Gramsci calls this sort of moment a "crisis of authority," where the old world is dying but the new is not yet ready to be born—a problem due in no small part to the revolutionary classes' disorganisation and fragmentation.

There is nothing novel about the claim that our disorganisation is a barrier to our power. But where revolutionaries have historically differed has been over the question of who needs to get organised: the *leadership* of the subaltern or the subaltern people *themselves*. Often, in debates, these two groups have appeared to be opposed to each other rather than a synthetic whole. Some Leninists, who constitute a branch of Marxist socialism, have argued that the organisation of a leadership group in the form of a party comes first. Leon Trotsky's first words in his 1938 *Transitional Program* are emblematic of this view: "The world political situation as a whole is chiefly characterised by a historical crisis of the leadership of the proletariat." Trotsky suggests that it is the *leadership* that is in crisis, not the proletariat itself, and that the problem of disorganisation can be resolved through the self-organisation of a new group of leaders armed with correct revolutionary ideas. Some Trotskyist groups in the US and Canada have taken this notion to an extreme and explained every setback in class struggle through the prism of the corruption and misleadership of either labour bureaucrats or the Stalinists. According to this narrative, the revolutionary consciousness of the working class is there waiting behind a door for a party with the right key—a correct slogan wielded by a correct leadership.

Anarchists, committed to the power of spontaneous worker's struggle, have often occupied the other side of this split in diagnosis. The most prominent and influential theorists of spontaneity today are in the "communization" tendency, assembled in their journals *Endnotes* (in the UK and US), *Théorie Communiste* (in France), and *Chuang* (whose dispersed editors write about China). Arguing that the Leninist vanguard party is a relic of an earlier period of industrial capitalism, before "industrialization itself...passed away," communization thinkers claim that communism is imminent in the very actions of worker's movements. Communizationists reject what they term the "programmatism" of parties that seek to articulate a revolutionary strategy and give voice to a future society through a set of demands and slogans, arguing instead that world revolutionary "conditions will emerge, not from internal development within the Left, but rather through the development of historically specific forms of class struggle."[1]

1    See Roger Rashi, Sam Gindin, Stephen Eric Bronner, Aaron B., and Richard Rubin, "Program and Utopia," *Platypus Review* 58 (July 2013).

Maybe it is slightly off to say that communizationists see the first task to be the organisation of the worker's movement, given that they see that organisation as imminent and not a task left undone. It might be more correct to say that they see the spontaneous activity of the working class as the expression of its already-existing self-organisation; that the revolution waits only on this spontaneous *expression*.

Both proposals—that revolutionary classes require only more intelligent leadership, and that the revolution is already and inevitably underway beneath the appearances of misery and alienation all around us—contain grains of truth. The self-emancipation of oppressed people requires their self-organisation. And this self-organisation must realise more than spontaneous moments of refusal and collective opposition to intolerable conditions; it must be able to articulate common goals, reach consensus, make compromises, and even organise strategic retreats. That means self-emancipation includes leadership and organisational cohesion. There is something offensive in the notion that the leadership and the masses are so radically different—as though the truest leaders do not emerge from the self-activity of those masses. Thinking and doing are not separate, discrete motions; they together make a whole.

In his 1902 book *What Is To Be Done*, written during a time of radical disorganisation in the Russian socialist movement, Russian revolutionary leader Vladimir Lenin famously wrote that "there can be no revolutionary movement without a revolutionary theory," and that "the role of the vanguard fighter can be fulfilled only by a party which is guided by an advanced theory." These quotes have often been wrenched out of context to imagine "professional revolutionaries" as intellectuals who, wielding theory, descend as outside agitators to manipulate the masses. I read Lenin differently, as pointing at the process of political action needed to develop the consciousness of the revolutionary classes from their "trade union consciousness"—which develops through the practice of struggle, arm in arm with other workers around them in a particular factory against a particular boss—to revolutionary consciousness—which is the abstraction of oneself not as an individual amongst other individuals but as part of a historic class with a shared set of interests. To feel yourself to be part of a class and a participant in a class struggle taking place on a global stage is an intellectual act that steps with others in collective struggle, not an act of some separate, disinterested group of intellectuals.

Gramsci explains this further in his *Prison Notebooks*, where he discusses the "progressive acquisition of the consciousness of one's historical identity" as a "cleavage" of oneself from the disorganising and mystifying swamp of everyday life. I think Gramsci's writing here is useful for shrugging off the various misinterpretations of Lenin's *What Is To Be Done*. Gramsci says revolutionaries have to have a clear assessment of the "relationship of forces" between the subaltern and the hegemonic bloc, including understanding the "objective" function of a group within production, and the "subjective" level of self-consciousness of that group. The revolutionary wants to fight and win at the objective level, against capitalism and colonialism, but to have any hope of winning, our side has to be powerful and united, which is a subjective problem. Gramsci presents three developmental categories of group-consciousness which he scales from lowest (most local and dependent on direct experience) to highest (most abstract and global). The lowest is *economic* consciousness, when unity is limited to the immediate economic interests of a local group, like a craft union. *Corporate* group consciousness is also bound by obviously common economic interests but is less locally bound, such as in industrial unions. The highest is *political* consciousness: a revolutionary global consciousness that breaks from the ideological limits of everyday identity to bridge superstructural concerns. From political consciousness, a group can develop a counter-hegemonic bloc with a complex ideological and organisational unity and the group-will to overthrow the dominant group.[2]

Gramsci explains:

> The metalworker, the carpenter, the construction worker etc.
> must not only think as proletarians and no longer as metal-
> worker, carpenter, construction worker etc; they must also take
> another step forward: they must think as workers who belong

2     Antonio Gramsci, *Prison Notebooks*, vol. 2 (New York: Columbia University Press, 1992), 53, 179.

to a class that aims to lead the peasants and the intellectuals, a class that can be victorious and can build socialism only if it is helped and followed by the great majority of those social strata.[3]

The work of a revolutionary intellectual, Gramsci says, is to encourage this process along; to "feel the rudimentary passions of the people, understand them, and explain them in the specific historical situation, linking them dialectically to the laws of history." Gramsci's revolutionary intellectual is the opposite of that outsider, "distinct and detached from the people." Instead, revolutionary theory and organisation is a product of the self-activity of the subaltern; the thought and leadership of the intellectual is inconceivable without a dialectical connection with that social base.[4]

Revolutionary organisation is an instrument in the hands of revolutionary intellectuals to actively contribute to the development of the self-consciousness of a subaltern social group from economic (your own local community) to corporate (all communities connected to yours) to political-revolutionary (your historic class). This means that the revolutionary organisation is necessarily not something imposed from outside by "distinct and detached" intellectuals; it is itself a synthetic production of this process of group consciousness development.

In this chapter I argue that the synthesis of subaltern self-activity and the theory-making and strategy-hatching leadership of formal organisation are necessary parts in a whole revolutionary process. But that does not mean that there is one true revolutionary class and one true leading party with one true idea. The process of leadership and organisation-making cannot emerge from outside of the process of the real movements and struggles in the everyday world. The revolutionary organisation must emerge as something more like a set of wheels turning a serpentine belt, powered by and powering an alternator of movements between the fractions of subaltern classes as they have been objectively formed and subjectively constituted in a particular moment. The test of the revolutionary organisation must be whether it can make its politics relevant to its social base, in their real-world

3   Gramsci, 557.
4   Gramsci, 173.

struggles. Through a historical process of class struggle, the organisation and its leaders emerge as an organic part of the many autonomies of reorganised subaltern institutions.

Working through the various critiques of socialist organisation, with the goal of clarifying the strategies and organisational structures I am proposing, this chapter begins with a critical review of the classic Hal Draper article, "Anatomy of the Micro-Sect." Then it looks back to the organisation of the working class today to argue for a multiple and autonomous—rather than single, centralised—approach to organisation. It concludes with a review of Red Braid's experience with organisational structure and a diagram of the revolutionary "organisation of organisations" around which revolutionary groups can regroup based on the politics demanded and defined by the real movement of people in struggle.

## Revisiting critiques of the micro-sect

When Hal Draper wrote "Anatomy of a Micro-Sect," the movements of the 1960s had hit their excited zenith and begun their fragmented descent—like a firecracker packed with gunpowder that explodes in midair, making a loud sound and sending only bits of paper to scatter the ground. The excited momentum of the mass movements ran aground, many of which included groups and parties with revolutionary commitments, but many of those committed revolutionaries continued their dedicated labour, either ignoring the changing circumstances or hoping that the flagging energy might only be temporary. Draper's foil is that committed revolutionary militant who soldiers on, redoubling their efforts with a smaller and more committed group of comrades, saying, "better fewer but better," as they make their turn to industry or into underground armed struggle. The durability of the influence of Draper's article is due to the historical problem that since he wrote this article in 1973 the situation faced by radicals has not significantly changed. If anything, the fragmentation and disorganisation of the working class has worsened, and the isolation of socialists from that class has only deepened.

There is some ambivalence about the question that haunts Draper's "micro-sect" article: What are revolutionary socialists supposed to do in a time of low-momentum or disorganisation in the working class? Draper recognises the need for organisation but rejects the idea that it can be initiated by socialists. This is where his term micro-sect comes from. "Whatever is formed by fiat will turn out to be a sect alongside the other sects," he writes. And while a socialist movement "cannot be created simply by an effort of will, it is also historically true that it is not simply a matter of spontaneous generation." But Draper here is leaping from "making revolution" to making a revolutionary party, which is not correctly understood as the same process, though there is a definite relationship between them.

Draper's conflation of the process of *making an organisation* and *making revolution* is what sets up his dismissal of all organisations that exist outside of revolutionary moments as a "sect." Draper writes:

> What characterises the classic sect was best defined by Marx himself: it counterposes its sect criterion of programmatic points against the real movement of the workers in the class struggle, which may not measure up to its high demands... The approach pointed by Marx was different: without giving up or concealing one's own programmatic politics in the slightest degree, the real Marxist looks to the lines of struggle calculated to move decisive sectors of the class into action—into movement against the established powers of the system.

The slippery thing here has been the question of what actions constitute "the real movement," who is included in "the workers," and what arena stages "the class struggle." Draper critiques those "neo-Stalinist (Maoist-Castroite-etc.) sects" that he says were a "danger to any healthy development in the working-class movement." He says these "neo-Stalinist sects are 'oriented' towards... the lumpenpoor, or the blacks, or the 'third world'... [because for them] the most suitable class is one with a minimum of capacity for initiative and self-organisation." Draper claims that these "elements" are "enemies to the revolutionary democracy of socialism."

Now, Draper doesn't cite examples or name names, but this was written in Berkeley, California in 1973. Certainly, critiqued here are the Black Panthers for their orientation towards the lumpenproletariat. Draper

derides as sectarian those groups that are not supporting the "real movement" composed of "the workers," and we must read the "real movement"
as the organisations and mass movements that include white men with jobs
in the "decisive sectors of the class."

Draper had been a leader in the International Socialists (IS) in Berkeley
when it was principally a campus organisation that was involved in the
free speech movement. Draper left the IS when it relocated its centre from
California to Michigan in order to focus on their strategic turn to industry
—to organise on the factory floor for direct worker's control. What was the
difference between the IS organising in the free speech movement in the
San Francisco Bay Area in 1968 as well as the multi-organisational, multiracial Peace and Freedom Party, both of which Draper supported, and the
IS organising in the factories of Detroit in 1971, which Draper denounced?

## The autonomism of the League of Revolutionary Black Workers

In his classic history, *The Origins of the Urban Crisis*, Thomas Sugrue shows
that not all workers in Detroit industry in 1970 were Black, but Black workers
were concentrated in industry. Between 1950 and 1970, about forty percent
of Black male workers in Detroit were employed in industrial labour. While
Black workers were not the majority in the factories (in 1960, about a quar-
ter of the workers in GM and Chrysler plants were Black, and closer to forty
percent in Ford plants), they were a significant set of the workforce, and they
formed a persistent vanguard in the workers movements.

For this vanguard, the class struggle, whether against plant owners and
managers or white auto workers and union bureaucrats, was waged through
race power. An article in the *International Socialist* newspaper in 1970 reports
that Black workers active in the Dodge Revolutionary Union Movement
(DRUM) "often refer to white workers at Dodge Main as 'Polish pigs.'" And
in the classic book about the League of Revolutionary Black Workers, *Detroit
I Do Mind Dying*, Dan Georgakas and Martin Surkin say that Black revolutionaries in Dodge and Ford plants would even refuse to distribute leaflets
to white workers.[5] This was certainly not a scene of Draper's unproblem-

5    See Dan Georgakas and Martin Surkin, *Detroit: I Do Mind Dying* (Cambridge,
     Mass.: South End Press, 1998).

atic class unity led by "the workers" in the "decisive sectors of the class." Detroit's industrial-class struggle was not led by formal, white-dominated trade unions, which were already beginning to accommodate the mass lay-offs out of Rust Belt factories that would continue through the following decades. The League of Revolutionary Black Workers fought against the conservatism and racism of the United Auto Workers (UAW) bureaucracy by forming their own autonomous worker's organisations called Revolutionary Union Movements, or RUMs, within and against UAW-organised plants. As for white radicals, League organiser Michael Hamlin recalled in a memoir interview that the League "advised the whites to go into the plants and organise in their communities." Through that level of parallel work, those white and Black revolutionaries oriented towards the self-activity of industrial workers maintained what Hamlin called a "limited relationship."[6]

These dynamics were described in the first issue of *Workers' Power*, the relaunched version of the *International Socialist* newspaper that was now based in Detroit and focused on organising worker struggles at the industrial point of production. In the issue's lead article, "Auto Strike 1970," Karl Fischer and James Coleman argue that the atmosphere in the factories and union hall was characterised by duelling dynamics of increased militancy amongst workers and the constrictive conservatism of the bureaucracy. They explain:

> Wildcats have hit GM Fleetwood, Dodge Main, Eldon Gear & Axle and Sterling Stamping in Detroit; Ford Mahwah in New Jersey, and many others. The rise in absenteeism, sabotage, and local work stoppages shows a rebellion—not yet organised—against the tightening work discipline in the shops.
>
> But the ability of the UAW international bureaucracy to wage a real fight is another question. In recent years, the union bureaucrats have done everything possible to dampen the militancy of the ranks, including placing locals in receivership to break wildcats. In 1967, taking over the Mansfield Ohio local to end a wildcat, an international rep told the strikers, "There

---

6   Michael Hamlin and Michele Gibbs, *A Black Revolutionary's Life in Labor: Black Workers Power in Detroit* (Detroit MI: Against the Tide Books, 2013).

is one vote in this local, and I have it. Get back in the plant tomorrow morning!"

Draper does not disagree that the union bureaucracy is a problem. As cited in the quote above, he characterises revolutionary movement as that which moves "against the established powers of the system," which he then defines as the "state and bourgeoisie and their agents, including their labour lieutenants inside the worker's movement." But he sees an organised preparation, coordination, and independent grouping outside of the bureaucrat-controlled formation as "dual unionism," and the hallmark of a sect. "The most important test" of a socialist, Draper says, "has always been the relationship of the self-styled Marxist and the working class organised on the elementary economic level, i.e. the trade-union movement." This formulation is interesting. It is almost as though Draper is rebuking the anti-racist struggle of the League of Revolutionary Black Workers for skipping past the unifying "elementary" of economics to the secondary academics of racism.

I am convinced by the approach that the League and the IS took instead. I see the IS, faced by the dynamics of struggle as it existed on the shop floor in auto factories, as straining against the limits of Draper's "elementary economic unity." Again, Fischer and Coleman write:

> A worker's movement can gain strength only through unity.
> But Black workers—and, increasingly, women workers—are already struggling against the discrimination they face on the job and in society. *We can unify only on the basis of the commitment to Blacks, Chicanos, and women, that we will all stand together in fighting against the special forms of oppression that these groups have always faced.* [Emphasis in original]

The IS call to action goes beyond the facile "Black and white, unite and fight" slogan that I expected to read. Instead, their call is more similar to Noel Ignatiev's argument in his "Black Worker, White Worker" article, published by the Sojourner Truth Organization in 1972, that white workers face white supremacy as a critical barrier to their own radicalization and to universal class unity. Like Ignatiev, in recognising Black and women workers' militancy,

Fischer and Coleman invert the classical socialist solution to working-class unity which calls for building coalitions around the oppressions that white men also experience. Instead they define the ideal strategic point of unity as coalitions around the class struggles experienced by those whose sub-jectivities are shaped by oppression under white supremacy and patriarchy, because their experiences come closer to representing the total problem-atics of capitalist rule.

The poet of African decolonisation Aimé Césaire defines this inverted, insurgent universality in his 1956 resignation letter to the French Communist Party. He rejects "walled segregation in the particular" and the "emaciated universalism" of the Communist Party, both of which, he says, place the struggles of "Black peoples in the service of Marxism and communism." Instead, he says in a slogan that should be etched across the highest skies:

> My conception of the universal is that of a universal enriched
> by all that is particular, a universal enriched by every particular:
> the deepening and coexistence of all particulars.

Césaire concludes his resignation letter by proposing organisational structures to accommodate this insurgent universalism: "Organisations capable, in sum, of preparing them in all areas to assume in an autono-mous manner the heavy responsibilities that, even at this moment, history has caused to weigh heavily on their shoulders." Césaire was explaining that organisation is necessary for freedom.

As the concrete manifestation of the radicalising consciousness of the militant vanguard of Black workers, Detroit's League of Revolutionary Black Workers was such an organisation. More durable and directive than the urban Black rebellions and spontaneous wildcat strikes, the League developed as an articulating layer of that collective consciousness, com-posed of sudden energy but made relatively solid—a permanent rank and file organisation of struggle. That the League's permanence was not long is not a condemnation of the idea. Who could know in 1970 that the gears of neoliberalism were turning and that the occasionally powerful-feeling explosions of workers' movements in the factories would find no ballast and dissipate instead into echoes that revolutionaries still listen for today?

Instead of the various autonomous factory organisations coalescing into a
great multiple party of the sort that Césaire called for, "capable in all areas"
of carrying heavy responsibilities "in an autonomous manner," the historical moment that compelled such an assemblage instead faded.

The League of Revolutionary Black Workers struggled under the blows
of a reactionary police unit formed under the incredible name "Stop the
Robberies, Enjoy Safe Streets—STRESS" that, in 1971, murdered the most
people per capita of any police department in the US and infiltrated auto
plants to spy on radical worker organisations.[7] This intense pressure exacerbated fractures inside the League, which Michael Hamlin says split along
three political lines: Black nationalism; local electoralism, which the League
had always opposed; and the national and internationally focused Black
Workers Congress.[8] A significant portion of the League's remaining leadership pivoted away from its social base in the factories, many of whom the
leadership tried to purge by pushing for a mandatory internal education
program, as well as by pushing towards building a US-wide Black political
party. James Forman, the preeminent leader of this turn, promised that the
Black Workers Congress would "link the vital poor people's movement of
one region to the new working class movement of the other, using some of
the personnel of SNCC and the League, the highest expression of each of
those struggles."[9] Michael Hamlin reflects years later that "the only reason we
weren't smashed entirely was because of our base," and displacing energies
from that base to an undeveloped and unrooted US-wide network knocked
the already-stumbling League off balance.

Reflecting back, Michele Gibbs, a Black woman organiser in the League,
said, "Precisely when the male-led organisations were disintegrating, the
women's movement was gaining ground in the Black community. Many
of us who were forced apart by organisational splits maintained our personal connections. We met in our own consciousness raising groups and
brought up children together." I read Gibbs's observations as a further com-
plication of this history that illustrates the thesis that class fractions must

7    Georgakas and Surkin, *Detroit*, 170–172.
8    Hamlin and Gibbs, *A Black Revolutionary's Life in Labor*, 30.
9    Georgakas and Surkin, *Detroit*, 133–135.

develop the organisational forms appropriate to their needs. The history of the League that is usually told is male-centric, but as Gibbs argues, Black women were pivotal to "building and sustaining a base of support, both organizationally and in the community."[10] When the male-centred organisational structures broke down, the informal and behind-the-scenes structures built by working-class Black women endured, showing themselves to be a deeper autonomous infrastructure of the class struggle.

The lesson I take from this story is that the power exercised by the League as a political force was directly proportionate to the vitality of its connection to its social base. This is consistent with the theme that I do think is useful in Draper's micro-sect article about the relationship between the revolutionary group and its "mass base." Draper says that the thoughts of super smart Marxists cannot, methodologically, be the material for the foundation of a party. "As long as the life of the organisation (whether or not labelled 'party') is actually based on its politically distinctive ideas, rather than on the real social struggles in which it is engaged, it will not be possible to suppress the clash of programs requiring different actions in support of different forces," he warns. I think that when the League turned away from the concerns and self-activity of its social base to focus on forming a US-wide revolutionary party, it suffered the effects of decentring the organising force of real class struggle to centre instead the ambitions and thought of intellectuals as a distinct group themselves.

Draper's binary definition of the sect versus the party with a mass base depends too much on his imagining of the working class as a singular, white masculine body, as opposed to Césaire's multiple class, alive with particularities. I prefer the term "social base," because "mass base" implies a certain quantity or generality of class expression as a condition for the legitimacy of the relationship between organisation and social group. The social base of the League was not "mass" in the sense that Draper means, but it was a powerful, grounding base that animated the League as a vital political force. The "real" social struggles that Draper refers to are radically multiple at their bases and in their so-called superstructural expression. There is not one

10    Hamlin and Gibbs, *A Black Revolutionary's Life in Labor*, 74–76.

single mass base that revolutionary parties must compete for or combine to represent in its totality. Instead, we must see that the working class is irreducibly multiple, composed of innumerable fractions that are real and part of the constitution of the class as it historically *is*, not superficial or inconvenient divisions to be unified away. The anti-identity, economistic Marxists are the ones that have it wrong: it is the recipe for "the" singular class struggle, not culture, that is the problematic fetish.

Gramsci's strategic word on discerning the meaning of the relationship between a revolutionary organisation and its social base is that revolutionaries must be sensitive to the real expression of the interplay between classes and class fractions that constitute our political world. He says that economistic Marxists imagine they can "forge an organism once and for all, something already objectively perfect," but this would be a misdirection, an interruption of organic processes.[11] Such a party, called into being on the basis of a superficial agreement between self-identified revolutionaries rather than an expression of the real appearances of multiple class fractions in multiple locations, would produce an ahistorical rigidity. Most importantly, "class representation" in an organisation or party has to recognise the multiplicity of oppressed classes and groups with distinct economic bases and relations within the overall universe of capitalist production, while also recognising the political significance of multiple cultural, racial, national, gender, and sexual expressions of class being.

Rather than the ahistorical rigidity of the "objectively perfect" but historically artificial party-form, what follows from this analysis is an outline for an organisation composed of organisations deeply rooted in and representative of different fractions of the working class and of Indigenous peoples. An organisation of organisations that each have a base in different fractions of the class has the advantage of synthesising their experiences and lessons of struggle and consequential thinking with the goal of producing deeper and richer mutual understanding between fractions and discovering Césaire's universalism of a thousand points of light.

Red Braid's experiences differ from the League of Revolutionary Black Workers because of our different historical and geographic location and

11   Gramsci, *Prison Notebooks*, 56.

because of significant differences between the class fractions that made up our social bases, but the method of rooting our revolutionary organisation in a social base, we had in common.

## Lessons from Red Braid's organisational experiments

In 2014, as Red Braid formed the core ideas that would become our basis of unity and political strategy, we started by identifying the fractions of oppressed classes that made up our social base, meaning those class fractions that our little collective had direct and reciprocal contact with through organising protests and direct actions. We called these "subaltern" groups—the radically excluded segments of the working class and of Indigenous nations, though the specific subaltern class fractions that composed our social base were unhoused or precariously housed, low-income people. Our decision to invest in organising with the subaltern groups that we came to call "street kin" was both circumstantial—it was the fraction of oppressed groups where we already had contact—and historical, because these communities are defined by a constant social struggle against domineering forces of capitalist and colonial domination. Based on that experience, we speculated that the subalternity of these fractions of oppressed groups meant that they made an appropriate base for revolutionary organising in terms of their historical situation relative to imperial and capitalist power.

Then we asked what form of organisation and activity these subaltern groups use organically. How do our people organise their struggles already and what forms do these struggles take? We found that subaltern groups have been badly disorganised after generations of attack by dominant society. *Indian Act* provisions had long outlawed Indigenous peoples' self-organisation, even making it illegal for Indigenous people to hire lawyers to advocate for their rights within Canadian law. Band councils appointed by the colonial state displaced and disempowered sovereign Indigenous governance structures. And, for Indigenous people living off-reserve, a rigorous apparatus of regulators and cops broke up families by stealing children into Christian assimilation schools and private white homes, locked Indigenous adults up in prisons, and held everyone in between in the restraints of terrible poverty and humiliating institutions.

Since its development as a class, sections of the working class have built and been represented by particular autonomous institutions—including parties, trade unions, and cultural associations—but these have been incomplete and "subject to the initiatives of dominant groups," as Gramsci explains, and are therefore vulnerable to historical situations that are not necessarily stable and enduring.[12] After a brief postwar high where white male workers experienced greater union densities and concurrent socialist organisation, the global restructuring of capitalist production since the 1970s has wrecked these institutions. Neoliberal restructuring has also meant government austerity policies—which means slashing social programs that make life easier for the poor and the transfer of public dollars to policing and prison institutions. And as day-to-day life has gotten harder, the organisations that subaltern people had used to resist and survive, when we had them at all, have been dissolved by increasing capitalist power.

That they lack combat organisations does not mean that subaltern people are not fighting back. In these conditions of desperation and scarcity, without self-directed combat organisations, subaltern people fight for survival spontaneously, in fragmented, partial, and often individual ways. We call these "survival struggles." Survival struggle includes petty crime like shoplifting and low-key drug dealing. It also takes on organisational forms like gangs—whether they are highly organised with semi-formal membership and leadership structures, or informal and more socially based like those common in street communities in the Vancouver suburb of Surrey, where discipline is kept through more sporadic violence.

Taking subaltern survival struggles as the baseline political activity of our social base, Red Braid's main strategy was to seek to politicise these struggles by revealing the political terrain that they exist upon. Survival struggles are waged individually across a political terrain thick with race, gender, and colonial difference and separated by geographies of historical isolation that include the breakdown of communication within this group that shares a common situation and a common enemy. While people in such survival struggles may feel that they are alone and even that their suffering is their

---

12    See Antonio Gramsci, *Subaltern Social Groups: A Critical Edition of Prison Notebook 25* (New York: Columbia University Press, 2021).

fault in one way or another, we see it differently. We see survival struggles as inherently political, though disorganised.

We designed Red Braid's organisational form to serve as an instrument for the exercise of this political strategy. We used our organisation to theorise, analyse, reflect, critique, and make decisions. We found that subaltern communities, because of their radical disorganisation at this point in history, need an organisation to support and give language to their organic collective struggles. And we found that we, as revolutionaries, need an organisation to put thinking into the contexts of collective struggle. The test of our political theories, theories which emerge out of discussions as well as out of reflection on our experiences, is their relevance to our social base communities in struggle. If we cannot be useful to those in struggle, then we have to change to be relevant. When each part in this structure works, the organisation can work as a two-way transmission belt between, on one hand, the general historical and international challenges of building counter-hegemonic power, and on the other, the local challenges of fighting to survive; or put in another way, between theory and practice.

But we encountered significant challenges that have tested the applicability of this strategy for a single organisation operating in just one local area with a small, all-volunteer membership, many of whom were themselves low-income and dispossessed. The classical model that we tried to follow is of organisations that have effectively supported and united the different local instances of class struggle into a general revolutionary political project. For example, the Bolshevik Party in 1917 was important because its leaders recognised the revolutionary potential of worker's councils, called Soviets, that workers had created in factories in every major city in Russia. The Bolsheviks invested in expanding the power workers exercised through the Soviets, uniting their energies between the factories as well as with other sites of class struggle to develop an analysis and program for action against the enemies that all workers shared. In Chile between 1970 and 1973, the Movement for a Revolutionary Left (MIR) organisation similarly tied together the efforts and organic organisations of students, unhoused people, and industrial workers through political education, mass demonstrations, and a common program, uniting these often spontaneous struggles in a common vision for a socialism based in self-activity. But what the Bolsheviks and MIR had in common that we do not have in our period is that they offered a revolutionary political vision to *already existing* organisations of practical, local, subaltern struggle.

Red Braid was able to perform some incredible feats of struggle, defending tent cities for years, starting and defending organised, public, political squats for days and in one case for weeks, and winning some important concessions like hundreds of non-market modular housing units in both Nanaimo and Maple Ridge, where local bigots had been blocking senior governments from building housing for the homeless for years. But we did not manage through these efforts to support people in struggle to build enduring subaltern institutions. We recruited leaders from these subaltern struggles into Red Braid membership, but this also did not translate into the development of autonomous subaltern organisations or other institutions. On reflection, that is because our historical situation forced us to go at this problem backwards. Where the Bolsheviks and MIR recognised and supported the organisations that people created spontaneously to meet their own needs, we had to create those organisations as part of our revolutionary strategy.

In those situations where subaltern people had created their own organisations, like tent cities, we were able to support, strengthen, and politically intervene to make those organisations more powerful, radical, and enduring. This work is consistent with the methods of the Bolsheviks and MIR and countless other revolutionary organisations in history. It is also consistent with the rule suggested by C. L. R. James in his 1958 book, *Facing Reality*, which presents an organisational strategy for socialist revolution that centres workers' self-activity. James argues that the central task of a revolutionary organisation is "to recognize the socialist society" in the lifeworld of workers, identifying and highlighting its existence mired and hidden in capitalist processes, "and to record the facts of its existence." James says, "The new society is to be found in the most unexpected places." He then goes on to describe a plant where workers organise their labour so that one worker, injured in a workplace accident and no longer able to perform the duties of the job, can continue on without getting fired. "Our task then is to *recognize* the new society, align ourselves with it, and *record* the facts of its existence… [We] can do this only by plunging into the great mass of the people and meeting the new society that is there. [The organisation] must live by this; there is no other way it can live." By recording "the fact of the existence" of the "new society," James says it comes more clearly into view and the workers come to recognise the broader worth of their activities and their connections to others like them around the world. In tent cities, we saw two features that made them autonomous subaltern institutions: tent cities are defiant spaces of collective resistance, where subaltern people refuse police orders to move along, and assert their power as a mass; and tent cities, when operated through the self-activity and under the autonomous self-control of residents, depend on mutual aid and cooperation, creating institutions of positive collective survival as well as refusal of the hegemonic order. They are, as James says of the self-organisation of the plant workers who help their injured comrade, the "latent socialism" of concrete subaltern social activity.

But once social workers have dragged the energies of tent city fighters into state processes of discipline and regulation, or once police operations have smashed and disorganised a camp completely, we have stumbled, unable to recognise subaltern social organisation in forms that we could engage. The formal organisations that do exist in street communities are usually state-run service organisations, sometimes with "peer" programs that incorporate organic leaders from communities into pseudo–social work positions with stipend payments. These are not organisations of subaltern autonomy; they are state institutions that invade and reframe organic survival strategies as programs of state power and regulation. Those autonomous structures of the everyday life of people on the streets are either borrowed from capitalist relations, though in illicit and irregular forms like drug dealing operations, or are organised through individual relationships and are extremely ad hoc and fleeting. Facing the disorganisation of subaltern communities and the desperate need to fight back, we tried to introduce organisational forms and strategies from the cookbooks of activism. Subaltern communities almost always planned and attended these protests, news conferences, and direct actions. But Red Braid members were also always at the centre of this organizing effort, organizing those community members to participate while also intervening to influence these events politically. Too much in the struggle depended on our group. Practically speaking, it meant that our small number of organiser-members bore too much responsibility for both the exercise of action on the ground and for the synthesis of resultant political problems into strategy and theory.

We encounter a paradox here. Subaltern groups are terribly disorganised and, as a consequence, are vulnerable to police brutality and the paternalistic manipulations of social service groups that wield soft force against them. Our revolutionary strategy to rebuild the autonomous organisational capacities of the subaltern begins with these miserable historical conditions we inherited. But the strategy we used to confront and correct against this crisis when it was expressed most clearly, was sometimes inflected with a substitutionist dynamic that slowed and misdirected the needed subaltern reorganisation. "Substitutionism" refers to activists who see an instance of oppression taking place, and rather than identify and support the struggles being waged by the oppressed group already, the activist steps in and takes on the struggle on the group's behalf—substituting their activist energy for the self-activity of the oppressed group. The paradox is that, when we build the organisations that we find the subaltern lack, they are not autonomous if they depend on our outside revolutionary organisation.

Rather than follow a substitutionist impulse to step in and introduce organisation where we can see it lacking, James suggests that we double-down on the central, political role of the revolutionary organisation: recognise and record. By disseminating (through publishing and distributing a newspaper that includes recording intimate struggles for subaltern autonomies) and discussing (through meetings, action planning, field education, discussion, and healing circles) this work in the disorganised subaltern community, we can, together, identify the inchoate forms of organisation that are an organic part of everyday struggle and intervene critically in these forms. So long as a revolutionary organisation is composed primarily of declassed intellectuals from activist backgrounds and other subcultures, and so long as the organisation is not led by the subaltern through immersive interaction with autonomous subaltern organisations, then it is not a revolutionary party and must not pretend to lead struggles outside of particular, local instances. But, given the level of disorganisation of subaltern groups today relative to the 1950s when James was writing, to restrict revolutionary work to *recognising and recording* would mean abstaining from subaltern struggles entirely, which could even mean passively observing harms that a revolutionary organisation could otherwise intervene in and counter. There is a lot to learn from the anti-substitutionist critiques of C. L. R. James' autonomist period, if only we can add to "recognize and record," strategic *reorganisation* and *resistance*.

A total revolutionary perspective and organisational apparatus can grow from this revolutionary organisation rooted down deep in a particular fraction of the subaltern, so long as we can find and make relations with similarly oriented groups rooted in other class fractions. Those groups could be organisations that we could unite with and make a new organisational form that, taken together, would link us to a more total spectrum of the world working class and of Indigenous peoples fighting for sovereignty. Such a united organisation would be able to coordinate resistance and power-taking actions that could threaten capitalist and colonial power and could be able to form a revolutionary programme. That would be a party.

What we can offer to this hypothetical group are lessons from our organising experiments. What we can gain is the critical, political feedback from these allied groups that would offer an outside perspective on our work. This work of synthesising each of our local experiences into a common, political organisational venue will, we hope, develop a unified, common language and set of goals out of which common strategies and the capacity to coordinate across class fractions and geographies can be created—therefore forming the basis for that party.

You can see here that the path from the pre-party formation of Red Braid to that party that could represent the working class and sovereign Indigenous fighters as a whole is not just a matter of organising in local struggles alone. In order to have anything meaningful to contribute to that potential party form, a revolutionary organisation would have to build the power of subaltern people and dutifully represent and honour their interests and desires. An essential part of that preparation is also in building relations with other pre-party groups that have similar designs on building power. But it's important to be real about what class forces specific groups represent. One reason the League of Revolutionary Black Workers was unable to pivot into a national organisation as the Black Workers Congress was because, with the pivot, the League broke its dialectical relationship with its social base of Black workers in factories. Other locals that were supposed to be animating part of that Congress had even less-developed connections to a social base. Connections with revolutionaries in other places can help insulate a single group from the dangers of exhaustion and demoralisation, but for these discussion networks to approach something like a party, each part must be actively, dialectically representative of the real struggles of a class fraction. To build a revolutionary organisation is to put together a puzzle out of historical conditions that include us, ourselves. The revolutionary organisation requires autonomous subaltern institutions, which demand the support of revolutionary organisations! The single revolutionary organisation needs relations with revolutionaries elsewhere, but to do useful cross-regional work between groups depends on the living existence of individual organisations! Nothing could be more complicated.

## Class fractions and the organisation of organisations

Organisations that are rooted in particular fractions of global working class and Indigenous sovereignty struggles have their own particular dialectical relationship to those struggles, determined by the level of self-organisation in the group's social base, the location of that fraction in the global process of capitalist production (including its imperialist expressions), and the maturity and fighting capacity of the organisation itself. But the role of the revolutionary organisation is similar in each case: in one motion, carrying, exercising, and expanding the role of revolutionary politics in those struggles, and in another, synthesising those experiences as informed revolutionary politics.

Revolutionary movements always include this tension in one form or another between the local, immediate needs of people engaged in direct struggle and the broad, longer-term and more abstract needs of a revolutionary contest for power generally. By virtue of the immediacy of their conflict with police or strikebreakers and the demands of the others around them, local fighters are more attuned to immediate needs. Meanwhile, leaders farther afield who have the advantage of distance from those immediate needs and therefore receive a broader range of information from a diversity of local struggles, can more dispassionately measure the relative importance and strategic value of a particular struggle as they focus on the more distant horizon of possibility. To emphasise a particular, local struggle too much can be myopic and lead a group into demoralisation when it does not succeed. But to direct a local struggle from afar can short-circuit the sensitivity of local fighters to their particular dynamics and lead to the use of rash, overstated, or ignorant strategies and tactics.

The first motion, where the guiding principle is to *make revolutionary politics relevant to people in struggle*, prioritises the particular needs of a particular class fraction. Leadership in this activity must be a composite of the local knowledge of the organisation embedded in its social base and the self-activity of the community involved directly in their own organic struggle. I'm using some key terms here: the *transmission belt process* refers to the dialectical relationship (meaning that the relationship itself is changed through the process of creating change) between the *revolutionary organisation* that has its politics and strategy to offer to its social base, and its *social base*–locked in particular struggles. This social base community, in turn, tests the usefulness and relevance of these politics and strategies through practice, and returns lessons to the organisation. It is a bit unfortunate that Lenin used the "transmission belt" metaphor a couple times, because his usage was more instrumental and top-down than what I mean here. He referred to trade unions and other mass organisations as a transmission belt to carry the party's ideas to the people, which sounds more like a delivery system than a dialectical connection between wheels that depend on each other for the organic functioning of an engine. The function of the activity of members of the organisation in this process is to serve as intermediary in both directions—in carrying the untested politics and strategy into the social base struggle, and in relaying self-critical lessons back to the organisation.

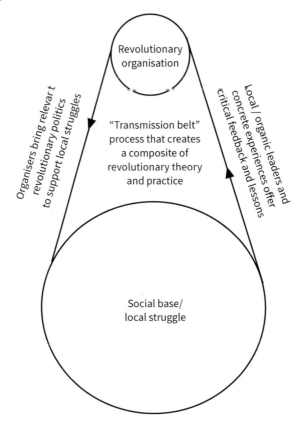

*Relationship between a revolutionary organisation and its social base*

But the strength of the revolutionary organisation, being embedded in a particular class fraction as its social base, is also its limitation. The description of these limitations and the way around them are usefully thought through by the US-based libertarian communist group CounterPower in their 2020 book, *Organizing for Autonomy*. Arguing that socialist organisations must both "defend the everyday interests of the proletarian and popular social groups *and* prefigure a communist alternative," CounterPower proposes a "party of a networked type" where "each organisation could operate as a complementary part of a more complex whole." They cite inspiring historical experiences of socialist movements in Latin America, including the five parties that together constituted the Frente Farabundo Martí para la Liberación Nacional (FMLN) in El Salvador's revolution and civil war of

1979–1992; the strategy of "zonalization," where each of four member revolutionary organisations controlled a particular base area in Guatemala's Unidad Revolucionaria Nacional Guatemalteca (URNG) in 1982; and, during the socialist Salvador Allende government years in Chile, the Movimiento de Izquierda Revolucionaria (MIR), which was composed, at a social if not formal level, of affiliated social movement and union organisations that carried out land seizures for the homeless and factory occupations, creating "communal forms of governance based on autonomous popular assemblies." Although CounterPower doesn't include Cuba in their examples, Fidel Castro's Movimiento 26 de Julio (M-26-7) is another example of a revolutionary socialist organisation organically composed of the multiple parts determined by and through the course of struggle. Though a difference with M-26-7 was that it did not start out as a necessarily socialist project. The combinations and adaptations of the Latin American movements and organisations of the 1970s and '80s cut new paths to revolution outside of the formulas dictated by historic political tendencies that tend to insist upon a single, intelligent leadership as the key to socialist revolution. There is a lot to learn from them.

No one organisation or party can represent all the multiple fractions of the working class, let alone of Indigenous nations. But an *organisation of organisations* can create a space where each revolutionary group can carry the results of their *local* synthesis into a common space with other organisations (each embedded in their own class fraction). This would make way for the creation of a *global* synthesis by combining these multiple experiences across the landscape of a broader mass base and a more complete class representation than any group could accomplish in a moment of class fragmentation, on its own. The following chart shows approximately how this kind of relationship could work, with revolutionary organisations grounded in particular class fractions collaborating to form a universal built not of a totalizing unity but of vibrant particulars. For the purpose of illustration, I have charted these class-fraction groups within their own individual circles. In reality, fractions will overlap between different class locations: the Black freedom struggle and teachers; unhoused people and retail workers; migrant farm workers and Indigenous #landback struggles; the fights of each fraction may be carried out together or in complicated interwoven ways.

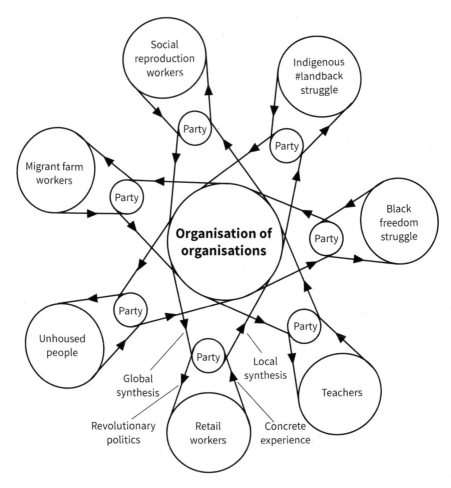

*Organisation of organisations is a space for*
*a universal composed of particulars*

The local "transmission belt" work of the political-practical organisation in the struggles of its social base demands a rigorous local attention to
the struggles on the ground in a particular class fraction; the organisation
of organisations demands abstraction from particular class fractions to a
revolutionary context that insists upon, as Aimé Césaire said, a universal of
particulars. Organisations, rather than individual activists, are essential to
this work because only an organisation—with developed political analysis

to synthesise with communities in struggle and a responsible membership base—can act as a transmission belt locally, creating the precondition for combination between localities. Regardless of the work done by a dedicated individual, an activist on their own lacks that space of local synthesis that is necessary in order to carry the consciousness of a particular class fraction into an organisation of organisations as contribution to the production of a universal of particulars. To extend the metaphor of the dialectical transmission belt between a local organisation and its social base, the organisation of organisations depends on a serpentine belt that combines the motion of each class fraction in struggle in a total class movement. Each, should they exist, powers the other.

## Conclusion: Two legacies of the last great socialist movement

There are two contesting legacies of the socialist movements of the 1970s and 80s—the last great period of global socialist revolution: Eurocommunism and autonomism. The first legacy, Eurocommunism, is of the parliamentary path to power anticipated by Salvador Allende's socialist Popular Unity government in Chile, which was defeated by a fascist coup in 1973. The premise of Eurocommunism was that the long period of capitalist expansion after the Second World War and the "labour peace" that was part of that boom was ending in a new capitalist crisis. Eurocommunists hoped to win electoral votes by promising to maintain and expand the gains and welfare-state reforms of the postwar period through continued negotiation and accommodation between workers and bosses rather than through class struggle.

The legacy of autonomism, the emergent alternative to Eurocommunism, is of a worker's reaction against the class compromises, abandonment of the revolutionary project, and the setbacks and weakening of once-powerful worker's movements under this Eurocommunism. Autonomism was also a recommitment to the fundamentals of communism expressed through the self-emancipation of workers in the Soviets of the Russian Revolution of 1917. Not all movements that I consider to have been part of the historic autonomist tendency under the banner of extra-electoral struggle and direct worker's power used the same terminology. According to the conditions in different countries, different forms, strategies, and political articulations of autonomism emerged in the 1970s and early '80s. In Italy, operaismo (often translated as workerism) emphasised the direct class struggle and power of workers in factories; in the UK, anglophone autonomism focused on feminist struggle, including the Wages for Housework movement; in the US, autonomist struggle was preeminently about Black worker's power through the League of Revolutionary Black Workers and a scattering of small socialist groups influenced by C. L. R. James; and in Latin America, revolutionary parties in Nicaragua, El Salvador, and Guatemala were composed of both the direct power wielded by guerrilla movements and their electoral wings, while in Chile the electoral and direct action groups were separate but had dynamic relations that overlapped in struggle.

It is easy to see Eurocommunism and autonomism as mutually exclusive political tendencies, even if they were established antagonistically against each other. But with the benefit of a historical perspective, I think it is more useful to see both as results of the sparks thrown out of the friction of a moment when the organisation of industrial production under capitalism was in the throes of transformation and the authority previously enjoyed by the Communist Party of the USSR had been irreparably stained by Khrushchev's revelations about Stalin's long terror, followed by the ostensibly post-Stalinist bureaucracy's military repressions in the Czechoslovak and Hungarian socialist republics. Eurocommunism was a response from the labour bureaucracy and Communist Party leaders, as well as those workers entrenched in the aristocracy of labour who hoped to use this moment of pivot to turn towards a greater socialisation of production. Autonomism was a response from those denied that tenuous toehold in respectable society, and especially of a generation of younger workers who had experienced the radical possibilities of the militant street movements of 1968.

A good example of a dialectical spark firing between these contesting movements was in Chile, where Movement for a Revolutionary Left (MIR) militants moved energetically into the space provided by the election of Salvador Allende's Popular Unity government. When Allende promised that his courts would not prosecute movements making socialist gains, MIR supported land seizures by homeless workers as well as factory occupations. Regardless of their limitations and strategic and political errors, in Chile a socialist response spanned and included parliamentary and class-autonomist strategies, and each leaped over the other in a dialectic of revolutionary development—until the process as a whole was arrested by General Pinochet's bloody coup of September 11, 1973.

The monopoly of left politics in Canada and the US today by democratic socialists, the inheritors of Eurocommunism, must be broken by those who follow the legacy of violent revolutionary rupture, from Russia in 1917 to the autonomists of the 1970s—whose political project was cut off by a global capitalist offensive before it could mature and be truly tested. I am not suggesting that social revolutionaries should depend on or welcome a Eurocommunist-style "political revolution"; to the contrary, part of our job is to expose the illusions of parliamentary socialists as false promises and dead ends. But rather than a critique from the balcony of history, it is through struggle—where we offer revolutionary politics as the only relevant instrument to make sense of and advance subaltern struggles, and exhaust and overcome the contained theatres of struggle available to us—that we can show that we either exceed the limits of social democracy, or die.

While spontaneous outpourings of collective rage will continue to shake and terrify the capitalists into their penthouse panic rooms, frightening the rich is, at best, an aggressive form of lobbying for more progressive politicians and stronger consumer stimulus packages. The promise of decolonial socialism is that each person will have what they need in order to develop their full human capacity, and that they will then be able to contribute back to the worlds of the past and future that capitalism threatens to obliterate. The organisational strategy that relies on and feeds a universal power based in each of our particular energies foretells a post-revolutionary world that is, likewise, not unitary, singular, or directive, but multiple—a world we all live in together through our combination.

But moving from protest and rebellion to the planned, intelligent, efficient, social coordination necessary to seize and operate the global forces of production requires a self-conscious and democratic organisational machinery. Because we are far away from that level of autonomous organisation today does not mean it is impossible. We must waste no time beginning.

# Who are the protagonists of climate justice?

## The Green New Deal and the dangers of building a citizen base

Isabel Krupp

*The following article was initially published in* The Volcano *newspaper in October 2019.*

Just over a decade ago, Al Gore was the face of climate action in the United States and Canada. His documentary, *An Inconvenient Truth* (2006), premiered at the Sundance Film Festival to standing ovations. It won two Academy Awards. The film closed with the message, "The climate crisis can be solved," and then promoted energy-efficient light bulbs, hybrid cars, and recycling.

Times have changed. It's no longer possible to frame climate change as an "inconvenience." The scale and urgency of the crisis drove six million people into the streets in September 2019 with the beginning of the latest wave of global protests. The face of this new era of climate action, sixteen-year-old Greta Thunberg, has a message that resonates with our times: "I don't want your hope. I want you to panic and then I want you to act. I want you to act as if our house is on fire." Today's generation of celebrity-activists wastes no time promoting ethical consumer choices—they call these tactics out for what they are: dangerous distractions. Instead, they demand bold, radical action. They call for revolution.

The Green New Deal (GND) is the answer to these demands. At least, that's what its advocates say. The GND is a developing set of policies aimed at reducing global emissions by forty to sixty percent by 2030 and achieving net zero emissions by 2050. Naomi Klein, a leading proponent for a GND in Canada, calls the GND "a transformational vision for the next economy"—an economy that places the needs of people and the planet ahead of profit, renounces exploitation and inequality, and respects the sovereignty of Indigenous peoples around the world.

But critics from the left argue that the versions of a GND being championed by progressive politicians and their allies come nowhere close to ending exploitation, dispossession, and oppression. In response to shortcomings in US Representative Alexandria Ocasio-Cortez's version of the GND, the Ecosocialist Working Group of the Democratic Socialists of America developed a set of guiding principles for what they refer to as "a radical Green New Deal." The Indigenous Environmental Network also released a critique of Ocasio-Cortez's resolution with the goal of pushing the GND further to the left. The Indigenous revolutionary organisation Red Nation has developed a platform they call the Red Deal, which seeks to "capture the momentum" of the GND and "catapult it into a full-blown mass movement" for anti-capitalist, anti-colonial revolution.

Calls for a "radical GND" miss the danger that the movement for a GND, radical or otherwise, presents: the delusion that we can accomplish our goals by mobilising US and Canadian civil society, electing "climate champions," and pressing for legislative and policy reforms. A GND is a shortcut—a way to dodge the work of organising and building the independent power of exploited, Indigenous, and oppressed people around the world. That fundamental misdirection, not the particular inadequacies of its recommendations or wording, is why the GND won't get us to where we need to go. By funnelling grassroots energies towards electoralism and reform, the GND has become a prop for the New Democratic Party (NDP) in Canada and the

Democrats in the USA, and it functions more broadly to legitimise the colonial and capitalist institutions of Canada and the United States, steering us away from the revolutionary path that it claims to represent.

## Recruiting people into the state

While its spokespeople refer to the GND as a grassroots movement to radically transform society, at the end of the day, it's a set of legislative and policy reforms. In Canada, all practical activity surrounding the GND is led by a horde of well-funded environmental NGOs and oriented towards politicians and government institutions. Greenpeace created a toolkit for winning a GND, which recommends talking to your MP, writing letters to the editor, and painting street murals to "show our politicians with our art that it's time for a Green New Deal." The Council of Canadians produced an organising guide, which outlines strategies for pressuring municipal governments to pass GND resolutions. Our Time, a youth organisation supported by the NGO 350 Canada, endorsed and canvassed for NDP and Green candidates for the federal election. The Courage Coalition circulated a petition calling on NDP leader Jagmeet Singh to run on a GND in the 2019 Canadian federal election.

The GND is oriented towards the state because, according to its proponents, only the state has the power to solve the climate crisis. In June 2019, activist and author Harsha Walia spoke at a cross-Canada tour promoting the GND. She told a crowd of more than 300 people gathered in Vancouver, "Canada is genocide." But when documentary filmmaker Avi Lewis took to the stage, he positioned the Canadian state at the centre of the fight for climate justice, arguing that "only a nation state, with the power to issue its own currency, will be able to marshal the vast resources necessary for a climate-saving transition at the scale and the speed that we need." While these two positions appear antithetical, they're reconciled within the movement for a GND, which argues that the people (a cross-class melange united around moral-climate outrage) can—and must—take the reins of the state through campaigning, voting, and protesting in order to steer it away from genocide and towards justice.

When Lewis said, "Neither governments nor markets are going to be the protagonists of this story—the people are!" he was met with thunderous applause. He continued, "We're talking about building a mass movement powerful enough to elect and hold accountable a government that will turn our vision into law. This is how we'll win a GND." That bears repeating: the role of the people, according to Lewis, is to elect politicians and hold them accountable.

This is what Lewis means when he says the people are the protagonists: the people vote, petition, campaign, and put pressure on politicians, but it's the politicians who make the decisions. Lewis tells us we can't trust the state, and he even questions "the legitimacy of those colonial structures," but ultimately, under the guise of building popular power, Lewis and other GND activists recruit people into state activity.

## Building a citizen base

Because it is oriented towards the state, the GND depends on a social base of "citizens" and "voters" who are invested, psychologically and materially, in the activities and institutions of the state. CBC reporter Laura Lynch gestured to the contradiction between the radical vision of the GND and the material interests of its citizen base when she asked Naomi Klein, "Are the citizens of the developed world ready for the kind of wealth redistribution that would come with this kind of climate action?"

In her response, Klein sidestepped the question of material interests while affirming the centrality of the citizen to the project of climate justice. According to Klein, "We have to decide: are we going to hoard or are we going to share?" In other words, the strategy to win a GND is to convince Canadian citizens to set aside their immediate material interests in favour of abstract ideals like "fairness" and "humanity." The problem with this strategy is that it relegates communities that are excluded from Canadian civil society—whether legally, by Canada's imperialist borders and citizenship regime, or de facto, by settler colonialism and race, gender, and class oppression—to the sidelines, where there is little to do but wait for the "citizens of the developed world" to decide, as Klein said, "what kind of people we want to be."

Laura Lynch could have posed a second question: are Canadian citizens ready to give back Indigenous lands? During the event in June,

Kanahus Manuel, a leader of the Tiny House Warriors, a group currently obstructing the path of the Trans Mountain pipeline through unceded Secwepemc territory, told the crowd, "The true Green New Deal means land back for Indigenous people." Later in the evening, Avi Lewis referred to Indigenous territories as "land we must give back," recasting Manuel's statement to centre the settler colonial state and its citizenry as the agents of decolonisation.

What could compel a state built on theft and genocide to "give back" the land on which its very existence depends? According to Lewis, "It begins with a revolution of respect for Indigenous peoples." But this is a failing strategy based on abstract ideals and undue faith in settler "goodness." While GND spokespeople pay lip service to Indigenous sovereignty, even suggesting that the GND could be expanded to encompass the Red Deal (making it, as Lewis quipped, "a rainbow deal"), at the end of the day, the strategic orientation of the GND towards the Canadian and US government and state as actors necessarily leaves colonialism intact.

Laura Lynch wasn't wrong to question whether "citizens of the developed world" are ready for revolution. The cross-class category of the citizen encompasses capitalists whose interests are diametrically opposed to revolution, as well as the Canadian working class whose consciousness is, in large part, corrupted by imperialist and settler colonial power. The white working class in particular experiences immediate benefits as a result of Canada's imperialist domination and exploitation of the Global South, and further benefits from the violence Canada enacts against Indigenous peoples within its borders in order to continue occupying and plundering their territories. This segment of the working class—with its ideological and material investment in the twin systems of capitalism and colonialism—finds a degree of power and belonging alongside bosses and landlords in the realm of the "citizen," "voter," and "taxpayer."

The GND adapts to the imperialist and settler consciousness that pervades Canada, with the hope of nudging it along the path of climate justice, and more. But by building a cross-class citizen base and affirming its faith in colonial and capitalist institutions, the GND leads us astray. To find our way, we need to build a base of working-class and Indigenous people around the understanding that our long-term interests lie in divesting from imperialist and settler colonial power and joining in the struggles of exploited, Indigenous, and oppressed peoples around the world.

## More than "people in motion"

Some socialists, including writer David Camfield, suggest that there's no contradiction between the revolutionary rhetoric and reformist strategies of the GND. Camfield warns socialists not to dismiss the GND, which has value, he argues, not as an end in itself, but as a means to "build a larger and more powerful movement for climate justice." The mass movement that Camfield envisions is expansive enough to encompass the GND plus "efforts on other fronts, including anti-pipeline campaigns, resistance to austerity, and anti-colonial struggles." Once it has been built, Camfield suggests, the movement can then be directed against the root cause of the climate crisis: capitalism. But Camfield's big-tent approach allows him to avoid reckoning with the contradictions between the movement for a GND and the revolutionary struggle against capitalism and colonialism. Camfield declares, "What we need is many more people in motion," but the character and direction of a movement is just as important as motion itself.

Camfield is right to recognise that the climate crisis presents a profound opportunity to the left—but alongside that opportunity comes the responsibility to develop an honest and accurate assessment of what is needed and how to achieve it. If we agree with Harsha Walia that "climate change is a devastating symptom of capitalism and colonialism," then it is clear that we can't look to the state to solve the crisis for us.

The movement for a GND tells workers to wait for progressive politicians to legislate a Just Transition, just as it tells Indigenous nations to wait for the settler colonial state to recognise their sovereignty and return their lands. The myth that only the state has the power to solve the climate crisis casts the people not as protagonists, but as secondary characters whose role is to demonstrate moral outrage and desperation in order to convince the state to act. The desperate, moral gestures of the GND match with Greta Thunberg's righteous indignation as the face of today's climate movement. We have to lay waste to this myth to become conscious of our own power—to see that, through our combined self-activity, we can bring the gears of capitalism and colonialism to a grinding halt.

## Workers' self-management: "We can carry on without them"

The GND takes its name from the New Deal of the 1930s—President Franklin D. Roosevelt's attempt to dull rising working-class militancy and the devastating effects of the Great Depression in the USA through massive investment in public works like housing, schools, and hospitals, as well as legislative and policy reforms like social security, union protections, and financial regulations. During this period, radicals led by the US Communist Party adopted a strategy known as the popular front, which involved building alliances with progressive Democrats like Roosevelt, trade union bureaucrats, and middle-class liberals, at the expense of building militant industrial unions and an independent labour party. According to socialist Charlie Post, the popular front strategy was a compromise that "undermined the possibilities for a militant labour movement, significant social reforms, and left-wing politics" in the US.

Instead of taking inspiration from this moment of class compromise, revolutionaries should look to examples of class struggle, like May '68 in France. For over a month, France saw mass demonstrations, street battles, university and factory occupations, and general strikes involving ten million workers—more than twenty-two percent of the total population of the country. The movement was not limited to bread-and-butter demands like better wages. One of its central rallying points was workers' self-management, known as autogestion.

In May '68, workers across France occupied factories. When 293 workers took over an electricity plant at Cheviré, they continued providing electricity to hospitals and other vital services, while paralysing local industry. The workers themselves organised production around the clock. After two weeks with no bosses or managers, one worker triumphantly declared, "Everything is going fine. We can carry on production without them." Another observed, "We wanted to prove that we were capable and therefore had a right to control the running of the means of production. And this we have proved."

What the workers in Cheviré and factories across France showed is that the working class has the capacity to seize the means of production and redirect them towards the social good, which in our moment must include the good of the climate, earth, and biosphere. Imagine workers today occupying factories, distribution routes, and resource extraction sites around the world, shutting down destructive and wasteful industrial production and producing to meet the needs of people and the planet. Suddenly the power of the state to mitigate the climate crisis through legislative and policy reforms seems pathetic in comparison.

## Indigenous sovereignty: "Necessary for the continuation of life"

While working-class self-activity has the potential to interrupt and replace the capitalist mode of production, the self-activity of Indigenous peoples confronts the colonial domination of land and life, and it charts a way for Indigenous land relations and life ways to persist and proliferate. In a recent article for *The Intercept*, Nick Estes argues that Indigenous land defence, from Standing Rock to Wet'suwet'en, is "necessary for the continuation of life on a planet teetering on collapse." Taking Unist'ot'en as an example, Estes demonstrates how land defenders not only block climate-destroying projects like the Coastal GasLink pipeline but also "bring the land and the community back to health" by restoring land-based economies and exercising sovereignty over their territories.

While the movement for a GND pretends that Indigenous sovereignty can coexist alongside the colonial state, what it promotes in practice is not sovereignty but subordination. No matter how many "climate champions" are elected, the bourgeois and colonial state will never legislate an end to colonial borders and property regimes or restrict capital's inborn need to discover and dominate new frontiers. As Estes writes for *Jacobin* magazine, these changes require nothing short of a "social revolution that turns back the forces of destruction."

This vision of social revolution is no more utopian than the fantasy that legislative and policy reforms can end the climate crisis. So why is the climate justice movement investing in reform, not revolution? Because for people like Klein and Lewis, the protagonists of climate justice are not working-class people at the point of production and Indigenous nations defending and nurturing their lands, but the middle class, the NGOs, the professional intellectuals and journalists, and the politicians they claim they can influence. This is the fundamental problem with the GND: it promotes the lie that those with power, the same people who created the crisis we're facing, are the ones who can reform the system to pull us out of crisis.

## Independent movements and antagonistic institutions

If we're serious about revolution, we need to start with communities that are radically excluded from Canadian and US civil society and have neither faith nor hope in existing political and economic systems. We need to build Indigenous and working-class power by establishing independent, militant, antagonistic institutions—not by capitulating to the priorities and constraints of bourgeois institutions like the NDP or the NGOs that funnel grassroots energies into the project of progressive electoralism.

When we look around, we can already see the germs of our power: homeless people are establishing and defending tent cities, drug users are launching unsanctioned overdose prevention sites, migrants are occupying airports to block the deportation of their comrades, and Indigenous nations are reoccupying their traditional territories. These struggles may not carry the banner of climate justice, but by building independent Indigenous and working-class power, they prepare us to extinguish the flames of our burning house and build a new one in its place.

*A Separate Star* Section 2

# Decolonisation

# Introduction
## Decolonisation

This section presents the *decolonial* part of our socialism. While other sections of this book are focused mostly on theory, this section on decolonisation is preoccupied with practice, or, more exactly, with the evaluation and critique of Red Braid's experiences with anti-colonial and decolonial struggles.

This section begins with "History of the Indigenous Leadership Council (ILC)," a chapter that tells the story of Indigenous organising in and with our organisation. Ours is a history of action, of fighting pipelines by blocking ports and railways and fighting for the sovereignty of inner-city and low-income Indigenous communities. But more central here is a history of thought and critique. The three periods of Indigenous struggle in Red Braid described in this history are defined by three developing ideas that directed the action and organisational structures of Red Braid by and for Indigenous members of the group: Indigenous and working-class unity, Indigenous autonomy, and finally, Indigenous sovereignty as organisational method.

"Decolonisation and the struggles of Indigenous street kin" is a programmatic document that establishes critical definitions of anti-colonial and decolonial terms as used by the ILC, written when the group was composed of low-income Indigenous women who organised in urban and suburban spaces in the Vancouver area. This document defines the role of organisation in low-income Indigenous peoples' struggles and what the ILC meant by Indigeneity, urban Indigeneity, kinship.

"Covid-19 Plus Colonisation Equals Death" is an important document from the second period of the ILC; a statement written by the Indigenous Warrior Women of the Hothouse Squat, a group started by the Indigenous Leadership Council at the outset of the COVID 19 pandemic.

Finally, "Indigenous sovereignty, Decolonial Internationalism, and the Settler Working Class," by Mercedes Courtoreille (Cree), is an adaptation of a speech they gave at a panel organised by the Marxist Center in April 2021. Courtoreille argues that while the struggles for socialism and for Indigenous sovereignty are intertwined, they are not identical. As well as differences between the destinations of each struggle, there are also important differences between how each is waged, and in who can lead. Working-class people can lead the socialist struggle against capitalism, but Indigenous people don't need non-Indigenous workers to build non-capitalist Indigenous worlds. For the working class in a settler colonial society to confront and overturn capitalism, they must walk an anti-colonial path, and for that path to be true depends on revolutionary Indigenous leadership.

The interaction between decolonial theory and practice—particularly for Indigenous people who live under the colonial conditions of crushing poverty, overcrowded slum housing, the constant threat of child apprehension, and homelessness, often on their own lands—is the driving force of the chapters collected here. This section of A Separate Star, like all the others, does not offer a perfect recipe for action. What it does offer is a history of thinking hard, of trying against all odds, and of lessons from where these experiments worked and built Indigenous sovereignty as a method of struggle, and just as importantly, where we fell short.

# For Decolonial Revolution

## A history of the Indigenous Leadership Council of Red Braid

Red Braid

When the group that would become Red Braid first started organising together, we found ourselves stumbling over contradictions between our claims that we opposed settler colonialism, and the slogans, demands, and methods of organising that we had inherited from the community organisations we had emerged out of. In *The Volcano* in 2016, then-member Natalie Knight (Yurok/Navajo) writes that we were sometimes guilty of trying to resolve these contradictions "with rhetorical acknowledgement rather than the careful attention they deserve." In the context of a settler colonial society, "demands for redistribution of wealth" against the impoverishment produced through capitalist production "can seem the same as demands for a share of Indigenous land." She concludes that it is not enough to "say that our struggles are united—we have to find better ways of practising what we preach and participating in both of the struggles against colonialism and capitalism."

That "practising what we preach" led to a lot of group thinking about organisational forms and identities, as well as political bases of unity, and to a series of organising experiments based on that thinking. Fundamental to this series of experiments was the Indigenous Leadership Council (ILC) of Red Braid, a group that emerged out of organisational experiments as an Indigenous-only space, responsible for organising decolonial (distinct from anti-colonial) struggles within and through Red Braid. This chapter reflects on these experiments by breaking them down into three periods: initially, we were an organisation that sought to unite Indigenous and non-Indigenous members; then we built autonomous Indigenous organising spaces; last, we arrived at sovereignty as Indigenous organisational method.

During our first experiment—organising a united Indigenous and non-Indigenous "we" in Red Braid—we tried to deal with differences between Indigenous and non-Native working-class members and political goals by speaking in and through both voices. Maybe because the majority of our membership was non-Indigenous and defaulted to a settler consciousness, or because we were straining to define and work out our political vision and agreements in both the decolonial and the socialist "strands" of our "braid," we were frustrated by a tendency of our non-Indigenous members to speak confidently and knowledgeably about capitalism and class struggles while reducing Indigenous peoples' struggles to a rhetorical add-on. Indigenous members found this organisational strategy tended to flatten Indigenous people into an indistinguishable mass along with the non-Indigenous working class, through a poverty reductionist unity that could not recognise or deal with the specific problems Indigenous people face, like the settler colonialism that results in Indigenous people's disproportionate representation in the ranks of the poor in Canada and the US.

Our second experiment—creating autonomous Indigenous spaces—was designed to address the limitations of organising through a united, hybrid organisation. Autonomy meant that the group as a whole prioritised the distinct operation of the Indigenous Leadership Council as a leadership body parallel in authority to Red Braid's non-Indigenous majority Coordinating Committee. The ILC formed a coordinating committee, held regular community meetings, drafted statements, organised talking circles, and coordinated demonstrations. But Indigenous members who sensed the possibility and pressing need for Indigenous community organising felt increasingly frustrated by the distractions of having to deal with non-Indigenous members and the socialist-focused politics of the rest of the group.

In hindsight, it was a mistake to apply the political and organisational framework of autonomy developed through Marxist theory about legacies of revolutionary class struggle to Indigenous sovereignty struggles. The limits of autonomy brought us back to a beginning, to Indigenous sovereignty as method of struggle for sovereignty, which, we quickly found, was not something that we could think of through the framework of a single organisation—particularly not one that was majority non-Indigenous.

Red Braid's experiments with decolonial struggle ultimately challenged us to rethink the premise of our group's strategic unity between Indigenous sovereigntists and non-Indigenous socialists. Our political premise, that Indigenous sovereigntists and socialists can productively unite against their shared enemies, was challenged by the depths of antagonism between settlers and Indigenous people that we plumbed in our group. We found that we could not afford to deviate, even temporarily or through a unity in action, from Indigenous sovereignty as practised method, without swerving our directed struggle away from that goal.

In our initial steps, our unified Indigenous and non-Indigenous organisation was challenged by the demands of sovereignty as an organising method. The problem, from a perspective of organisation, is that a sovereign Indigenous people, however constituted, cannot depend on non-Indigenous people for its survival, political articulation, or collective activities. In Red Braid, that was too often the case. To adopt sovereignty as method, Red Braid aspired to turn outward, to learn from and support Indigenous sovereignty struggles located outside our group. For Indigenous members of Red Braid, the Indigenous Leadership Council remained critical in this work, reaching into and organising those low-income and street kin Indigenous communities who are under-represented in land-based sovereignty struggles, using Red Braid's organisational resources to heal, and strategizing and building the sovereign power of low-income, street kin, urban Indigenous peoples to lead powerful movements against colonialism.

In this chapter we first outline an argument for decolonial socialism based on a rejection of colonial socialism and a commitment to the distinction between anti-colonial struggle against the settler colonial state—which we think workers can contribute to alongside Indigenous sovereigntists—and decolonial struggle—which is the purview of Indigenous nations. Then we examine Red Braid's three periods of experimenting with organisational forms that can actualize these principles.

## The principles of Indigenous and non-Indigenous unity in Red Braid

Red Braid modelled our strategic unity of Indigenous and non-Native people on the social structures created together by Indigenous and non-Native people in low-income communities where our organising work had always been based. In these communities of unhoused and precariously housed people, Indigenous and non-Native people often have deep and interdependent relations. Red Braid member Linda Mama Bear Whitford, who was killed by the health effects of colonialism in her supportive housing room in May 2020, discussed this interwoven Indigenous and non-Native community as her "street family," and as an extended, practical reach of her kinship relations. Following Mama Bear's thinking, we referred to this community as "street kin."

In street kin communities, Indigenous and non-Native low-income people defend each other and collaborate in informal and illicit economies for mutual survival. But these are not utopian communities. Although Indigenous and non-Native low-income people collaborate around the shared interests of their common survival, non-Natives in these informal and spontaneous alliances tend to disappear the particularities of colonial dispossession that produce Indigenous poverty and homelessness, and pressure Indigenous people in these alliances to "act white" in the course of the struggle, emphasising only those demands that include non-Indigenous poor people. We thought of this flattening of Indigenous people into the white-dominant street community as "poverty reductionism," a form of class reductionism that emerges from the under-developed and local form of class consciousness that exists in many street communities.

Our inheritance, therefore, was complicated. In one sense, Indigenous and non-Native low-income people unite through common survival struggles. This unity is practised in the daily lives of low-income communities because it arises organically out of the conditions that Indigenous and non-Native low-income people share on the streets, in supportive housing buildings, and in illicit and informal economies of survival. It comes about through the simple mathematics of having greater strength in numbers and of having powerful shared enemies—police, property owners, business owners, landlords, local governments, and anti-homeless vigilante gangs. The organic character of this unity prefigures conscious political organisation and makes for a powerful model that, we found, can be translated into political organisational form in tent city councils, street kin self-defence organisations against police and vigilante violence, and activist campaigns.

But we had to oppose the poverty reductionist political character of this unity, where low-income whites tend to decentre Indigenous peoples' sovereignty struggles against colonialism by insisting on uniting around experiences and forms of colonialism like poverty and homelessness rather than the colonial causes of poverty and homelessness. Decolonial socialist unity inverts this dynamic, decentring white men and centring Indigenous women's struggles as the universalizing politic. In the spring of 2021 Red Braid organised a "Justice for Georgia" campaign in support of Ali Colligan, an Anishinaabe mother whose daughter Georgia had been moved through fifteen foster homes since being apprehended by the Ministry of Children and Family Development (MCFD) in 2016. The demonstrations led by Colligan in front of the MCFD office and the Surrey RCMP detachment were focused on Indigenous sovereignty and the defence of Indigenous families as an essential aspect of decolonisation. But these actions, and their decolonial emphasis, represented the interests of non-Indigenous low-income women as well, who enthusiastically rallied behind Colligan. While that may have been because there can be a "we're all the same" reductionism from working-class women even when confronted with Indigenous women articulating the unique position of facing colonial oppression, it also indicates that the particular character of decolonial struggle has universal implications for the non-Native working class. The inverse is, however, not true.

## Legacies of colonial socialism

Revolutionary socialists who have a class analysis more sophisticated than the poverty reductionism of street communities also tend to flatten Indigenous peoples into their default revolutionary subject: a European working-class man. Socialist organisations, by virtue of their hegemony of whiteness, tend to over-emphasise a supposedly universal working-class unity against capitalism and have often treated gender oppression and racism as secondary to a limited version of class struggle that centres the experiences of white men. Those socialists who see the working class as universal, either in fact or as historical destiny for all oppressed people, will have a hard time understanding Indigenous sovereignty as distinct from class struggle against capitalism.

The record of revolutionary socialism in theorising settler colonialism in the US and Canada is dismal. The classic Trotskyist text about settler colonialism is George Novack's 1970 pamphlet "Genocide Against the Indians," which argues, like Marx's articles on British colonialism in India, that European conquest is brutal but ultimately progressive because it will bring Indigenous people into the ranks of the world proletariat. Marx was wrong about India, where, rather than eliminating non-capitalist hierarchies of modes of oppression, capitalists made use of caste oppression by paying lower castes lower wages and, as Marxist historian Vijay Prashad points out, dispatched them into clogged sewers below the streets of Mumbai as human pipe cleaners. And Novack was wrong about the US and Canada, where the masses of Indigenous peoples were not proletarianized or assimilated as the architects of residential and boarding schools claimed, but instead have been targeted for destruction.

Fifty years later, some dogmatic socialists remain immune to evidence that the particularities of settler colonialism cannot be reduced to the internal laws of capitalist production. In 2020, in the wake of the movement that—through the power of Indigenous nations uniting in defence of Wet'suwet'en sovereignty—shut down ports, railways, and highways in Canada for weeks, the Canadian section of the International Marxist Tendency, known as Fightback, published a long analysis ending with the prescription:

> Marxists place primacy on the class struggle because it is the sole means by which the capitalist system and the Canadian state can be defeated. It is through the class struggle, through the overthrow of capitalist property relations and the creation

of new socialist relations, that the legacy of colonialism and racism can be tackled.[1]

Fightback is wrong on two fronts. Firstly, Fightback is wrong that class struggle is the "sole" means of defeating the Canadian state. Indigenous land defenders have proven that the expression and practice of their national sovereignty is a means to defeat the Canadian state in battle. Far more effectively than class struggle, during a long period of working-class quiescence and despite the passive indifference—or worse, the hostility of working-class groups—Indigenous nations have pushed back invasions by the settler colonial state and stopped legal and political attacks by Parliament.

Secondly, Fightback is wrong that it is "through…the creation of new socialist relations" that "the legacy of colonialism…can be tackled." This formulation repeats the earlier problem of placing primacy on class struggle as the sole means of defeating the Canadian state, and continues the problem—endemic to class reductionist socialists—of answering strategic problems of fighting white supremacy, patriarchy, and in this case, colonialism, by waving it off until after the revolution. Worse, their description of these "new socialist relations" are even more colonial than the liberal democratic version of reconciliation promised by Prime Minister Justin Trudeau. Fightback explains:

> Socialism aims to socialise that [land] wealth under democratic control. Through this, Indigenous communities would be genuinely involved in all levels of production and development. A socialist society, which organises production and exchange to meet the needs of the people and not profit, would be able to resolve all the outstanding issues and injustices inflicted upon Indigenous people. The immense resources of this land would be able to be put in motion for Indigenous peoples to provide a decent and sustainable standard of living for their people.

1   Fightback, "Indigenous Struggle and the Fight for Socialism: Revolution, Not Reconciliation!" September 30, 2021, https://www.marxist.ca/article/indigenous-struggle-and-the-fight-for-socialism-revolution-not-reconciliation.

It is precisely by freeing up all the wealth of society that the challenges and injustices faced by Indigenous communities can be meaningfully addressed, as they would be guaranteed the funds and resources needed to implement programs and services to meet their needs, and could democratically decide how to go about doing so without outside imposition.

Such "democratic control" over Indigenous lands and nations, in a settler colonial context where Indigenous peoples have been reduced to about five percent of the overall population, is a vision for settler colonialism to continue under the name of socialist planning. "Freeing up all the wealth" stolen from Indigenous peoples as "the funds and resources needed to implement programs and services to meet their needs" means the trapping of Indigenous nations in the paternalistic grip of a new socialist state that sounds not much different from the promises made by the new capitalist state under John A. MacDonald, Canada's first prime minister. Canada already promised to meet the needs of Indigenous people, and it dealt them instead starvation in the name of food, torture institutions in the name of residential schools, and prisons in the name of housing.

## Anti-colonial and decolonial

Colonialism, no matter how benevolently packaged, blocks, undermines, and disorganises the self-organisation and self-actualization of Indigenous nations. It is these interwoven problems of social being and national self-determination, the decolonisation of Indigenous selfhood against the invading inferiority complexes of the colonising world that Yellowknives Dene scholar Glen Coulthard calls to arms through self-recognition; an epistemological framework that expresses Indigenous sovereignty as antagonism to colonial power, while also preceding and exceeding that colonialism. In his 2014 book *Red Skin White Masks*, Coulthard explains Black Martiniquan decolonial theorist and Algerian anti-colonial revolutionary Frantz Fanon's thinking about total social revolution:

What ultimately needs to be realised in both cases [of cultural renaissance and national liberation] ... is that the "native's hand-to-hand struggle with his culture" must be geared toward "the total liberation of the national territory." According to Fanon, it is only under these radically transformed material conditions that a truly *national culture* can emerge; a "fighting culture" that "does not leave intact either the *form or substance*" of previous cultural practices but instead strives toward the construction of a *totally new set of social, cultural and economic relations.*[2]

Here, Coulthard fundamentally rejects the offer of the coloniser's recognition of Indigenous humanity on the coloniser's terms—an offer made by the Royal Commission on Aboriginal Peoples in 1996 and frequently and energetically since, through Canada's Truth and Reconciliation process. If the fundamental problem with colonialism is the domination of Indigenous lands and peoples by an occupying force, which has drawn great scars across the land and the collective psyche of Indigenous people, then changing the languages and administration of that power modifies but does not address that fundamental problem. Decolonisation cannot arrive as a gift from the coloniser, Coulthard writes. Decolonisation breaks forever the subordination of the Native to the settler by the smashing of settler power by Indigenous nations themselves. This action is fundamental to liberation because it is, as Coulthard explains in his telling of Fanon's thinking, only through revolutionary activity that the revolutionary comes to know themself and to define the free world they are building.

Coulthard distinguishes anti-colonial action from decolonial action, arguing that anti-colonial action is necessary to the cultural and social development of Indigenous sovereignty, because it drives the coloniser off the land. He cites Michi Saagiig Nishnaabeg writer Leanne Betasamosake Simpson, who says, "I am not so concerned with … which set of theories we use to critique colonialism; but I am very concerned with how we (re)build our own house, or our own houses." Critiquing and fighting colonialism is anti-colonial revolution; the struggle of Indigenous peoples to "(re)build our own house" is decolonial revolution.

2    Glen Coulthard, *Red Skin White Masks* (Minneapolis and London: University of Minnesota Press, 2014), 148.

The stock socialist solutions to colonisation cannot recognise the distinction between anti-colonial and decolonial activity because they imagine, as the verse in *The Internationale* goes, "the international working class will be the human race." One of the unfortunate and historically unproven enlightenment ideas unpurged from Marx's critique of the Hegelian dialectic is that, because capitalism tolerates no economy or social life outside of its purview, it inevitably liquidates previously multiple histories, forcing all the world's people into its service as proletarians—industrial workers. All stations, no matter of which nation, are but stops on this unitary rail route. This perspective is mistaken because it overestimates the power of capitalism, misrepresenting it as an unstoppable juggernaut, rather than a world system that is necessarily incomplete and prone to crisis, and therefore precarious in its hold over the forces it commands. Marx does not celebrate this worldwide domination of capital. Dialectically, he sees in this spread of universal power its universal undoing. That's why he wrote in 1853 that British colonialism in India, however brutal, self-serving, and hypocritical, would ultimately play a progressive historical role.

Lenin and the Bolsheviks applied Marx's recipe-book method towards historical development in their thinking about what they called the "national question" when they wrote that socialists must defend the "self-determination" of oppressed nations because resistance to colonialism would, ultimately, move those "backwards" peoples more rapidly through the march of history, clarifying and enunciating national class divisions out of which the proletariat of the colonised nation would emerge as soldiers in the world army of the working class. Not a bad principle—to support the national movements of those fighting colonialism. But the premise that self-determination struggles must inevitably lead in the direction of capitalist (and then socialist) development has distorted the socialist view of what constitutes a national struggle for liberation, creating theoretical ambiguities that produced contradictory policies towards anti-colonial struggles globally and within the Soviet Union, depending on whether Soviet leaders thought those movements aligned with the interests of the industrial working class in oppressor nations.

These thinkers paint a hermetic portrait of capitalist production, as though it is a whale that swallows up every life force it encounters. From her vantage point at the outset of the First World War, Rosa Luxemburg challenged this view. Rather than keeping its workhouse in a whale's belly, Luxemburg painted a portrait of capitalism as a many-headed hydra—one hungry, gnashing monster's head thrusts outward to swallow the wealth of new lands and new markets to feed the unrelenting demands of the production process, which is simultaneously presided over by another accountant's head, adjusting the moving components of commodity production towards Taylorist perfection. Luxemburg argues that Marx's recognition of the great theft of land and "divorcing of producers from the means of production" as the origin of capitalist production does not go far enough. In her classic 1913 critique of imperialism, *Accumulation of Capital*, Luxemburg writes that "the second requirement of accumulation is access to material elements necessary for expanding reproduction," which capitalism accomplishes through imperialist means—"between capital and a non-capitalist environment."[3] This means that the capitalist world wages an ongoing war against the non-capitalist world through mechanisms like settler colonialism. While capitalism is totalizing, swallowing up all non-capitalist economies it encounters, all life on the planet can never be finally totalized under capitalist rule, because it would mean capital would have run out of fuel.

## Decolonial socialism

Decolonial socialism means that decolonisation is the concomitant and constituent activity of socialism. There can be no socialism without Indigenous sovereignty, and without socialist revolution that ends capitalism, Indigenous sovereignty—which requires the end of settler colonial nation states and the end of capitalism—will always be under threat.

While many Indigenous people work wage-labour jobs in the settler colonial nation states of Canada and the US, Indigenous peoples have not been proletarianized as nations; they face capitalism as an invading force that attacks them in order to steal and commodify their lands, as the invasion of their non-capitalist world by capital that Luxemburg talks about. This colonial invasion, and its power nested in the settler colonial nation state that dedicates

3    Rosa Luxemburg, *The Accumulation of Capital* (London and New York: Routledge Classics, 2003), 335.

its existence to guaranteeing capital access to Indigenous lands, can only be overthrown by Indigenous nations. As Coulthard and Simpson explain, and as we saw with the Wet'suwet'en Shut Down Canada movement of 2020, the exercise and expansion of Indigenous sovereignty is both a vehicle for anti-colonial struggle and for the (re)emergence of decolonial Indigenous worlds.

Indigenous struggle against colonialism is objectively also against capitalism, but the Indigenous struggle against colonialism is not a substitute for the working-class struggle against capitalism. Workers occupy a privileged position within the gears of capitalist production as the producers of the forms of value that are legible to and appropriated as capital. A more powerful workers' movement would weaken capitalism and, if it did not appropriate colonial mechanisms of wealth production into an emergent socialism, also weaken the settler colonial state. But there is also the more pressing and immediate problem that Indigenous solidarity movements in Canada and the US tend to be dominated by the middle class and its environmental NGOs. Meanwhile, established working-class groups, like private-sector and especially oil and gas extraction related labour unions, tend to lobby for more aggressive, anti-Indigenous state policies in the name of jobs. There is a lot of potential for decolonial socialism, especially for working-class anti-colonial solidarity with Indigenous decolonial movements, but that potential remains mostly unrealised.

While we modelled our "braid" of Indigenous and working-class unity in action on the unities practised in our subaltern social base, we fought to centre Indigenous sovereignty as the precondition for our revolutionary struggle, and Indigenous sovereigntists as unobstructed protagonists in our organisation and the community struggles we supported. Our experiments with organisational forms were focused on this latter problem—to decentre white hegemony, poverty reductionist assumptions, and class reductionist socialisms within actions that continue the strategic unities of Indigenous and non-Native working-class people.

### First period: The Indigenous and non-Native "we" in Red Braid

Our first efforts to bolster the leadership of Indigenous people and the centrality of Indigenous sovereignty struggles in our campaigns were to intervene in shared organisational spaces and struggles and correct against settler biases. This initial form was called the "Urban Indigenous Campaign."

Inside Red Braid, which at the time was called Alliance Against Displacement, we did not have a distinct, Indigenous-only organisational space. The responsibility of producing anti-colonial analysis, theory, and strategy rested on the shoulders of Indigenous members of the organisation. Organising urban Indigenous people into a coherent group proved immensely challenging, and Indigenous organisers saw a big part of the problem in the colonial dynamics that were proving difficult to root out of the group internally. The group was mixed in every sense: Indigenous members had the same communications channels, the same membership meetings, and the same leadership structure as non-Native members. A consequence was that members of the Urban Indigenous Campaign spent a lot of their time and energy educating non-Natives—explaining how their behaviours and default beliefs were informed by colonialism—rather than organising with other Indigenous people.

Indigenous leaders identified two problems that emerged out of this structure where anti-colonial action and politics depended on the constant attention of Indigenous leaders in a group of mostly non-Native people. On one hand, non-Native members tended to defer to Indigenous leadership to answer all the questions that came up about colonialism and anti-colonial struggle. This pattern of "deference," which a subsequent Indigenous leader would call "white deference," demonstrated that non-Indigenous members of Red Braid felt anti-colonial struggles to be Indigenous peoples' responsibility. We characterised this attitude, which was common in Indigenous solidarity movements outside the group, as "allyship politics," where guilty-feeling whites work to assuage their own guilt by performing support for Indigenous leaders. The goal of such allyship is for the white ally to feel better and like they are a "good" white, not to build fighting organisations and power capable of overturning colonial structures.

On the other hand, there was overt racism through the privileging of discussions of class and the reducing of anti-colonial struggles to little more than rhetoric. One Indigenous member complained that he could not relate to discussions in meetings, which he referred to as "walls of text" with little cultural life to them or social relevance for him or for other low-income Indigenous people in his life. This racism assumed and treated the subjectivity of the organisation as white and working class and fostered an internal culture that excluded Indigenous people.

We tried to correct against these problems, following the leadership of Indigenous members in the group, by doing internal education work about colonialism and anti-colonialism, and by centring Indigenous members in the writing of organisational statements. This is why our basis of unity and other documents use "we" in reference to both Indigenous and working-class communities. We felt that using "we" for both groups would connote a central belonging and fluid identity of the group as both Indigenous and non-Indigenous. The point of adopting this language of what we called "multiplicity" was to disrupt the settling-in of a default white subjectivity to the organisation, which we felt would be even louder if we removed all overtly subjective language, which would also mean barring Indigenous members from expressing their subjectivities through organisational writing.

The united "we" form of managing our strategic unity ended with the resignations of those Indigenous leaders in the group who had been central to this first period of united struggle. The political lesson that the organisation ultimately took from their resignations was that the organisational demand to merge Indigenous and non-Indigenous fighters into united "we" placed heavy burdens on Indigenous members in the group. We needed a better way.

## Second period: Fighting for autonomous Indigenous spaces

The pivot away from a "unity" strategy for coordinating Indigenous and non-Indigenous alliance happened while the group was hard at work on a new basis of unity, a more developed and focused political strategy, and a new name and framework for organising. Part of this new framework was a new organisational structure that set out internal institutional space for Indigenous organising as an autonomous Red Braid group.

An Indigenous leader who organised this turn argued that "urban Indigenous" was too broad a category because it flattened Indigenous people in the city into one indistinguishable group. The truth, she argued, was that some Indigenous people in the city were forming into a relatively influential and power-wielding Indigenous middle class, which had found opportunities in Trudeau's phoney reconciliation agenda.[4] For Canada to pull off this reconciliation scam and continue its colonial domination over Indigenous peoples and lands, it required the participation of this Indigenous middle class, composed of a very tiny minority of Indigenous people to act as administrators of government-Indigenous programs; social workers to continue seizing Indigenous children under a cynically "Indigenised" public relations spin; cops hired to "diversify" police departments and create a myth that Canada's racist institutions had changed; and Indigenous professors, cultural critics, journalists, and advocates to perfect the discursive "Indigenisation" and "decolonisation" of universities, city halls, planning departments, and social service agencies.

Red Braid's Indigenous leadership said that those low-income Indigenous people who were not included in this new Indigenous middle class were essential to it because managing, regulating, policing, and representing the great majority of Indigenous people—contained in prisons and social service institutions and dying on the streets in horrifying numbers—was the purpose of this middle class. By this principle, they set out the basis for organising with poor, subaltern Indigenous people.

The Indigenous Leadership Council was started as an Indigenous-only, autonomous Red Braid space in order to build a social base in Indigenous street kin communities. Starting around the same time as the mass Shut Down Canada movement at the beginning of 2020, which was also when Alliance Against Displacement relaunched as Red Braid, the ILC started meeting to bring together Indigenous members of Red Braid in an autonomous group with Indigenous people from low-income communities where we were organising. The organisational strategy was to create Indigenous-only discussion, healing, and planning space within the organisation itself, and within the organic organisational spaces of tent cities and struggles against police violence, institutionalisation, evictions, and criminalisation.

4    Ma Maa Tea, "Beyond the White Problem: Racialized and Indigenous Middle-Class Power and the Regulation of the Poor Native," internal Red Braid presentation, June 10, 2020.

Where those meetings happened, members of the ILC, as well as the women from communities who attended (it tended to be Indigenous women who took part), said the meetings were spaces of healing and also of political intervention. During the Wet'suwet'en Shut Down Canada movement of early 2020, the ILC supported low-income and unhoused Indigenous women to take part in rail blockades in Maple Ridge and Abbotsford. They then formed an ad hoc group called Maple Ridge Indigenous Warrior Women and planned a demonstration outside Maple Ridge City Hall in solidarity with Wet'suwet'en land defence.

While this demonstration had to be cancelled because of the outset of the COVID-19 pandemic, the work of low-income Indigenous women organising in the suburbs of Vancouver as Indigenous sovereigntists was proof that the ILC's political goal of organising Indigenous decolonial actions within and from the mixed street kin community struggle was in reach and could be powerful. The same group that organised the cancelled Wet'suwet'en solidarity demonstration then pivoted into organising against the devastating effects of the COVID-19 pandemic on Indigenous street kin.

Starting in April 2020, Red Braid organised two squats to create space for unhoused people to seek sanctuary from the pandemic and the disastrous policies of the government that continued the use of congregate shelters despite COVID dangers. The ILC, with the Maple Ridge Indigenous Warrior Women group, intervened and took leadership within those squats, foregrounding the colonial power relations that made Indigenous people especially vulnerable to the pandemic and arguing for the necessary centrality of decolonial Indigenous self-activity in a fighting solution. They wrote:

> The Warrior Women of the Hothouse Squat are holding down COVID safe space for Indigenous people because our struggle for health and survival is our struggle for sovereignty against Canada's colonial invasion.
>
> One month ago, we were planning rallies in defence of Wet'suwet'en sovereignty. We were defending the land against mining companies. Today we are rallying for the sovereignty of our people and our people's bodies again. We are defending our kin against another virus that Canada has brought us.

In the Hothouse Squat, we can create sovereign Indigenous space, space for our family to be together and support each other, while also being safe from COVID-19. We need to have Native space to survive. Canada is refusing us that space. [See the full statement later in this section].

But this work was also frustrated by barriers erected by settler colonialism, both external and internal to Red Braid. The lives of subaltern Indigenous people are constantly interrupted by attacks on their nations by regulatory forces of the colonial state, like police, supportive housing, child apprehensions, gender violence, medical discrimination, and the criminalised drug supply poisoning crisis. During the COVID-19 pandemic, these disorganising attacks intensified.

In May 2020, just after writing the Warrior Women of the Hothouse Squat statement, Linda Mama Bear Whitford died alone in her room, stuck there because of a guest ban illegally and arbitrarily enforced by her so-called "supportive" housing provider, Coast Mental Health. Her words in that statement were suddenly terribly prescient:

COVID-19 is frightening. To fight it, we want to stay together as family and friends; to be there for each other. We want homes now for all our family. We want no surveillance. We want health care in Indigenous ways, without the racism and colonial paternalism. We want to sit in the sun.

If you have your family beside you when you pass away, you are free to move on with no bad feelings. It's good to be together to the end. Being together is the medicine we need. Family is medicine.

We don't know how many Indigenous street kin members we lost in 2020 in so-called British Columbia, but the Provincial Coroner reports that 1,716 people died in the drug poisoning crisis that year. We know that Indigenous people are over-represented amongst those killed by drug poisoning, so we can figure that we lost hundreds of people alongside Mama Bear, who was killed by a health condition exacerbated by a racist health care system and by institutionalisation in BC's supportive housing system. The deaths of Mama Bear and others in our communities made organising meetings increasingly difficult, and meetings did not happen as often as needed.

At the same time, as Red Braid's Indigenous leadership argued, settler colonial ideology was still rearing its head within Red Braid spaces. Like the experience of the generation of Red Braid Indigenous leaders before them, by the end of the year, Red Braid's Indigenous leaders complained they were frustrated that they had spent too much energy and time combating anti-Indigenous racism while bearing too much of the weight of analysing and strategising anti-colonial struggle.

One year after the founding of Red Braid and the Indigenous Leadership Council, we found ourselves revisiting the premises of this structured strategic unity. We found that structuring a separate Indigenous space within Red Braid, regardless of its level of autonomy, had not removed from Indigenous members the burden of educating and correcting the colonial attitudes and behaviours of non-Natives.

### Third period: Indigenous sovereignty as method

To strategically overcome the problematic persistence of settler consciousness and hegemony we had found in our mixed Indigenous and non-Native socialist organisation, Red Braid developed an answer that was political and organisational: first, Red Braid determined that there is a fundamental difference and strategic division of labour between *anti*-colonial and *de*colonial politics and struggle; and second, we decided that our "braided" unity must support, not interrupt the decolonial work of Indigenous sovereigntists, no matter whether those sovereigntists were inside or outside the organisation.

The principle underlying these ideas is that Indigenous sovereignty is not a far-off goal, but a necessary method of struggle for subaltern Indigenous survival, revolutionary decolonial self-consciousness, and freedom. The "sovereignty as method" principle was drawn from the totality of Red Braid's three periods of Indigenous struggle. Indigenous sovereignty is fought for and exercised on *the land*, where Indigenous nations directly blockade resource extraction and development projects that are the practice of land theft colonialism. For example, in January 2020 the Unist'ot'en and

Gidimt'en clans asserted Wet'suwet'en law forbidding Coastal GasLink's trespass onto their territories as a method of struggle in order to fight for Wet'suwet'en sovereignty against Canada's colonial claims to their lands. Sovereignty, as Leanne Betasamosake Simpson argues, is a unified means and end.

Indigenous sovereignty is also fought for and exercised in cities and towns, on the land that has been cleared and suffocated in concrete (which is itself made of crushed stone stolen from lands devastated by gravel quarries), claimed as property, zoned by the banal colonial administrations of city planning departments, and traded on global markets. On these sites of sovereignty struggle, the fight is centred on the lives of Indigenous peoples who have been dispossessed of their lands and often also displaced from their territories, their direct relations with their nations strained or severed. This intergenerational plague of genocidal dispossession and displacement is why Indigenous peoples are so drastically over-represented amongst the impoverished and unhoused on the streets of settler colonial cities.

As Mama Bear explains, having had nationally based kinship ties strained or severed, Indigenous street kin create new kinship networks out of the survival conditions imposed on them. Between Indigenous peoples, these street kin groups are multinational, and they often include non-Native people who have arrived in similar situations of radical social disorganisation and poverty through distinct processes of capitalist exploitation and disposal. For Indigenous street kin, sovereignty struggles centre immediate survival demands like fighting drug poisoning, malnutrition, illness, racist vigilante violence, intimate partner violence, and the danger of exposure to the elements. But for these struggles to be decolonial—rather than get stuck in superficial anti-poverty demands—requires the self-organisation, radical self-recognition, and political self-articulations of Indigenous street kin themselves, through their own sovereign institutions.

Autonomy proved inadequate to this task. As an autonomous group within Red Braid, the Indigenous Leadership Council could develop analysis and make decisions about political actions that they could count on the rest of Red Braid to back up. But the entry point for Indigenous people to join Red Braid was through the group as a whole, and to participate in the life of the organisation, including accessing information about Red Braid's campaigns, internal education, and political critiques, Indigenous members had to work in and through mixed organisational spaces that were dominated by non-Native socialists.

Autonomy refers to the independence of communities, but it falls short of sovereignty because autonomy is an independence forged through antagonism. For example, an autonomous working-class organisation is valuable to the working class as a group oppressed under capitalism, because it can express the politics, desires, and power of the working class despite and against capitalist domination. Autonomy means independence, but independence from a powerful force that shapes the oppressed group through domination. Without that context of domination, an autonomous class would lose its relevant footing and need to develop a new subjectivity and sense of unity. So the goal of socialist struggle against capitalism is for the working class to abolish itself, becoming freed from its subordinated class position.

Indigenous nations existed before the invasion of British settler society, and their sovereignty does not need the antagonism of that settler society to be relevant. Sovereignty, for Indigenous nations, is a more complete project than autonomy is for the working class. Sovereignty is the method of struggle against colonial domination, and sovereignty is the goal to be realised on the other side of that struggle. Victory will enlarge, not eliminate, the relevance of sovereignty for Indigenous nations. In our experience, autonomy, which suggests independence within a unity, maintained a thread connecting the Indigenous Leadership Council—and Indigenous sovereignty struggles outside Red Braid—to the class struggle as the primary political field against which others are measured and oriented.

## Decolonial revolution

Red Braid's turn to sovereignty as method had radical implications for how we understood the strategic unity between Indigenous and non-Indigenous working-class peoples and struggles. Internally within Red Braid, sovereignty as method placed the onus on non-Indigenous Red Braid members and committees to give Indigenous Red Braid members a reason to take part in shared spaces. We decided that Red Braid's structures must not be set up to compel Indigenous members to take part in non-Indigenous dominated spaces as the only or default way to take part in Red Braid. If member meetings, campaign meetings, and coordinating committee meetings only existed as majority non-Indigenous spaces, then Indigenous members would be put in the position of either accepting those majority non-Indigenous spaces as they were, even if they were thick with settler consciousness, or investing their energies in improving their settler comrades, reforming them through education in one form or another.

Rather, sovereignty as method meant that non-Indigenous Red Braid committees and members were expected to provide political and infrastructural resources to the Indigenous Leadership Council without the right to participate in the ILC's decisions or work, affirming the ILC's sovereign power to recruit and make decisions as Red Braid. Sovereignty as method allowed Red Braid to form a strategic unity between Indigenous and non-Indigenous members that included the carrying out of everyday strategies like meetings, publishing, and outreach work as a cluster of groups, not as a single group totalized under a universal class struggle.

Our shift from autonomy to sovereignty relieved Indigenous members of Red Braid and our social base of having to participate in non-Indigenous spaces while ensuring access to the organisational support that ILC members described as "crucial." We saw the ILC's dependence on Red Braid as a whole to practically exercise sovereignty as both necessary—given the powerfully disorganising forces of colonialism in subaltern Indigenous communities—and limiting, in as much as this dependence was an expression of the very forces the ILC combated.

A hard accounting of the effects of Red Braid's decolonial strategies suggests that we were not able to make sustained, consistent contributions to Indigenous sovereigntist movements, nor were we able to support an increased influence of low-income urban Indigenous people in those movements. Where our decolonial organisational structures and political strategies were effective was in community struggles with low-income Indigenous fighters themselves, on their own terms and in their existing spaces. Red Braid was able—supporting the formal initiative of the

Indigenous Leadership Council and supporting the spontaneous initiative of low-income Indigenous women in community spaces—to boost the leadership and increase the power of low-income Indigenous people in their street kin communities, and to organise actions that united mixed Indigenous and non-Indigenous low-income community members behind the leadership and demands of Indigenous women—against the apprehension of Indigenous children by the government Ministry of Child and Family Development, for example. When we were talking about lessons from our decolonial organising efforts in a Red Braid meeting, Karen Lane, a low-income Black and Indigenous member agreed with supporting sovereignty fights led by people outside our group with more emphasis, but said, "That does not mean we don't need the Indigenous Leadership Council. We have our own fights that no one else is going to lead for us. And we have our own healing to do."

Lane's "we" here is not the "we" that Red Braid identified in our first period of decolonial organising; it is not the unified, mixed Indigenous and non-Indigenous subaltern. But Lane's "we" is also not referring to an imagined united Indigenous sovereigntist movement that includes the front lines of the land-based struggles and the front lines of the Indigenous tent city. Lane's "we" is referring specifically to the low-income, Indigenous street kin group that Red Braid always, throughout three periods of struggle, looked to as our social base. It is that low-income Indigenous street kin group whose power Red Braid was committed to building in particular, because we saw their healing, self-organisation, and sovereign power as essential to decolonial revolution overall.

Sovereignty as method means that Red Braid's organisational purpose was to build this sovereign Indigenous street kin power as an expression of the decolonial revolution that we aspired to be a useful part.

# Decolonisation and the struggles of urban Indigenous kin

Indigenous Leadership Council

*This programmatic statement was written by the Indigenous Leadership Council in 2020, soon after the relaunch of Red Braid, in the context of the Shut Down Canada struggle in defence of Wet'suwet'en sovereignty. We are republishing this document as originally written as a record of the thinking and activity of the ILC during those militant days.*

"Decolonisation and the struggles of Indigenous street kin" is a programmatic document that establishes critical definitions of anti-colonial and decolonial terms as used by the ILC, written when the group was composed of low-income Indigenous women who organised in urban and suburban spaces in the Vancouver area. This document defines the role of organisation in low-income Indigenous peoples struggles and what the ILC meant by Indigeneity, urban Indigeneity, kinship.

Red Braid is an Indigenous sovereigntist organisation. We see the rematriation of all lands occupied by the settler colonial nation states of Canada and the United States as the first and most meaningful step towards developing a decolonial, socialist federation in their place.

Our work within Red Braid as the Indigenous Leadership Council (ILC) is to build Indigenous leadership within struggles that often include non-Indigenous communities. In subaltern communities, and particularly in low-income communities that are unhoused and extremely criminalised, state and civil society pressure on the community as a whole can make it difficult for Indigenous people to identify as Indigenous in general, and to name and struggle against settler colonialism in particular. Defending the low-income community as a whole, including Indigenous and non-Indigenous people, can make it difficult to name and fight against colonial ideas, racism, and anti-Indigenous gender violence within the community.

Our organising carves out space for low-income Indigenous people to identify and fight colonialism—to decolonise the urban Indigenous community alongside parallel struggles against capitalism. We think of these struggles as Indigenous community defence and home defence struggles.

To be Indigenous and exercise Indigeneity is to defend Indigenous sovereignty no matter where we are. To struggle for sovereignty is to defend the land, Indigenous homes, lives, communities, and therefore, nationhood.

## Indigeneity

To be Indigenous means we have not been colonised. We have been here since time immemorial. If colonisation defined Indigeneity—or if Indigenous peoples were fully colonised—then that would mean Indigenous peoples had been assimilated into the class structure of capitalist society. Despite hundreds of years of trying, the settler colonial project has not assimilated or eliminated the many nations of Indigenous people.

Indigeneity is not defined by colonial dispossession, because Indigenous nations retain relations that have been practised for thousands of years between members of each nation and between different nations. Consensual, non-colonial relations between Indigenous nations and non-Indigenous inhabitants of Indigenous territories can be nurtured only by recognising and practising these Indigenous national relationships, not by continuing to refuse and repress them.

Indigeneity is kinship. Indigenous relationships are defined by reciprocity, not antagonism. The spirit world is a space of language and interaction between one and another, sidestepping the "self and other" binary that structures European methods of understanding being. Indigenous economies interact with lands as non-human relations essential to, not oppositional to, human being.

Reciprocity and kinship, including with the spirit world, sets Indigenous laws and ways of being on a different footing than European thought, including Marxism. But the arrival of European power—its thought, property forms, state power structures, and murderous violence—has interrupted Indigenous nationhood, social structures, and economies, transforming Indigenous being forever.

Capitalist property forms are also knowledge systems. Fluid networks between humans and non-humans have been disrupted and replaced with private property and extractive economies, which are one-way relationships. Likewise, recovering Indigenous ontologies, ways of being, knowledge systems, and relations with each other and the land is synonymous with defending the earth. Neither capitalist profit motives nor enlightenment ideals of industrialisation present in European-style communism can address the apocalyptic climate crisis.

As nations, Indigenous peoples are outside the regular production and reproduction of capitalism. Every aspect of our lives, nationhood, and community is attacked because our land relations are antagonistic to the capitalist economy. Indigenous nations in Canada and the United States have their lands and communities imprisoned within the borders of the empire, so their relationship to Canada-Euro-American imperialism is different than their relationship to Indigenous peoples in other parts of the world. So, while individual Indigenous people may be working class or petit bourgeois, Indigenous nationhood and the struggle for decolonisation is outside and inimical to the settler colonial national projects of Canada and the USA.

The violence of colonialism produced the setting for how we must understand Indigeneity today, against and through the settler colonial reality imposed by Canada and the USA, and by settler majority populations.

If not for settler colonialism, Indigenous peoples would be Squamish, Musqueam, Tsleil-Waututh, Kwikwetlem, Nuu-chah-nulth, Gitxsan,

Mi'kmaq, and hundreds of other nations. To be Indigenous is for these many national identities to share a singular opposition to the external threat of an imperialist power that threatens to separate the people from the land, destroy them, dispossess them, and displace their land-relations, replacing reciprocity with property.

## Urban Indigeneity

There is a difference between our claim that Indigenous nations are all united in opposition to settler colonial nation states and the "pan-Indigenous" claims popular during the Red Power movements of the 1970s. Red Braid understands decolonisation as a national project that must be carried out by each Indigenous nation on their own lands, in relation to other Indigenous nations around them, through the expression and practice of their own national sovereignty on their own terms. But the common problem faced by each and every one of these nations—so long as they pursue their full sovereign nationhood, including economically, and not a form of assimilated recognition or reconciliation with Canada or the USA—is the settler colonial nation state. Urban Indigenous people, who make up more than half of all Indigenous peoples within the borders of both Canada and the USA, play an important role in this anti-colonial and decolonial project.

Indigenous peoples from territories in the Global South, whose lands are within the borders of nation states that are also dominated by Euro-American imperialism, are also displaced into cities and towns on Indigenous lands that are not their own. Indigenous peoples displaced by military and economic pressures from continents of the Global South into what George Manuel called the "fourth world" of Canada's colonial occupation raise possibilities of defining urban Indigeneity as global, and of global anti-colonial alliances. But our discussion here is limited to considering the already complicated problem of relations between Indigenous peoples who share the problem of their nations being directly occupied by the settler colonial nation states of Canada and the United States.

Like all Indigenous people, urban Indigenous people have been dispossessed of their lands and the full exercise of national sovereignty by colonial occupation, but urban Indigenous people have also been displaced from their home territories and therefore cut off from the everyday practice of direct land relations.

But although urban Indigenous people are forced to sell their labour power, it would be flattening their ongoing colonial relationship to capitalism to call them working class. The difference between Indigenous workers and the working class is that an Indigenous worker's relationship to capitalism is mediated through the broader structure of their legal and national relationship to colonial power.

Neoliberal, financialized capitalism does not have the same imperative to reproduce the labour power of a local working class that national-industrial capitalism once did, but colonialism is worse than indifferent to the reproduction of Indigenous peoples: colonialism is exterminationist.

The Indigenous work of continuing to fight for sovereignty makes urban Indigenous people different than the working class even though they have to work, or have to buy things to eat and pay rent to stay indoors.

Urban Indigenous peoples have an uninterrupted unity with the land, and Canada knows this. Colonial violence targets Indigenous people for destruction regardless of whether we are in the streets of cities or on the land. The genocidal gender violence directed at Indigenous women does not differentiate between whether we are on reserve, on the land, or sleeping unsheltered on the streets. Indigenous people represent the land, unconquered and still living, even in the city.

The colonial system steals the land. So, with it, Indigenous people are stolen. But urban Indigenous people are fighting to get away from the colonial and capitalist system, to escape from the grasp of the system trying to steal Indigenous people and lands.

## Anti-colonial struggle in the city

Anti-colonial struggle is the more straightforward part of this Indigenous national project. Anti-colonial struggle is the opposition to all forms of settler colonial power, anti-Indigenous racism, and imperialist theft of sovereign lands.

Every city and town in Canada and the USA is Indigenous territory.

Suffocating the earth under pavement does not erase Indigenous land title. And also, the built form of cities and towns is possible only through the coalescing of Indigenous lands into a single place, as "dead" relations. The stone, crushed and processed into the concrete of Vancouver's streets, and the iron and lead that pipes waters routed from the aquifers of the Squamish and Tsleil-Waututh nations, has been mined in quarries on the unceded lands of the Skwah nation in the Sto:lo territory. The natural gas pumped into the heaters and stove units of each home is stolen from the grounds of Treaty 8 Nations, the Dog River, Fort Nelson, Halfway River, Prophet River, Saulteaux, and West Moberly First Nations. The lumber used to frame those homes was logged from the lands of the Nuu-chah-nulth. Electricity comes, travelling across the lands of innumerable nations, from hydroelectric plants on the lands of the Sekani. The grain for breads and cattle for meat come from farmlands stolen from Cree, Assiniboine, and Blackfoot nations. The coffee that helps us make it through our days is grown on lands stolen from Indigenous people in Latin America and Africa. Settler colonialism and capitalism have already produced each city as a space composed of many Indigenous nations.

There is a strategic advantage to anti-colonial struggles in the city because the city is not only a destination for stolen land wealth, it is also a transfer point on to global markets. Urban Indigenous people organise anti-colonial actions when they blockade rail lines, ports, and highways. Choking off the transfer of stolen Indigenous wealth into capitalist markets is the exercise of the strategic slogan that "the front lines are everywhere." As a strategy of blocking the theft of Indigenous lands, there is a continuum between the front line of Indigenous nations blockading the passage of a pipeline through Indigenous territory at Standing Rock or Unist'ot'en, and the front line of urban Indigenous people blockading—along with the Squamish and Tsleil Waututh nations whose lands Vancouver occupies—the shipment of bitumen from the port of Vancouver.

Anti-colonial struggle is led by Indigenous nations who lead and often bear the entire burden of fighting colonial power and extraction, but its character is expansive. Colonialism is a braid in the global process of capitalist production that makes each Indigenous nation's anti-colonial struggle objectively also anti-capitalist and anti-imperialist, forming a central part of an international struggle against imperialist domination of the world.

## Decolonising the city

Decolonisation is a more complicated problem for urban Indigenous people. Because, while anyone, Indigenous or not, can get involved in anti-colonial activity, decolonisation is more than refusal; it means the substitution of colonial power for Indigenous sovereignty, of colonial dehumanisation for Indigenous self-realisation. There appears to be a contradiction here. If Indigenous sovereignty is necessarily national and not a single, pan-Indigenous project, then how can urban Indigenous people who are not living on their traditional territories and not involved in their own particular national resurgence decolonise?

It would be a mistake to think of Indigenous nations as fixed, either in cultural time or in population. Indigenous nationhood has never been static or free from outside interruption and influence. Indigenous peoples have always interacted with other nations, exchanging at all levels culture, trade, and migration movement of individuals between nations.

The trans-national presence of emissaries from many Indigenous nations in cities and towns presents a challenge for decolonisation, and the contributions that these multinational relations can make to decolonial struggle will differ from the contributions made by members of a particular nation. Displaced, urban Indigenous people must make contributions to decolonial worlds through the ways available to them in each circumstance.

Cities and towns are points of resistance that bring Indigenous people together by strategic necessity, and in those interactions, decolonial possibilities arise. In discussions of decolonial relations to Indigenous lands, there is a tendency to centre concerns about white settlers. To centre the relationships between nations of Indigenous peoples, including those displaced to a certain nation's lands, means approaching these relational problems as an anti-colonial alliance with the possibility of developing decolonial relations. Urban Indigenous people displaced from other territories occupied by Canada or the USA share political understandings of histories of facing a common enemy's singular strategies of domination, and these relations can be organised around contributions to anti-colonial struggle.

## Kinship

The reason that urban Indigenous leadership of anti-colonial struggles can lead to decolonial relationships is because these struggles are theatres for new forms of kinship practices, and therefore relations. Urban Indigenous people continue traditional, national kinship structures, beliefs and spiritual practices when displaced into cities. And we also adapt to urban contexts and to social contexts along with peoples from other Indigenous nations, creating resistant forms of kinship.

Agents of British and then Canadian and US American colonialism set out to destroy Indigenous kinship structures with missionaries, the introduction of European patriarchal gender roles and power, organised starvation and immiseration, residential schools, child apprehensions, foster care, homelessness, and criminalisation and mass incarceration.

The social service, police, army, and judicial agencies of the Canadian nation state are colonial and remain exterminationist, targeting Indigenous kinship relations. Generations of land theft and poverty have inflated the numbers of Indigenous people amongst the urban poor and unhoused. Urban Indigenous people have been fed into the jaws of Canada's disciplinary, punitive, and soft power reformer institutions.

In 2020, thirty percent of men and forty-two percent of women in federal prisons in Canada are Indigenous. Forty percent of people recorded as unhoused in Vancouver identify as Indigenous. And more than fifty percent of children in foster care are Indigenous. A Ministry of Family Development report from 2016 said that forty-three percent of apprehensions of Indigenous children were because the parent was "unable/unwilling to care." According to MCFD's own report, only 0.7 percent of kids were apprehended due to sexual abuse. Indigenous kids are stolen by the state because of the settler colonial impoverishment of Indigenous peoples.

Indigenous people dragged into colonial institutions suffer attacks on their kinship relations. Most homeless shelters are segregated by gender and do not allow children. The same goes for so-called "supportive" housing, which is the only form of social housing in British Columbia. Children are not allowed in the tiny, single rooms of supportive housing, so to get a room off the streets means being institutionalised away from your kids.

Other kinship ties are also broken by these institutions, like street families. Supportive housing usually does not allow guests, and almost always forbids overnight guests. And housing agency interrelationships with police mean that residents are highly surveilled, policed, and likely to be arrested. Supportive housing, like other Canadian institutions, is designed to maintain Indigenous homelessness and isolation, fracturing kinship relations.

Anti-colonial struggle has decolonial possibilities because urban Indigenous people organising together as Indigenous people immediately establishes kinship ties. Talking circles create a space for communal healing that treats the trauma any Indigenous person has suffered as a political problem. One person's feeling of pain and shame can become a problem for all Indigenous people; a problem of colonialism; a problem to fight all together. To unravel something that has been wrapped into your brain by colonisers is to take away something they have tried to do to you.

Taking action together in struggle continues the work of the circle. That's the difference between bourgeois therapy and a revolutionary talking circle. Therapy is a professional relationship or a confidential process where each person speaking and being witnessed and supported is the goal. The revolutionary talking circle creates collective Indigenous subjectivities that become stronger and surer through action.

## The inheritance of urban Indigenous power and the role of organisation

The Indigenous Leadership Council's goal is to organise urban Indigenous communities in order to be able to exercise anti-colonial power and defend our lives against the murderous machinery of settler colonialism, and to contribute towards the total project of decolonisation: the dissolution of Canada and the United States as occupying settler colonial nation states; the rematriation of all lands to Indigenous nations; and the creation of a world that contains multitudes, in consensual, cooperative harmony with each other and the non-human world.

In this work, we inherit a tradition of Indigenous resistance against colonialism that has always been the clearest definition of what it means to be Indigenous, as we, individuals and nations and displaced urban communities, survive Canada's genocide. Urban Indigenous people were the leaders of the groups that organised the Red Power movement in the 1970s. We were the ones who organised the Native Youth Movement in the 1990s and *RedWire Magazine* in the 2000s. We were the ones who fought for decades against the genocide against women in the Downtown Eastside. And whenever nations on the land face down the RCMP, we are the ones who rise up and shut down the streets, the ports, and the rail lines in cities, alongside our relatives.

Indigenous communities have a deep rooted national consciousness that binds us together, with or without formal organisations. It is the land and the spirit world that coordinates our sustained resistance, which erupts suddenly in brave disruptions and points of resistance. But in between our moments of beautiful resistance, urban Indigenous people can be consumed by the everyday problems of surviving colonial occupation. We are everywhere, but we can be hard to find.

ILC is an Indigenous-focused space first, where Indigenous revolutionaries who are dedicated to fight within the international, braided movement against colonialism, capitalism, and imperialism can learn and teach protocols for our own work, and guide the strategic unity between our sovereign organising space and non-Indigenous revolutionary fighters both inside and outside Red Braid. We will protect Indigenous spaces for people inside the ILC and in our urban spaces, as we must also for the Wet'suwet'en and all Indigenous nations on their territories.

We also organise to support and advance struggles to defend the land against resource extraction, dispossession, and colonial domination. We think of these struggles as land defence. Urban Indigenous people are not *allies* in land defence struggles; we are part of land defence because Indigenous people and communities are inseparable from the land. As urban Indigenous people, we can use our tactical advantage in cities and towns to shut down the transit hubs, financial office towers, and city centres that direct resource extraction.

Urban Indigenous people are surviving a long moment of everyday crisis. Colonial violence against urban Indigenous people is defined by monotony and predictability, not by dramatic events. We know the police will stop us and steal our belongings and harass us and beat us and then arrest us for assault of a police officer. We know the white men at the bus stop will sneer or whisper or yell or follow us. We know that bosses will fire us, landlords will evict us, social workers will apprehend our kids. The Indigenous Leadership Council adds to our long, powerful inheritance of Indigenous resistance, by fighting to understand and fight this urban colonialism together.

# COVID-19 + Colonisation = Death

Indigenous Leadership Council and the Indigenous Women Warriors of the Hothouse Squat

*This statement was collectively written on April 1st 2020 by the Indigenous Women Warriors of the Hothouse Squat, a group convened by the Indigenous Leadership Council just before Red Braid started a short-lived squat of a vacant recreation centre in Surrey. The Hothouse Squat, a direct action to fight back against the closure of shelter spaces and the abandonment of unhoused people at the outset of the Covid-19 isolation measures, was shut down by a police raid just hours after it started, but this statement continued to guide the collaboration of Indigenous and non-Indigenous low-income communities in a series of actions against the devastating effects of Canada's mismanagement of the Covid-19 crisis for poor and unhoused people.*

We are a group of poor Indigenous women from the Nuu-chah-nulth, Gitxsan, Cree, and Mi'kmaq nations. We have been displaced from our home territories by colonisation and want to be good guests on the territories of other nations where we live. We acknowledge that the Hothouse Squat is on the unceded and occupied territory of the Kwantlen, Katzie, Qayqayt, and Kwikwetlem nations.

We want to begin by saying that the colonisation hasn't stopped; COVID-19 is just the newest crap on the block. It's not just one virus, it's one *more* virus that Canada has brought to us.

We were clean. We were healthy. We were indeed warriors. The food we ate wasn't tainted. And now the colonisers come in here and mess up our lives. As poor Indigenous women, our lives and bodies are etchings of how Canada rips us apart: by poisoning our blood.

When settlers moved west, they brought viruses that killed us and then their doctors quarantined us so that our genocidal sickness would not inconvenience white Canadians. Today Canada is again isolating us because of a virus that they brought to us.

Look how the government responds to the virus: their response is to break up our communities, not to help us. The provincial health authority says that we must isolate, but for Indigenous people, isolation is death. They say we must stay in our homes, but we don't have homes.

We're supposed to have interaction; we're supposed to be with each other. But our people live on the streets where police roll up and move us along if they see a group of Indigenous people together. We live in so-called "supportive" housing where we're not allowed visitors, not allowed to see our children.

Our street family is our kin. When we talk about family and blood, we don't mean the white nuclear family, with just two parents and children. Our family is not an inventory of possessions a man has as the head of the household. Our family includes all our people. The colonisers are always trying to break up our families, to cut us off from everything: from our heritage, from our kin.

BC Housing says that because of COVID-19 we can't have visitors, but what colonisers call visitors, we call kin. Our unhoused relatives live on our couches and floors. When they ban visitors, it hurts us. It hurts us to sleep on the streets, and it hurts us to know our relatives are on the streets.

The cops are telling people to go isolate. But if we listen to the police and run and hide in abandoned buildings all on our own, then we will die alone there from overdoses.

We help each other. We don't isolate. If you need help, I'll help you. We don't go, "mine-mine-mine-mine-mine." Our survival depends on our kinship networks, our kin. They say it's necessary for our survival from COVID to be alone, but being alone is threatening our survival as poor Indigenous people.

To survive COVID-19, we have to keep on protecting Indigenous spaces. We have to protect our physical spaces where we can see and care for each other. We have to defend all our relations against being controlled by building managers, surveilled by police, and killed by coloniser violence.

The Warrior Women of the Hothouse Squat are holding down COVID safe space for Indigenous people because our struggle for health and survival is our struggle for sovereignty against Canada's colonial invasion.

One month ago, we were planning rallies in defence of Wet'suwet'en sovereignty. We were defending the land against mining companies. Today we are rallying for the sovereignty of our people and our people's bodies again. We are defending our kin against another virus that Canada has brought us.

In the Hothouse Squat, we can create sovereign Indigenous space, space for our family to be together and support each other, while also being safe from COVID-19. We need to have Native space to survive. Canada is refusing us that space.

COVID-19 is frightening. To fight it, we want to stay together as family and friends; to be there for each other. We want homes now for all our family. We want no surveillance. We want health care in Indigenous ways, without the racism and colonial paternalism. We want to sit in the sun.

If you have your family beside you when you pass away, you are free to move on with no bad feelings. It's good to be together to the end. Being together is the medicine we need. Family is medicine.

The decolonised world we imagine is where we can be with our family and kin, with our people, safe, and healthy. Some of us feel like a life where you're safe and happy and have everything you need in the afterlife. But our spirits are the most powerful. Our spirits are here and in the spirit world all at once, with those we have passed and those still here. With our spirits we can change the world.

# Indigenous sovereignty, decolonial internationalism, and the settler working class

Mercedes Courtoreille (Cree)

*This chapter is an adaptation of a presentation Courtoreille gave on behalf of Red Braid for the Marxist Center, a network of revolutionary socialist organisations that Red Braid was part of, in April 2021.*

In this article, I take up the relationship between the working class and Indigenous nations in settler colonial societies and argue that workers need Indigenous leadership to build socialism, but Indigenous peoples do not need workers to decolonise their territories. This discrepancy is the opposite of how power relations appear to many socialists, who act as though Indigenous people either don't exist or are helpless victims who need non-Native support. Socialists have to come to terms with this discrepancy because in it we can see the limits of the classical socialist forms of organisation, and what kinds of organisational forms socialists need to wage a revolutionary struggle against capitalism, which requires a fight against colonialism too.

Indigenous nations precede colonial contact by thousands of years and will continue to exist after capitalism is eradicated. But large sectors of the working class are invested in and identify with colonialism, and that is a barrier to a socialist revolution. Workers need Indigenous leadership in order to divest from settler colonialism, but the same is not true of Indigenous people. We do not need settler leadership to decolonise. To build effective revolutionary organisations, socialists need to grapple with the fact that anti-colonial struggle cannot be advanced by a socialism that holds, at its core, settler working-class power.

The year 2020 was momentous for decolonial Indigenous movements—the Tiny House Warriors fighting to stop the Trans Mountain pipeline from crossing Secwepemc territory, land defenders on Wet'suwet'en territory fighting against Coastal GasLink, the Six Nations of the Grand River at 1492 Land Back Lane defending their territory against Foxgate Developments, the Algonquins of Barriere Lake enforcing a moose hunting moratorium on their lands with blockades, the Kanehsatà:ke people resisting the Municipality of Oka's attempted land grabs, and the Mi'kmaq people defending their treaty right to fish against commercial fishers and the Department of Fisheries. These ongoing struggles by Indigenous people show the many fronts of Canada's ongoing assault on Indigenous nations. They also demonstrate that sovereignty struggles are independent from settler society, including from the non-Native working class.

Across all the territories occupied by Canada, Indigenous people are defending their lives against racist violence, their inalienable right to the land and water against settler hunters and fishing industries, and their extended kin (human and non-human) against resource extraction and property development. What aligns all these enemies of Indigenous nations—from the government to private industry to settler workers—is their shared stake in Canada's settler colonial project. So while each Indigenous nation is fighting for their own, distinct nationhood, they are also united in struggle against Canada.

## Mi'kmaq sovereignty and working-class defences of colonialism

In the case of the Mi'kmaq struggle to exercise their sovereign right to fish, working-class organisations like the Maritime Fishermen's Union function as a part of the settler colonial and capitalist state, vociferously defending their interests. They make up part of the obstacle to sovereignty that Indigenous people face. In September 2020, the Sipekne'katik First Nation launched a self-regulated lobster fishery, run according to Mi'kmaq laws and practices, outside of the colonial regulatory regime of the Department of Fisheries and Oceans. Non-Indigenous commercial lobster fishers in Nova Scotia responded with a campaign of anti-Indigenous violence, attacking Mi'kmaq rights, livelihood, and sovereignty. Non-Indigenous fishers vandalised several Mi'kmaq lobster pounds and burned one to the ground. They torched Indigenous fishers' vehicles, destroyed their catch, and tampered with their gear. In mid-October, an Indigenous man was forced to barricade himself inside a lobster pound while a mob of 200 non-Indigenous fishers demanded that he relinquish the lobster he had harvested and threatened to burn the building down. In November, the Department of Fisheries and Oceans joined in the attack on Indigenous fishers, seizing 500 traps in St. Mary's Bay, including many belonging to Sipekne'katik fishers. The Nova Scotia Assembly of Mi'kmaq Chiefs issued a statement condemning the "colonised approach" of the federal government.

In October 2020, at the height of settler fisher attack on Indigenous people, the president of the Maritime Fishermen's Union Local 9, Joel Comeau, announced he was stepping down from his position. In an interview with the CBC, he explained that the "unrest" had taken "too much of a toll" on his family, and that he no longer felt safe.[1] Throughout the interview, Comeau portrayed himself, his family, and his settler organisation as victims, not instigators and beneficiaries of colonial terror and domination. He was joined by his wife Cindy, who mobilised her white woman's tears ("we cry daily") and the image of white childhood innocence ("to see our kids are scared…") against Indigenous resistance. Both Joel and Cindy Comeau denied the racism underlying the actions of non-Native commercial fishers. They claimed that they were not against Indigenous people's right to fish but expressed a colonial entitlement "to see their harvesting plans" and regulate the exercise of Indigenous rights. Joel and Cindy Comeau blamed the media for making the dispute a "race" issue and "crucifying" settler fishers as "racists," "criminals," and "terrorists."

1   "N.S. fishermen's union head quits, says lobster dispute is 'too much of a toll' on his family," *CBC Radio: As It Happens*, October 16, 2020.

As the union president, Comeau's opinion reflects the overarching allegiance of extractive industry unions and the settler working class broadly to colonialism, including the theft of Indigenous lands and denial of treaty rights for the purpose of "creating jobs." The benefits that non-Natives receive from the dispossession of Indigenous lands are not benefits that large sectors of the working class are going to willingly relinquish without strong and deep anti-colonial struggle that results in an understanding and respect for Indigenous sovereignty.

In 1999, the Supreme Court of Canada's Marshall decision confirmed the Mi'kmaq treaty right to fish for a "moderate livelihood." But in March 2021, Fisheries and Oceans Canada (DFO) said that they will not licence any "moderate livelihood" fishery in the Atlantic outside of the commercial season, siding with the key demand from the commercial fishing industry.

In response, Sipekne'katik First Nation Chief Mike Sack urged Mi'kmaq bands in Atlantic Canada to reject the government's position, stating that his nation will continue to exercise its sovereignty by "determin[ing] what our season is going to be and how we're going to fish." Bands that agreed to operate under DFO regulation according to DFO-approved "moderate livelihood fishing plans" were offered licences that would allow them to sell catch in 2021. (Under provincial rules, only fish products harvested under federal commercial licences can be purchased by shore processors.) Chief Sack correctly characterised the DFO as trying to divide and conquer the Mi'kmaq with their offer of "low hanging fruit." Meanwhile, the Executive Director of the Maritimes Fishermen's Union said in an interview that commercial fishers expected the DFO to crack down on Indigenous fishers operating outside of the season, including pulling traps and "potentially arresting individuals that are not keeping up with the law."[2]

The attacks on Mi'kmaq sovereignty by settler fishers are not exceptional: they point to the deep challenge and necessity of building an anti-colonial socialist movement that can alienate non-Indigenous workers from their investment in Canadian nationhood. While the spoils of colonial theft and occupation provide a material incentive for the settler working class to take

2    Paul Withers, "'Moderate livelihood' fishermen must operate during commercial season, DFO says," *CBC News*, March 3, 2021.

it upon themselves to defend colonialism, when workers line up behind the robber barons of extractive industries, union bureaucrats, and state agencies like the DFO, it is ultimately their own exploitation as workers they are defending. The working class can learn how to mount its own anti-colonial socialist struggles by learning from Indigenous sovereignty movements and their opposition to the bourgeois and settler colonial state.

## Indigenous solidarity as decolonial internationalism

In 1997, the Supreme Court of Canada ruled that the Wet'suwet'en people, as represented by their hereditary leaders, had not given up rights and title to 22,000 square kilometres of Northern British Columbia. For over a decade, the Wet'suwet'en people have been exercising sovereignty over their territories by blockading and fighting against the Coastal GasLink pipeline being forced through Wet'suwet'en lands without their free, prior, and informed consent. In February 2020, the Wet'suwet'en people called for solidarity actions in response to a militarised police raid of their territories.

The Wet'suwet'en call ignited a social movement under the banner Shut Down Canada, which shot a direct blow to capital. Indigenous people organised rolling actions all across the country from February 2020 to mid-March 2020, including blockades and disruptive actions at railways, ports, and highways. Most notably, the Mohawk people held a rail blockade for nearly a month on Tyendinaga territory. In the first six days of the blockade, at least ninety-two trains were cancelled, impacting over 16,000 passengers on one of Canada's busiest rail corridors.[3] Dozens of freight trains were stopped, stalling shipments of everything from propane to feedstock for factories.

Indigenous people have organisations, including nations and kinship networks, that are completely separate from settler society. The Shut Down Canada movement involved disruptive, anti-capitalist chokepoint actions, which were carried out as a coordinated offensive against the Canadian state and economy. These actions and blockades were spearheaded by the organised, formal leaderships of Indigenous nations, which

3   Jorge Barrera, "Mohawks prepare to enter 6th day of railway shutdown in support of Wet'suwet'en," *CBC News*, February 10, 2020.

are geographically separated but were connected through the Wet'suwet'en call for action and the fight for Indigenous sovereignty.

The Shut Down Canada movement, then, had an internationalist character: the Gitxsan nation, the Mohawk nation, and the Listuguj Mi'kmaq answered the Wet'suwet'en call for solidarity by blocking rail lines on their own territories. Workers have much to learn from the decolonial internationalism of the Shut Down Canada movement, which demonstrated the revolutionary consciousness and power of Indigenous people. As Indigenous land defender Harrison Powder told the CBC from a rail blockade outside Winnipeg in February 2020, "Our people have been saying for years 'we can shut down this country, we can stop the economy, we can cause major economic damage'—and it's happening now." Recognising Indigenous sovereignty as a core component of total revolutionary struggle, it is ultimately in workers' own interests to divest from colonialism and contribute to decolonial internationalism by staging anti-colonial actions from their strategic position within capitalist production.

### Sovereignty as method and the problems with unitary organisation

When large sectors of the working class identify with and enthusiastically defend colonialism, what does that mean for socialists? Big-tent socialists say we are all "on the same side" because we're all for workers, but which workers are we for? We can't take anything for granted. Socialists need to work out these political disagreements and positions within our social bases and organisations, otherwise white colonial hegemony will continue—even with the fall of capitalism. The stakes are high for me and for other Indigenous revolutionaries who organise alongside non-Native socialists. If socialist organisations don't take a stand against working-class colonialism, then why would Indigenous people join settler workers in the fight against capitalism?

Red Braid's experience organising in street kin communities has been that poor white workers, even when they are largely left out of the material benefits of settler colonial nationhood, maintain their investment in settler colonialism. One expression of this investment is the tendency of poor white workers to treat their Indigenous peers as "just like them," which means that they can react with hostility to assertions of Indigenous sovereignty and difference. At a tent city summit in 2018, with representatives and past residents from twelve tent cities in British Columbia in attendance, we discussed the necessity for Indigenous fighters to have sovereign spaces. During that conversation, a white homeless man asked, "Isn't that just segregation?" He was promptly scolded by an Indigenous woman, who definitively shut down his "colourblind" racism. The success of her intervention shows the importance of Indigenous leadership, for which non-Native activists are no substitute. Non-Native Red Braid members had tried raising this point in tent cities and homeless community spaces before, but poor white workers had consistently resisted it because it wasn't coming from Indigenous people within or adjacent to their own communities. We require Indigenous self-organisation and leadership in order to decolonise, and non-Indigenous working-class fighters need revolutionary Indigenous leadership to follow in order to fight against colonialism, including the colonialism in the heads, hearts, and wallets of the settler working class.

Red Braid's Indigenous Leadership Council (ILC) serves as a vehicle for decolonial power, giving organisational form to the political truth that only Indigenous people's self-activity can constitute decolonisation. The ILC does not need the leadership of non-Native working-class fighters in Red Braid in order to launch our own fight against colonialism, rather the opposite is true: it is the working class that needs *us* in order to realise a more total revolutionary struggle against the settler-colonial, imperial, capitalist state.

While capitalism and colonialism have a symbiotic relationship, it is only Indigenous people who can free themselves from colonialism. Even though that is true, the working-class anti-capitalist struggle *must* be anti-colonial as well, because one of the central barriers to waging revolutionary war against capital is the investment that white workers have in whiteness, settler colonialism, and imperialism. If socialist organisations want the leadership of Indigenous people, then settler dynamics, ideologies, and structures in the working class and its organisations need to be addressed.

Red Braid isn't trying to create a single, centralised body, because we believe no single organisation can wage a struggle against capitalism for socialism *and* against colonialism for sovereignty. Those things are not the same, which is why we need a parallel organisation, where we have a unity in action premised on sovereignty as a method, not just as an end goal. That is why our name is Red Braid—the "braid" represents the interwoven but distinct struggles of our people against colonialism and the working class against capitalism. In a settler colonial context, an organisation that focuses only on class struggle, with one single politics and decision-making structure, is a settler colonial organisation. Class struggle needs socialist organisations that take the fight against colonialism seriously, follow Indigenous leadership, and defend sovereign space—not just temporary caucuses where Indigenous people can advocate for their perspectives until a single unity is achieved.

If our goal is to build decolonial Indigenous power and anti-colonial working-class power, then we need clear, political analysis of what stands in the way of building these forms of consciousness and political activity, and organisations that are pliable and able to experiment with different forms. Revolutionary base-building organisations must shape and be shaped by their relationships to people in struggle—at times leading and at other times following. Our struggles are multiple, and so should be our organisations.

*A Separate Star* Section 3

# Gender power and women's revolution

# Introduction
## Gender power and women's revolution

A fundamental premise of Red Braid's politics was that revolutionary change requires a united struggle that includes working class–led struggles against capitalism, Indigenous-led struggles against settler colonialism, and struggles of Black people and nations of the Global South against imperialism. This was somewhat of a departure from the socialist feminism of other groups and eras, where the emphasis in socialist groups was on bridging movements against patriarchy with class-based movements. So where does gender figure in our "strategic unity"?

In Red Braid's basis of unity, we explained it this way:

> Feminism is not included alongside the "braided" struggles against colonialism, capitalism, and imperialism because we see gender power as a wire within each cable, and as the intimate power that completes the circuitry between them. Gender power encompasses the patriarchal and colonial processes that code, sculpt, and police us into a gender binary.

In other words, we didn't say we're united against colonialism, capitalism, imperialism, *and patriarchy*, because we believed that would be redundant. As we explain in this section of *A Separate Star*, gender power, like race, is fundamental to the organisation and operation of capitalism through the unwaged reproductive work assigned to women by gender, to colonialism through genocidal violence against Indigenous women, and to the maintenance of imperialism through the concessions and repressions of the bourgeois-patriarchal family. Gender power is everywhere and in everything; it can't be reduced to a distinct system like patriarchy alone.

In 2020, Red Braid held an internal education series called "Gender and Socialist Revolution," in which we studied experiments and theories of socialist feminism. We began with a critical reading of Friedrich Engels's *The Origin of Family, Private Property and the State*, and then traced how socialists active in the Russian, Chinese, and Cuban Revolutions, as well as the autonomous feminist movement of the 1970s, threaded their efforts to combat patriarchy with Engels's ideas. The first chapter of this section outlines and develops the contributions and shortcomings we've identified in Engels's foundational contribution to socialist feminism. We argue that a revolution limited to the realm of "thing-production," which neglects the patriarchal power that dominates "species-production" under capitalism, is not a socialist revolution at all. We concluded this study group with a reading of the 1977 Combahee River Collective statement, the conclusions from which Listen Chen incorporates in "The Birth of Radical Multiculturalism" in section 4 of this book.

"Revolution in the Factory and Reform in the Family" is followed by a companion piece—a group statement about gender power. In "Towards a Subaltern Feminism: Strategies for Adversarial Reproduction," we identify gender violence as having a triple function under settler colonial capitalism—disciplining working-class women to perform unwaged reproductive labour, carrying out genocide against Indigenous women as part of the settler colonial genocide upon which empire depends, and eliminating trans women and anyone who threatens the gender binary. Against the logic, power, and danger of gender violence, we call for "adversarial forms of social reproduction" that can defend our communities against gender violence as part of a struggle to abolish the systems of colonial land theft and capitalist production that organise and demand the oppression of women.

Finally, in "Cultural Ascendancy is Not Gender Liberation: The Imperial Recuperation of Queerness," Listen Chen analyses the class politics of the contemporary mainstream celebration of queerness. Following in the footsteps of radical critiques of the emergence of homonormativity out of the folding of gay liberation into Gay Pride, Chen argues that a queernormativity is the result of a queer politics that centres individual identity and cultural expression over solidarity and collaboration with other oppressed people against colonialism, capitalism, and imperialism.

# Revolution in the factory and reform in the family

## Revisiting Engels's two houses of production

Red Braid

Patriarchy is nothing if not persistent. While gender gaps in both wages and housework narrowed significantly in Canada during the second half of the twentieth century, women's gains have stagnated since 1990.[1] Men continue to dominate the public sphere, jealously guarding it through sexual harassment and violence, while women continue to bear the brunt of unpaid labour in the home, where they are disciplined through more violence still. The "girl boss" is more a cultural figure than an actual social phenomenon, with men holding over ninety percent of top-level executive positions in Canada in 2019.[2] Real advances made by professional and business women are dependent on the low-waged, racialized, and feminized service sector,

1  Melissa Moyser, "Measuring and Analyzing the Gender Pay Gap: A Conceptual and Methodological Overview," *Statistics Canada*, Catalogue no. 45200002, August 2019; Evrim Altintas and Oriel Sullivan, "Fifty Years of Change Updated: Cross-national Gender Convergence in Housework," *Demographic Research*, 35 (2016).
2  Catalyst, "Quick Take: Women in Management," August 11, 2020.

which provides a way out of housework for those women who can afford to offload their domestic responsibilities onto other women. Twenty-first century liberal feminism, which prioritizes cultural interventions and the representation of women in business, does not have answers for working-class women who face gendered exploitation and violence at work, at home, and in all spheres of life.

Socialist feminists follow another tack, setting their sights not just on the observable *effects* of women's oppression but on the underlying *social relations* that produce them, identifying the nuclear, heterosexual, male-headed family as the *material foundation* for patriarchal social relations. The socialist feminist call to abolish the family, which appeared in *The Communist Manifesto* in 1848, has become fashionable once again (if you run in the right circles), evinced and advanced by the popularity of Sophie Lewis's *Full Surrogacy Now*. But when we consider twentieth century revolutionary socialist experiments, from the Soviet Union to the People's Republic of China, we see that, while women made important gains, the patriarchal family persevered despite socialists' expectations that it would "wither away" and despite their efforts to quicken its demise.

There is a clear need to reassess theories of women's oppression in order to inform strategies of women's liberation. In this chapter, we return to a foundational work in the socialist feminist canon, *The Origin of the Family, Private Property and the State* by Friedrich Engels, which, at its best, offers a materialist analysis of patriarchy, grounded in historical conditions of production. Engels's insights and errors, taken together and brought to bear on revolutionary socialist history, suggest that gender liberation can only be achieved through social revolution in the totality of production: in the factory *and* the family.

## Engels's insights

In the Preface to the First Edition of *The Origin of the Family, Private Property and the State*, Engels makes a theoretically dense but important claim with far-reaching implications for socialist feminist politics. He writes, "According to the materialistic conception, the determining factor in history is, in the final instance, the production and reproduction of immediate life."

The materialist conception to which Engels refers is the premise that "life is not determined by consciousness, but consciousness by life," as he and Karl Marx write in *The German Ideology*. In other words, we make our own history, but not as we please. It is not our ideas, words, or dreams alone that matter, but how we confront already-existing circumstances, and how we organise social life and our collective survival, which are historical and material questions. We make our own history *through the production and reproduction of immediate life*, which is to say, through human activity, through our active relation with the world.

The production and reproduction of immediate life, Engels continues, is of a "twofold character: on the one side, the production of the means of existence, of food, clothing and shelter and the tools necessary for that production; on the other side, the production of human beings themselves, the propagation of the species." This second form of production, to be clear, extends far beyond procreation. Once we are born, human beings cannot survive past infancy without constant care, and even when we reach adulthood, our production is never complete: we need to sleep and eat, we need hygiene and health care, we need pleasure, intimacy, and a sense of meaning. Human life is not produced in a single moment but through an ongoing process that depends on the production of its *means* of existence, just as that means must be continuously produced and reproduced through human labour. The two sides of production, then, are dependent upon each other, and neither can exist without the other. While they are not identical, they form a unity: the two parts make a whole.

Engels's provocation is that social organisation, the shape and texture of our daily lives, is "determined by both kinds of production." In the example of the Russian Revolution, we can see the determining factor in history—production with its twofold character—in motion: the contradictions of production in both the factory and the family gave rise to a moment of historical rupture, unleashing the energies of not only waged workers, but also women struggling to feed their families. As historian Judy Cox writes, in the February revolution of 1917, the "anger of the women queuing for food coalesced with the grievances of women in the factories and exploded onto the streets of St Petersburg." Women in the thousands expressed their anger over the conditions under which they laboured, over the exploitative and inhumane mode of production of immediate life, through demonstrations, strikes, and clashes with police. Through their own activity, these women sparked revolution and actively *made history*.

A half-century later, in the 1970s, social reproduction theory emerged at the intersection of Marxism and feminism, challenging the orthodox Marxist belief in the factory as the primary site of class struggle, and the white, male industrial worker as its protagonist. Social reproduction theory foregrounds how the work involved in the production of human life is constitutive of capitalist relations, arguing that without the unwaged physical, emotional, and sexual labour performed by wives and mothers in the so-called "private sphere" of the home and family, the gears of capitalist production in the public sphere would grind to a halt. Social reproduction theory takes issue with the ways in which feminized forms of labour are devalued and rendered invisible, and challenges the myth that women possess a natural faculty and passion for reproductive labour, declaring instead that housework is economic activity.

While we owe a great debt to social reproduction feminists for drawing the foundations of our critique, in revisiting Engels and socialist feminist history we have found the phrase "social reproduction" or "reproductive labour" inadequate because it cedes the mantle of "productive labour" to the production of *things*: of food, clothing, shelter, and tools. As Engels at his most prescient makes clear, *both* forms of human activity are *kinds of production*. To emphasise this unity, we have opted to use the terms: "thing-production" and "species-production."

The distinction between these two forms of production, while real, is the outcome of historical developments, not the result of an inherent difference between two distinct forms of human activity. Consider the work of raising livestock, slaughtering, processing, preserving, cooking, and serving it. Where is the line between the production of livestock *as a thing* and the work of producing *human beings*? The distinction between these two forms of production only becomes meaningful with the development of commodity production, which splits production into two spheres: public commodity production for exchange, which is the decisive site of surplus value extraction within capitalism, and private production for use by workers, including in their development into sellers of the commodity of labour power that they, in turn, sell in the public market.

As Marxist feminist Eleanor Burke Leacock argues in her 1972 introduction to *The Origin*, prior to the development of class society, "the distinction did not exist between a public world of men's work and a private world of women's household service. The large collective household *was* the community, and within it both sexes worked to produce the goods necessary for livelihood." While there were, in most circumstances, gendered divisions of labour in this community organisation of production, those divisions typically did not have the power relations that private property would later usher in. French feminist theorist Monique Wittig extends Leacock's premise, arguing that a materialist feminist analysis must denaturalize the very categories of "man" and "woman" and recognise that "both sexes" are produced through social forces and, in particular, gendered class relations. "Man" and "woman," Wittig writes, "are political and economic categories not eternal ones."

Through definite historical processes, species-production was cleaved from thing-production, and the latter became known as production proper, while the former was subordinated in its service and naturalised as women's innate labour of love, not part of organised production at all. This transformation began, according to Engels, when societies developed the ability to produce a surplus, to produce more than was needed to survive, and the possibility emerged for individuals to start grasping, accumulating, and hoarding that surplus as their own private property. Engels argues that it just so happened that, in the development of bounded property forms under feudalism and then capitalism in Europe, men were in the position to grasp and hoard, because their role, generally, was to produce *things*, which could be owned and accumulated as property, whereas women had the job of producing *people*, of managing the kinship systems upon which their societies were based.

When men became property owners, there emerged an incentive for them to overthrow those kinship systems that were led by women and develop a family form that ensured their property would be passed on to their descendants. That family form, the nuclear, monogamous, heterosexual, male-headed family, which organises contemporary social life in the West, with its origin in property relations, is imprinted with the supremacy of men and the subordination of women. Most people living under this family form today, even if they stand to inherit nothing from their father, or from his father before him, probably have his name, while their mother's and grandmothers' names are lost to history.

Engels writes, in no uncertain terms, that the "overthrow of mother right was the *world historical defeat of the female sex.*" The family, at least in the West, became the presiding system for species-production, a system "completely dominated by the system of property" wherein man reigns supreme, and woman becomes a "mere instrument for the production of his children." Today the family is a site of capitalist production. And, like the factory, it is not just dominated by property: *the family is capitalist property.*

Under capitalism, as Engels correctly explains, species-production is dominated—not just symbolically but materially—by thing-production. That does not mean that species-production is less important than thing-production; without species-production, thing-production would have no use value, and the commodity-form would collapse. As Engels says, in the final instance, both forms of production, taken together as a dynamic whole, are the determining factor in history. But the fact of the domination of thing-over-species matters; it is the crux of the problem of socialist feminism.

## Engels's errors: Matriarchal production as natural, not historical

According to Marxist feminist Maria Mies, Engels's description of the twofold character of production is an analysis with which "every materialist feminist would happily agree." But Mies argues that Engels gives up his materialist conception in his analysis of the production of human beings and the family. For Engels, social life in any given time and place is determined by "the stage of development of labour on one hand and the family on the other." The separation of the concept of *labour*, that cornerstone of Marxist thought, from the *family* leads Engels down a path where his analysis of the two-sided character of production is lop-sided: thing-production is figured as historically determinate and species-production, natural.

Throughout *The Origin of the Family, Private Property and the State*, when Engels describes the development of matriarchal systems of species-produc-tion, Mies says he "does not apply an economic analysis but an evolutionary one." For example, he explains the introduction of the incest taboo as a prod-uct of "natural selection" and the transition from group to pairing marriage as an outcome of women's natural "longing for the right of chastity," rather than as historical developments conditioned by the political and economic leadership of women. For Engels, the introduction of monogamy—not coincidentally inaugurated by men—reflected a turning point from nat-ural to "social forces." Monogamy, he claims, was the "first family form based not on natural but economic conditions—on the victory of private property over primitive, natural communal property." And while Engels's description of the "world historical defeat of the female sex" powerfully underlines the historical significance of the development of patriarchy, his account of men's triumph through a "simple decree" imagines that women yielded without struggle, just as his all-too-final announcement of women's "historical defeat" obscures their ongoing resistance and corollary regimes of patriarchal, col-onial, and imperialist violence and discipline required by patriarchy to put down women's assertions of power.

When Engels describes the development of matriarchal forms of spe-cies-production as "natural" and therefore outside of history, he gives up his materialist methodology and falls back on idealism. He contradicts his earlier claim that the determining factor in history is the production and reproduction of immediate life—as well as his fundamental claim in the first paragraphs of *The Communist Manifesto* that the history of all known society is the history of class struggle—failing to see how *women have made history* through their own labour, as matriarchs responsible for the kinship systems upon which their societies were based.

Engels's teleological method, which sees human history as moving pro-gressively through a series of stages from savagery to barbarism to civilisation, undermines his capacity to analyse so-called "prehistoric culture" through a materialist lens. The outcome is a double error: a Eurocentric, imperial-ist, and false assumption that societies develop along the same linear path with European models of social organisation representing the pinnacle of development, and a failure to see, let alone understand, women's political and economic leadership in pre- and non-class societies founded on kinship, not property relations.

## Patriarchal family as effect, not cause

When Engels turns his attention to the patriarchal mode of species-production, the nuclear, monogamous, heterosexual, male-headed family, which he refers to simply as "the family," his materialism is uneven. Engels traces the historical emergence of the family as a product of material forces—in short, as the "victory of private property." For Engels, women's oppression cannot be explained in terms of biology or ideology, but requires a materialist explanation that grounds male supremacy in a family form that arises from and is dominated by property relations. However, while Engels advances material *causes* that explain the rise of the patriarchal family, he forgets his own argument that species-production is itself a *determining factor* in history.

Engels writes, "The supremacy of the man in marriage is the simple consequence of his economic supremacy, and with the abolition of the latter will disappear of itself." He presents the patriarchal family form as effect, not cause; as constituted by, not constitutive of productive forces. His logic is linear, against the dialectic that the production of the *people* needed to produce *things*, and of the *things* needed to produce *people*, are two parts of a whole. Engels's methodological error matters because it leads him to imagine the family as a superstructural effect of an economic base that will automatically vanish with the abolition of capitalist property, dismissing species-production as itself a site of power and struggle, as well as a potential site of revolutionary transformation.

Chinese revolutionary leader Mao Zedong continues Engels's mistake in his "Investigation of the Peasant Movement in Hunan," written in 1927. In the report, Mao describes and defends the spontaneous uprisings of peasants against feudalism and astutely ties the authority of the husband to that of the landlord in what he terms a "feudal-patriarchal system." However, he mistakenly concludes that inequality between men and women will be abolished as a "natural consequence of victory in the political and economic struggles." He locates patriarchy in the same category as superstition: as a superstructural effect of the economic base. And he imagines that when the peasants overthrow feudalism, patriarchy will lose its foundation and the "authority of the husband will begin to totter."

Mao's famous quote, "a revolution is not a dinner party," immediately follows his description of peasant men raping the daughters of local gentry as an act of revenge or attack against their fathers. While Mao is by no means indifferent to gender, he sees patriarchy as a secondary contradiction, which leads him to excuse peasant men's gendered violence against the daughters and wives of landlords as a rough expression of class struggle. But Mao misses the truth that gendered violence against any one woman is collective violence against all women. When a peasant rapes a member of the gentry, he is attacking feudalism by expanding the patriarchal power of peasant men. Peasant men's patriarchal power is wielded first and foremost against peasant women, ultimately undermining the peasant movement against the whole of the feudal-patriarchal system.

Mao's mistake is to imagine patriarchy as a cultural effect of class organisation, rather than as a form of class organisation per se, with a life of its own. He is unable to foresee that the defeat of the landlord class, rather than set patriarchy tottering, has the potential to clear the way for peasant men to expand their own authority as patriarchal heads of the household. If feudalism and patriarchy together comprised the mode of production in rural China in the 1920s, then the path to overturning the feudal-patriarchal system *as a whole* was not through a struggle against landlords alone, but through attacking *both sides* of production at their bases.

### Working-class patriarchy

In *The Origin*, the methodological error that takes the patriarchal family as an effect of the capitalist system of production, not cause, is perhaps most blatant in Engels's analysis of the working-class family. He writes:

> And now that large-scale industry has taken the wife out of the home onto the labour market and into the factory, and made her often the breadwinner of the family, no basis for any kind of male supremacy is left in the proletarian household, except

perhaps for the brutality toward women that has spread since the introduction of monogamy.

Through linear, mechanical, causal logic, Engels reduces the patriarchal family to a "simple consequence" of direct economic power. He romanticizes the working-class family, where men do not have access to the plain economic lever of controlling access to the household income as a potential site of heterosexual love and equality between women and men. But we know that the working-class family is a site of oppression, discipline, and routine violence for women and children. The "brutality toward women" that Engels breezes over is a structural aspect of the patriarchal family and is as material and consequential as the economic power to which Engels gives primacy, whether that power takes the form of the property that bourgeois men hoard or the higher wages that working-class men earn.

The patriarchal family is, as Engels says, "dominated by the system of property," but that system does not enter the family home *from the outside,* from the public realm of production, to shape the domestic sphere in its own image and for its own purposes. If we understand property not as an objective *thing* but as a social *relation,* we can see the family itself as a property relation, like that between the boss and worker but with its own particularities. Would Engels say that the domination of the boss over the worker is conditional, and that brutality at the site of production is merely an effect? The boss's domination over the worker is a social and historical appearance of the position that each occupies within capitalist production. And if we understand the family, including the working-class family, as a site of production, we see that it is an active and essential part of the totality of property relations under capitalism, and that the relations of domination within the family are also a property relation, an appearance of the social relations of species-production under the domination of the capitalist mode of production.

Marxist feminist Silvia Federici explains the property relation between wife and husband like a nesting doll within the property relation between the working class—including both husband and wife—and capital. In her 1975 polemic "Wages Against Housework" Federici writes, "In the same

way as god created Eve to give pleasure to Adam, so did capital create the
housewife to service the male worker physically, emotionally, and sexually,
to raise his children, mend his socks, patch up his ego when it is crushed
by the work and the social relations (which are relations of loneliness) that
capital has reserved for him." The relationship between husband and wife is
shaped by this property relation to such a degree that it becomes this property relation, dictated by the demands of capitalist thing-production at its
nexus with species-production. A March 2020 article in *Harvard Business
Review* titled "What's Really Holding Women Back?" shows that these nested
property relations cannot be reduced to an economic problem alone, where
the hypothetical husband is freed from housework simply because he makes
more money than the wife. Asking why, after two decades of advancement,
women's "progress accessing positions of power and authority" slowed in
the 1990s and stopped completely in the first two decades of the twenty-first
century, the authors suggest that it's *not* because women uniquely struggle
with balancing the demands of work and family life, as is commonly believed.
Rather, the accommodations offered by corporate employers, like reducing
work hours, are targeted to women workers rather than all workers, and lead
to stigmatization. While both men and women in the study expressed profound ambivalence over having to take time away from their family lives in
order to pursue a career, that ambivalence is disproportionately carried by
women. Men, the authors found, defend themselves against feelings of guilt
from prioritizing work over family by projecting those feelings onto women.
This tacit division of emotional labour, wherein both men and women make
immense psychic investments in the narrative that it is women's "nature" to
care more about family, is the subjective imprint of a patriarchal-capitalist
property relation.

Because it bridges social needs to intimate desires, the property relation of
the bourgeois family is a nexus where all historical forms of property relations
under the totality of capitalist production meet. The bourgeois-patriarchal
family relation serves thing-production and species-production by taking of
and reproducing imperialism and settler colonialism as well. In her 1986 book
*Patriarchy and Accumulation on a World Scale*, Mies argues that the transition
to capitalism required the "pacification" of European wage workers through

both economic and political concessions. The expansion of the bourgeois family relation was a delivery method that shared land wealth stolen from Indigenous nations through colonialism and imperialism with sections of the working class in a way that also disciplined and pacified working men and women to bourgeois-patriarchal social and gender norms. Mies writes:

> These political concessions are not, as most people think, the male worker's participation in the democratic process, his rise to the status of a 'citizen,' but his sharing the social paradigm of the ruling class...His 'colony' or 'nature,' however, is not Africa or Asia, but the women of his own class. And within that part of 'nature,' the boundaries of which are defined by marriage and family laws, he has the monopoly of the means of coercion, of direct violence.

Mies argues that it is within his own family that the European, working-class man exercises direct, immediate, and unrivalled power. But insofar as he identifies and acts as a citizen of the imperialist core, he also relates to Africa and Asia as territory under his domain. And in the settler colonial context, where the family home—the settler homestead—is the practical unit of colonial occupation, the white working-class man's monopoly on violence finds new frontiers and expressions, from Black lives stolen by lynch mobs to anti-Chinese race riots to missing and murdered Indigenous women, girls, and two-spirit people.

There is a dialectical relationship between the power of the white patriarch, which is secured by the nation-state, and the colonial and imperialist power of the nation-state as a whole. The white patriarchal family, as the basic economic and political unit of settler society, both produces and is produced by colonial, imperialist, and capitalist social relations; it is base and superstructure, cause and effect.

## Revolution against capital, reforming patriarchy

Engels's methodological error leads him to an erroneous conclusion: he pronounces that socialist revolution, in eliminating private property in the sphere of thing-production, will automatically free women from patriarchal power in the sphere of species-production—as long as they become work-ers in factories. He writes:

> To emancipate woman and make her equal to man is and remains an impossibility so long as the woman is shut out from social productive labour and restricted to private domes-tic labour. The emancipation of woman will only be possible when woman can take part in production on a large, social scale, and domestic work no longer claims to be anything but an insignificant part of her time.

Instead of advancing a revolutionary approach to the *totality of produc-tion*, he argues that the answer to patriarchy is the reduction of the sphere of species-production to a minimum and for women and men to devote themselves equally to the work of thing-production.

Since the 1950s, when women in Canada and the USA began joining the workforce en masse, we have seen that women's mass participation in wage labour is not a route to liberation—far from it. The property relations of the home follow women into the workplace, where they face gendered exploit-ation, harassment, and worse.

Since the women's liberation movement of the 1960s, liberal femin-ists have sought and won representation as professionals in bourgeois and colonial institutions. This movement of middle-class white women into demanding office jobs has produced a boom industry of personal service work, where predominantly women workers reproduce the capacities of entrepreneurial women and their families. The women who perform this low-waged personal service work are themselves stuck in a double-shift: because they can't afford maids and nannies, they perform unwaged work at home after doing their low-waged service jobs for yuppie families. In Canada, women primarily work in the broad field of jobs that constitute the personal services industry and, according to a 2015 Statistics Canada survey, continue to do an average of forty percent more unpaid household labour a week than men, irrespective of what kind of household they live in.[3]

3    Melissa Moyser and Amanda Burlock, "Time use: Total work burden, unpaid work, amd lesire," *Statistics Canada*, 2018. https://www150.statcan.gc.ca/n1/pub/89-503-x/2015001/article/54931-eng.htm

Engels is evidently mistaken when he claims that bringing the "whole female sex back into public industry" will necessitate the abolition of the family as the economic unit of capitalist society. But what if we imagine a socialist society where women will be welcomed into men's sphere as equals? The problem with this approach is that it leaves aside the relations of species-production and pushes them to the margins of socialist society. It amounts to the revolutionary overthrow of capitalism and the reform of patriarchy.

Russian revolutionaries continued Engels's mistakes by treating species-production as a secondary site of struggle, as an effect of capitalist production and not itself a space of power. In "Communism and the Family," published in the early years of the Soviet revolution, Alexandra Kollontai argues that the family is already "ceasing to be necessary to its members or to the nation as a whole," and that with the victory of communism, housework will wither away, giving way to collective housekeeping organised by the state. Like Engels, Kollontai's interest lies in reducing the sphere of species-production to a minimum because the "family distracts the worker from more useful and productive labour." And like Engels, she believes gender liberation can be won through women's participation in what she terms "productive labour." Kollontai writes, "The woman in communist society no longer depends upon her husband but on her work." In this way, she follows Engels in pursuing revolution in the relations of thing-production, while advocating reform for species-production.

It must be acknowledged that the family reforms implemented in the Soviet Union were far from insignificant. The Soviet government was the first in the world to decriminalise abortion and homosexuality, made divorce freely available to all, abolished the legal distinction between legitimate and illegitimate children, and created social wage institutions that reorganised aspects of women's labour out of the home and into state programs, such as community kitchens and cafeterias, laundries, sewing and mending centres, and universal child care.

But the family is more than a set of tasks. While taking a bulk of housework out of the home may reduce the amount of time women have to spend cooking, cleaning, and caring for children, a *quantitative* reduction in the demands placed on women does not automatically *qualitatively* transform their social role. It should come as no surprise, then, that it was women who performed low-waged work in Soviet kitchens, laundries, and daycares, and it was women who filled remaining gaps in the home.

Reflecting on the lessons from the first years of the Russian Revolution, Leon Trotsky says that "you cannot 'abolish' the family; you have to replace it."[4] He argues that because of the state of its economy, the Soviet Union simply did not have the resources needed to create a real alternative to the family. Kollontai's feminist dream of surrounding working-class women with the "same ease and light, hygiene and beauty that previously only the very rich could afford" was dashed by harsh reality: cafeterias were of such poor quality that only those with no other choice used them; people who relied on social laundries had their clothes and linens ruined or stolen; and abortion, while legal, was killing women because health care was inadequate. This is the consequence of a socialism that subordinates species-production to thing-production (while struggling with famine, profound national poverty, and against constant imperialist sabotage): when the revolutionary project is under threat, the subordinated and feminized form of production suffers, and women suffer along with it.

As in Russia, revolution in China brought important reforms to peasant family life. Peasant women were active participants in revolutionary struggle in the ways that were available to them, and the revolution opened new doors for their self-activity and organisation, including through joining mutual aid teams, co-operatives, and the war effort. As sociologist Judith Stacey highlights, peasant women, many for the first time, were able to earn remuneration for their work and "relate to one another outside of strict familial confines," which translated into "improved status, self-confidence, and a larger voice in family affairs." But while peasant women made gains, the status of peasant men increased more rapidly, leading Stacey to conclude that the "gap in social power between men and women may have widened despite the absolute gains women made."[5]

4   See Leon Trotsky, *The Revolution Betrayed: What is the Soviet Union and Where is it Going?* (New York: Pathfinder Press, 1972).

5   See Judith Stacey, *Patriarchy and Socialist Revolution in China* (Berkeley: University of California Press, 1983).

Revolutionary socialists recognise that social revolution requires the working class itself to take power into its own hands, overthrow capital, and seize the means of production. Or, as Mao writes in his report on the peasant movement in Hunan, "It is for peasants to cast aside the idols...it is wrong for anybody else to do it for them." But because they deal with patriarchy through reform, not revolution, these same socialists set aside the principle of revolutionary self-activity when it comes to questions of family and gender relations.

## Socialist expediency

If the rise of property was made possible through cleaving production into two gendered spheres and subordinating women's sphere to men's, then the destruction of property demands the end of this division. Otherwise, as history shows, socialism too will make use of gendered labour and fall back on the patriarchal family as an economic and political unit when expedient.

In the 1930s when the Soviet economy was suffering the effects of economic isolation and embargo, sabotage, and civil war, the socialist feminist project of family abolition was abandoned. By the mid-1930s the Soviet Union pivoted towards the recuperation of the family, while, in Trotsky's words, "covering its retreat with false speeches about the sacredness of the 'new' family." Women's rights were clawed back, including the right to abortion and contraception, and homosexuality was re-criminalised. The state extolled the "joys of motherhood" and even gave women medals for bearing children. But as Trotsky observed, there was nothing new about the "new" Soviet family: while men in the nascent socialist society gained opportunities to grow, develop, and acquire new tastes in life, "the wife, crushed by the family, remained on the old level."

The turn towards the strengthening of the family was not only an expedient answer to an economic crisis. The crisis in the Soviet Union was also social in character. As Marxist trans feminist Leslie Feinberg writes, "Famine, and military and economic warfare by world capital, were burning the revolutionary fuel of the population." The revolution was exhausted and gave way to a bureaucratic counterrevolution led by Joseph Stalin. In this context, as Trotsky argues, the family provided for a "stable hierarchy of relations, and for the disciplining of youth by means of forty million points of support for authority and power." While Stalin retained a *symbolic* commitment to women's liberation—even formally enshrining women's economic, social, and political equality in the constitution of 1936—the Soviet Union under his leadership restored formal foundations for the patriarchal family that the revolution had earlier attacked, and therefore reoriented the revolution away from its promised destination of women's liberation.

During the New Democratic period, Chinese revolutionaries likewise shored up the structural foundation of patriarchal authority, even as they reformed peasant family life. The Communist Party relied on the patriarchal family as the basic unit of the New Democratic Revolution: land title, taxes, and class status were all assigned to families rather than individuals. As landlords were overthrown and dispossessed, the principle of land-to-the-tiller was practically realised as land-to-the-families-of-tillers, producing what Stacey calls a "radical redistribution of patriarchy" and securing a renewed economic basis for peasant family life. The solidarity of the family unit was maintained, and women's political identity was submerged in that of her patriarchal family. While feudalism was directly confronted through revolutionary struggle, the patriarchal system was, Stacey argues, "reformed substantially at the same time that patriarchy was made more democratically available to the masses of peasant men."

The Chinese Communist Party's concessions to patriarchy should not be understood in terms of revolutionaries bowing to the "backwards" culture of the peasants. Patriarchy in rural China was not a mere "feudal remnant," an ideological hangover from the feudal-patriarchal system. It was, as Stacey argues, "simultaneously base and superstructure." Just as the survival of the patriarchal peasant family hung on the Communist Party restoring its material basis through land reform, the Party too depended on the peasant family as the "most viable basis for People's War" and therefore its rescue became pivotal to the party's economic strategy and a precondition for its victory.

Under socialism, as under capitalism, the patriarchal family derives its ever-persistent power and utility from its role as the basic economic and political unit of society. To break the back of patriarchy, socialist revolution must break from the family mode of species-production, which means creating, unearthing, and sustaining life-affirming modes of production based not on property but on kinship, broadly defined as reciprocal relations with the human and nonhuman world.

## Conclusion: Adversarial reproduction and the pursuit of many houses of production

From Engels to Kollontai to Mao, socialists throughout history have recognised that thing-production must be transformed at its base, but they have treated species-production as an auxiliary or contingent site of struggle—in sum, advancing revolution for capitalism and reform for patriarchy. The continued hegemony of thing-production over species-production is bound to undermine the socialist goal of the full development of all human potential. Socialists condemn capitalism for making life itself appear "only as a *means to life,*" as Marx writes in the *Economic and Philosophic Manuscripts of 1844*—but the same can be true under socialism if species-production is devalued and organised around the bleak and utilitarian question: what are the minimum requirements for a person to survive and work another day?

The hegemony of thing-production reflects an alienated relationship to labour, nature, and kinship. It is no surprise that Engels only conceives of a relation to the natural world in terms of subjection or domination. In *The Origin*, he misreads non-alienated relationships to nature among Indigenous peoples as "complete subjection to a strange incomprehensible power," which must be reversed in man's favour, just as the kinship relations of "the primitive community" are "naval strings" that must be severed. Under socialism, to continue the hegemony of thing-production over all of life is to continue the horrorscape of capital under a new name, which is also the violence of Engels's racist teleology insofar as development of thing-production is precisely the axis along which "progress" is assumed to move.

We cannot pretend to know precisely what is required to end the many co-constitutive forces that carve production into two and alienate us from labour, nature, and kinship, let alone what a world created through non-alienated modes of production will look like. One thing is certain: the family cannot be abolished in the absence of alternative modes of producing and reproducing immediate life unless we plan to let ourselves starve and our species go extinct. But rather than working towards a single, hegemonic mode of species-production, socialist feminists should instead strive to make room for multiple, co-existing systems for the production of human life—including those that have persevered through centuries of colonial, imperialist, and capitalist assault—as well as new systems created organically through struggle and experimentation.

In the subaltern communities where Red Braid organised, we saw the work of species-production undertaken in ways we refer to as "adversarial reproduction," that resist the disorganising, life-threshing forces of colonisation and capitalism. We saw adversarial reproduction in the collective efforts of our street kin to survive evictions, homelessness, bad dates, police violence, vigilante attacks, and the opioid overdose genocide. These forms of species-production, which are currently scattered, often desperate efforts, produced through sheer necessity, are among those experiments that we hope will form the basis for a subaltern feminism with the power and vision to challenge the patriarchal blind spot that splits the production of people from the production of things.

# Towards a subaltern feminism
## Strategies for adversarial reproduction

Red Braid

Gendered violence is integral to maintaining capitalist, imperialist, and colonial power. The World Health Organization reports that one in three women are subjected to physical or sexual violence over their lifetime, a rate that has remained stable over the past decade. The Canadian Femicide Observatory and the US-based Violence Policy Center report that in 2018 in Canada, a woman or girl was murdered every 2.5 days, and in 2018 in the USA, an average of over five women were killed every day. Statistics Canada reports that nine out of ten reported sexual assault victims in Canada are women. The Native Women's Association of Canada estimates that over 4,000 Indigenous women and girls have gone missing or been murdered in Canada over the past three decades. The 2015 US Trans Survey reports that four in ten trans people living in the US have attempted suicide in their lifetime.

Red Braid argues that this gendered and sexual violence, whether carried out by state bodies or by people exercising oppressive gender power in their intimate relationships, is always a representation of the formation and main-tenance of the oppressive gender roles integral to settler-colonial, imperial capitalism. Gender violence is *disciplinary* against working-class women, *genocidal* against Indigenous women, and *eliminatory* against trans women.

But far from helpless victims, each group of women also has the potential, through anti-violence struggles, to flip their exploitation and elimination into adversarial forms of power that are capable of smashing colonialism, capitalism, and cisheteropatriarchy.

For working-class women, social reproduction—behind-the-scenes, unwaged (or poorly paid) domestic labour that keeps society moving to and through workplaces—is the compulsory work assigned to them as part of their gendering as women. Gendered violence has a *disciplinary* function against working-class women. Intimate partner violence is the looming threat that adds compulsion to the gendered assignment of keeping the house clean and having dinner ready. Husbands and fathers use gendered violence to teach wives and daughters to accept the gruelling, thankless, endless toil of the housewife, and to accept the patriarchal dominance of the man at the head of the household. Sexual harassment and the danger of violence from men in public, on the streets and in workplaces, reinforce this patriarchal order by unrelentingly reminding women, with violations on their bodily sovereignty, that the public is the world of men, and that women's assignment is the care of the home. But working-class women's reproductive work has a double character. While this unwaged work is appropriated by capital and put into the service of men, it has an emancipatory counter-direction, in that in this unwaged labour we can see, occasionally, the roots of a new world beyond capitalist exploitation, where caring for one another will not serve the pursuit of surplus value, or profit. Working-class social reproduction has the potential of *transforming* labour appropriated by capital into counter-hegemonic structures of anti-capitalist struggle.

Violence against Indigenous women is not disciplinary as much as it is *genocidal.* Violence against Indigenous women is the most common, every-day appearance of the settler colonial genocide against Indigenous nations. Indigenous nations are attacked by Canada's imperial, settler colonial forces with the intention of seizing and converting Indigenous lands into property and commodities, and the elimination of Indigenous women and the scattering of Indigenous kinship structures is the foremost strategy of eliminating the Indigenous territorial sovereignty that opposes this colonial land theft. The Canadian state, including its committed settler population, attack Indigenous women with sexual and gendered violence as part of its campaign of genocide, with the goal of eliminating Indigenous nations' sovereignties and monopolizing Canada's claim to territorial sovereignty. Indigenous social reproduction, then, has a fundamentally revolutionary character. Indigenous women's survival and furthering of Indigenous generations is *decolonial* because the wellbeing of Indigenous kinship networks are the building blocks of Indigenous sovereignty.

All trans women, Indigenous and non-Indigenous, are vulnerable to the *eliminatory* violence faced by people who trespass the rigid laws of the patriarchal gender binary. Working-class trans women do socially reproductive work, in families and in community spaces, that can be appropriated to meet the needs of capital. And in that work, they are vulnerable to disciplinary violence, but never free from eliminatory violence. Trans women's self-defence responses to eliminatory gender violence, whether by fighting back against state violence or gendered and sexual assaults, or by creating nurturing, celebratory spaces that strengthen the overall existence of trans women's communities, is a *resistant* form of social reproduction.

For the subaltern, social reproduction is carried out in the shadows of civil society, under conditions of constant attack and privation. Red Braid organised with subaltern communities to politicise those survival struggles, including fights against evictions, homelessness, police violence, vigilante attacks, the opioid overdose genocide, gendered and sexual violence, child apprehension, and any other form of violence that plagues, punishes, and seeks to eliminate our communities. We see the development of adversarial forms of social reproduction, transformative, decolonial, and resistant, as an integral revolutionary strategy.

Subaltern social reproduction, however, can be individualised, scooped into the regulatory power of the state, and used to appropriate the adaptive, organic genius of community knowledge in order to cut off the revolutionary possibilities that are latent there. For example, in 2016, deaths from opioid overdose in British Columbia leapt to a record 992 deaths province-wide, double the number from the previous year (to go up by another fifty percent the next year). Drug users responded by creating autonomous self-defence spaces, like tent cities, where members of communities were better able to respond to overdose incidents and save the lives of their kin. The provincial health authority responded by picking off "peer" leaders, providing funding and resources and creating government-approved spaces. Resistant repro-duction was partially assimilated into a reproductive arena of public health, which included police surveillance and activities contained by social workers. While the health care wing of the state appropriated the resistant reproduct-ive techniques developed through drug users' self-activity, another, armed wing—the police—swept those autonomous spaces and scattered them.

The insidiousness of capitalism is in its ability to quietly and persistently appropriate our loving care for each other for its own benefit. But it is the ubiquity of this appropriated reproductive labour that makes reproduction a field for decolonial and socialist struggle. We need revolutionary organi-sations in order to identify and amplify the adversarial politics inherent to subaltern survival struggles and guard against their recuperation into the reproductive needs of capitalist processes. A strategic challenge facing revo-lutionaries is how to nourish and encourage the development of adversarial forms of reproduction towards revolutionary ruptures that face down patri-archy in its disciplinary, genocidal, and eliminationist appearances.

Subaltern communities exercise adversarial forms of social reproduction that defy hegemonic gender norms. Homeless women, for example, are per-ceived as "failed women" because they live their lives in public and have no homes to keep, whereas homeless men are perceived as failing to fulfil the patriarchal role of protecting and sheltering their families. But patriarchal power still operates within subaltern communities, where it is expressed through disciplinary, genocidal, and eliminatory gendered violence. Part of the revolutionary work of encouraging existing practices of adversar-ial reproduction includes defending women's leadership and taking hard stances against all instances of gendered and sexual violence and lingering fantasies of men's supremacy.

Because women are gendered into social reproduction work, they are often leaders in these spaces of adversarial reproduction. In our experi-ence, subaltern women take on leadership in the day-to-day maintenance and defence of survival spaces, like tent cities and the Whalley Friendship Corner, a street-run drop-in centre in Surrey, BC, that was coordinated by

Red Braid member Wanda Stopa. But the leadership of women in organising resistance to cops and property owners, in service of the survival and
well-being of their broader communities, does not in and of itself combat
patriarchy. For adversarial reproduction to challenge men's power, women
must consciously exercise their power as women *for women*, and they must
be able to command enough resources to free themselves from economic
dependence on men.

Crucially, we must decouple reproduction from gender. Bourgeois
reproduction is innately violent and misogynist because it is gendered as
women's work. While a revolutionary anti-capitalist reproductive practice
would value and hold up the sort of work that patriarchy has assigned to
women, revolutionary reproduction must be detached from gender and
reorganised in irreconcilable opposition to genocidal, eliminatory, and
disciplinary violence. A decolonial Indigenous reproduction is that which
reorganises Indigenous family, kin, and national structures outside of and
in opposition to Canada's colonial interests. A revolutionary working-class
reproduction must reject the fundamentals of liberal individualism and the
imperial, patriarchal family.

Social reproduction does not have an inherently negative or oppressive
value; it is the context of colonial genocide, patriarchal power, capitalist
production, gendered and sexual violence, and gender roles that invest it
with terrible meaning. But unshackling reproductive labour and its requi-
site gendered violence from bourgeois production and colonial domination
can make reproduction a political strategy, and a point of principle in a fight
against patriarchal-capitalism and colonial gender domination.

# Cultural ascendancy is not gender liberation
## The imperial recuperation of queerness

Listen Chen

> "The Society believes homosexuals can lead well-adjusted, whole-some, and socially productive lives once ignorance, and prejudice, against them is successfully combated, and once homosexuals themselves feel they have a dignified and useful role to play in society."—Mattachine Society statement of purpose (1951)

> "Crime has been the core of queer since queer came into existence."—*Queer Ultraviolence* (2013)

### Queernormativity and the ghosts of Gay Liberation

In the past two decades, terms that identify different gendered and sexual subjectivities have proliferated. When I created a profile on the dating site OkCupid in 2008, there were two options for gender (man/woman) and three for sexual orientation (gay/straight/bisexual). Today there are twenty-two options for gender and twenty for sexual orientation, reflecting the growing list of letters that tail the founding LGB acronym. Younger generations are increasingly identifying as queer, culture industries are representing more queers, and the number of celebrities coming out as queer or trans seems to have been rising ever since *Time* published its famous 2014 cover story "Transgender Tipping Point," featuring Laverne Cox.[1]

In 2021, US President Joe Biden announced his pronoun preferences in a television interview and on his first day in office, signed an executive order targeting discrimination against queer and trans people (a countermove to Trump's transphobic order banning trans people from the military). The same day, the White House updated its online contact form to allow visitors to specify their pronouns from a drop-down list, which includes "they/them." The year before marked a watershed moment for trans politicians, as four trans people—three trans women and one nonbinary person—were elected to office: Sarah McBridge as Delaware's state senator, nonbinary person Mauree Turner in the Oklahoma House of Representatives, Taylor Small in Vermont's House of Representatives, and Stephanie Byers in the Kansas House of Representatives.

Queerness is culturally ascendant, but with its ascendancy comes questions about the relationship between self-expression and power. It is impossible to imagine an end to compulsory cisheterosexuality that does not change gendered and sexual subjectivities through the rise of queer forms of expression and relations. But that does not mean that queer culture is inherently hostile to imperialist gender and sexual power. Queer cultural forms also diversify civil society, neutralise modes of queerness that resist representation and subsumption, and result in the expansion of liberal individualism to include queer forms of subjectivity that have historically been criminalised or subaltern.

Cultural intervention for the sake of cultural intervention isn't liberation: it's reformism. Thus, liberal progressives battle fascists and reactionaries by

1    A 2017 GLAAD report found that twice as many Millennials identify as trans or gender nonconforming (12%) as Generation X. A database of queer representation in children's media by *Insider* found the number of explicit and implicitly queer characters exploded between 2010 and 2020. GLAAD's "Where We Are on TV" survey of queer representation in US television found that 9.1% of TV characters in the 2020–2021 TV season were queer. While this is a dip from 10.2% the year before, GLAAD reports that from 2005 to 2008, queer TV characters hovered between 1–2% of characters, with the number steadily rising over the past ten years.

advocating for incremental progress: the step-by-step amendment of legislation, policy, and culture that ostensibly will, as the Mattachine Society theorised seventy-five years ago, remove the discriminations that bar predominantly white, middle-class queers from integrating into imperial civil society. Rather than going backward, which is the purview of the right, liberal queers want to move forward, and in so doing fetishize cultural ascendancy, cloaking it in a radical aesthetic that mystifies its political function: the queering of capitalism.

The goal of a subaltern queer politics is something else entirely: not the reform of the death machines of the US and Canada, but their abolition. Culture will necessarily be part of struggles to abolish compulsory cisheteronormativity in its colonial, bourgeois, and imperialist iterations, but cultural and language expressions cannot be an end goal without leading us into the cul-de-sac of liberal individualism. Queers and queer consciousness must be part of struggles against capitalism in order to challenge the dominance of the nuclear family and generate alternative forms of sexual and gendered kinship. But queer culture today is monopolized by middle-class activists and institutions that, in abstracting gender and sex from history and economy, are paving the way for the queering of homonormativity, appropriating the aesthetics of liberation to reformist ends.

The term "homonormativity" was developed by queer communist feminist Lisa Duggan, who critiques the assimilation of gay culture into neoliberal capitalism as sustaining, rather than destroying, heteronormative institutions. "Normativity" refers to the development of new socially accepted norms that are gained through the assimilation of, in the case of homonormativity, predominantly cisgender, white, gay men with purchasing power. While queers are quick to critique the assimilation of white gay men into colonial and capitalist institutions (for example, see the *New Yorker* article, "The Queer Opposition to Pete Buttigieg, Explained," which describes the 2020 presidential hopeful as "a straight politician in a gay man's body"), the pursuit to fill those positions of power with people who are *more* queer because they are not white and not cis merely seeks to perfect the goals of homonormativity through its same strategy: mobilising queers as declassed consumers to shape the commodities capitalism produces to fit their lifestyle needs, and rallying for greater representation of queers in petit bourgeois and bourgeois positions.

Just as the capitalist recuperation of the gay rights struggles of the '60s and '70s resulted in homonormativity, today's queer struggles for inclusion in capitalism are paving the way for queernormativity. The relationship between those subaltern queers fighting for inclusion—and their critiques of the queers who are already in—demonstrate the ever-shifting contours of gendered normativity. Subaltern women and non-men find themselves radically excluded by hegemonic masculinity and femininity, forming the abject backdrop that normative genders depend upon for their definition. But these are not fixed positions; rather, they are shaped by social processes that include the demands of capitalism, colonialism, and imperialism, as well as class forces—like the reformist pursuits of a queer petite bourgeoisie and aspiring petite bourgeoisie.

Starting in 2021, the number of anti-trans bills introduced yearly in the United States began to surge. In 2023, anti-trans offensives reached a boiling point, with Republican-controlled state legislatures churning out a record number of bills that seek to erase trans people from public spaces, with a special focus on schools. Proposed bills restrict gender-affirming medical care and bathroom access, criminalize drag performances, and effectively eradicate recognition of trans genders.

A queer liberation movement must be prepared to defend against such attacks without ceding the horizon of what constitutes queer politics to counter-mobilization alone. While reactionary right-wing forces need to be fought, including on the battlegrounds of cultural representation and legal inclusion, it would be a mistake to limit queer emancipatory politics to these arenas, which struggle to grapple with the structural, material basis of homophobia and transphobia. Queerness needs a mode of expression to contribute to decolonial, anti-imperial, and socialist struggle, but without decolonial, anti-imperial, and socialist politics, queer expression is a dead-end project, funneling subaltern energies into the ruts of civil society.

## We're all women in the struggle against patriarchy

In the West today, the normative way of understanding gender, which is a proxy for gender *power*, is to attribute women's subjugated positions to their biology, a mistake that trans-exclusionary and liberal feminists both make. Biological essentialism is misogynistic, identifying women's positions in patriarchy as a matter of natural differences between men and women rather than the outcome of social processes that uphold colonialism, capitalism, and imperialism. But trans-inclusive defences against biological essentialism can be just as essentialist, static, and simplistic when they substitute "biology" with "identity" as the thing that determines and causes transphobia.

Identity, when understood as fixed, innate, ahistorical, and individualised, reinscribes the boundaries of gender defined by biology with the no-less socially constructed boundaries of gender defined by expression, invisibilizing gender oppression against social groups who do not fit neatly into the analytic of identity. While identity can be a tool that helps social groups form a common understanding of their subjugated positions in society and develop counter-hegemonic practices and knowledge, it can also be appropriated by the state in an effort to better manage and identify subaltern populations, as well as by petit bourgeois and bourgeois actors interested in defending and expanding their class power. Both biological and identity essentializations obscure how power shapes the production of subjectivity, abstracting "gender" from fields of violence, capitalist production, and hegemonic power.

The terms "queer," "transgender," and "non-binary" all increased in frequency within Google Books' text corpora between 1990 and 2019, and "homosexual" and "lesbian" have been declining since the late '90s. There are multiple interpretations of the meanings of this trend. Trans-exclusionary feminists and adjacent thinkers complain that lesbians are going "extinct" because women who would otherwise identify as lesbians in another historical period are fluttering like moths to the flames of trans culture. There's probably some truth to that, but where trans-exclusionary feminists falter is in fetishizing language and culture as having inherent political value—as if some forms of gender expression are *more* arbitrary than others, a claim that reinstitutes "nature" as a category outside of history.

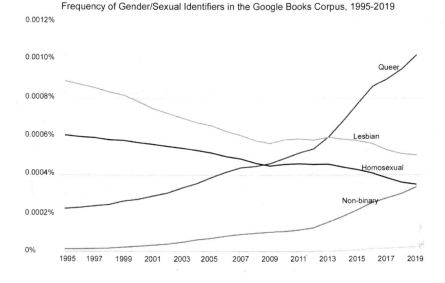

*Google Ngram chart*[2]

The liberal queer rejoinder to the trans-antagonistic smear that trans-ness is a trend is that trans people have "always existed." These trans-defensive positions are no less fetishistic because they overlook how different economic and social processes *produce* gendered relations in any given time and place. They essentialize social relations in the container of identity, instead of biology, but still explain gender as a naturalised and individualised, rather than as historically and politically determined. Thus, a white nonbinary woman argued in *Teen Vogue* in 2018 that non-binary is "a real identity that's existed for thousands of years," ahistorically flattening countless social groups disciplined, punished, and cast as sexually deviant while

2   Google's Ngram Viewer shows how frequently a given word or phrase appears in Google's corpus of books over a selected period of time. Between 1995 and 2019, the frequency of terms "transgender," "queer", and "non-binary"/"nonbinary" grew exponentially, while "homosexual" and "lesbian" decreased. Whereas "gay" (not pictured in the graph) has remained relatively stable over this time period, increasing in frequency by only 12%, "homosexual" and "lesbian" have both decreased by roughly 40%. "Queer" increased by nearly 350%, "nonbinary" or "non-binary" by 490%, and "transgender" by 1780%. Source: Google Ngram Viewer.

also obscuring how class, nationhood, and race have always animated the casting of sexual transgression by Western empire. None of these processes hinge on identity, although they shape and constrain it.

For example, the exploitation and oppression that early Chinese immigrants to western Canada experienced in the nineteenth and early twentieth centuries were shaped by racializing, classed, and gendering social processes. The infamous Head Tax was designed to severely restrict immigration in a discretely gendered way, as whites did not want Chinese labourers establishing roots in Canada by starting families, which is why there was a gender ratio of twenty-eight Chinese men for every one Chinese woman in British Columbia in the 1920s. Chinese working-class men lived in close proximity to one another, stimulating white anxieties about racially coded homosexuality as well as miscegenation with white women. The moral panic over opium dens in the late nineteenth century sensationalized them as shadowy places where young white women, referred to as "white slaves," would be corrupted by their contact with Chinese men, who were figured both as competitors with white men as well as gendered deviants because of their social location outside of white, Canadian patriarchy. Without an attention to the fluid processes that produce white, bourgeois, imperial patriarchy, we miss how the reproduction of that patriarchy relies on the exclusion of social groups, like Chinese men, that cannot be retroactively wedged into the so-called "real identity" categories of trans, non-binary, or queer.

If trans-inclusive liberalism posits identity-essence in order to dislodge the hegemony of biology-essence, then it similarly attempts to replace the gender binary (man versus woman) with another binary: queer/trans/non-binary versus cis. But this binary, detached from an analysis of how gender serves capitalist production and colonial domination, conflates gender as a *socially and historically created political category* with gender as an *identity*. Thus, NonbinaryWiki defines cisgender as an "aspect of a person's gender identity," defined in contrast to trans and nonbinary identity, rather than a system of gendering that has never waited on self-identification. The new gender *identity* binary splits the feminist terrain of struggle, according to an abstract definition of gender power that fixates heavily on identification as a determiner of gendered experience.

Queer liberals and revolutionaries are likely to agree that compulsory cisheteronormativity should be abolished, but we differ in how to envision that struggle strategically, and in who its protagonists are. If patriarchy scaffolds capitalism, imperialism, and colonialism, then it is only through waging wars against these modes of production that queers can hope to abolish the gender binary; cultural escape chutes are, at best, private coping mechanisms and at worst, a means of assimilation. And because each of these modes of production produce and reproduce womanhood through relations of production which overwhelmingly benefit white, propertied men in the imperial core, queers have a natural stake in overthrowing these relations alongside women more broadly, which is a category that is *not* contingent on identity.

A 2019 article by white, nonbinary social psychologist Devon Price called "Was I Ever a Woman" conflates identity with social relations in order to conclude that there is something essentially different between cisgender women and nonbinary people who were assigned female at birth (which is 80% of nonbinary people in the US, according to the 2015 US Trans Survey). Price argues that "as much as cis people like to assume that I had a woman's life in the years before I came out, the truth is I never did … I was a piece of 'assigned female' hardware, running mostly male software." Price's essentializing split between biology ("hardware") and gender expression/identity ("software") sidesteps how *both* our bodies and our subjectivities are historical productions, substituting one binary for another.

As proof of their "male software," Price points to how they behaved in ways that violate "female socialisation," including "manspreading" on public transit, feeling entitled to personal space, and confidently asserting their boundaries "without any fear of recompense." In other words, they summarise, "In my mind, I have always had the security and confidence of a stereotypically privileged dude." They conclude that due to their "male-ish" privilege, they do not belong in women's spaces, while also implying that women who know how to say "no" are less "female" than women who don't.

Price's theory of how subjectivity is produced displaces the centrality of men's power over women by essentializing differences between people who were assigned female at birth (AFAB) and identify as non-binary and people who are AFAB and don't, and in so doing reinscribes a patriarchal story of how power is produced through "traits." Feminist theorist Martha Gimenez argues that the typical liberal mistake of locating gender power in men's "traits" or "intentions" as the cause of women's oppression "diverts attention from theorising the social relations that place women in a disadvantaged position in every sphere of life and channels it towards men as the cause of women's oppression." Price, while following this same logic, merely constructs men's traits as autonomous from male embodiment, ascribing them to Price's own personhood as proof that they are essentially unlike cis women.

In Price's worldview, queer and trans people are products of nature, coded with gendered hardware and software. Their argument stands in stark contrast with the vision of the lesbian described by Monique Wittig in her classic text, "One Is Not Born a Woman," as "something else, a not-woman, a not-man, a product of society, not a product of nature," who violates a gendered division of labour that produces "womanhood" as the property of men. Wittig argues that for those subjected to the condition of womanhood (which is not at all contingent on *identifying* as a woman), what stops them from "becoming" men is not that they lack essential male traits, but a property relation that defines manhood not as an "identity" or "software" but a position in relation to a capitalist mode of production.

Womanhood is a material condition conferred on women and feminized others whether or not they identify as such. Subaltern feminist struggles against capitalism, colonialism, and imperialism cannot afford to conflate womanhood with a narrow definition of identity, just as we cannot afford to mistake "identity" as the source of men's power over all those who experience the material conditions of womanhood. Doing so flattens the classed, colonial, and imperial logics that define womanhood, and—when appropriated in service of queer reforms—constructs a static picture of queerness as an identity rather than gendered social position that violates patriarchal-capitalist property relations.

Recognising womanhood as a social position rather than an identity allows us to sound out the basis of a feminist unity, but that does not mean ignoring shades of power within the broad category of womanhood. Rather, it means teasing out how patriarchy is wielded by both subaltern and bourgeois actors of all genders, *within* subaltern communities to their own detriment, *and against* subaltern communities for the benefit of an imperial, colonial, and bourgeois social order.

## The imperial repercussions of queer-normativity

Hegemonic queer culture, produced by middle-class institutions and activists, suffers from a radical cleavage between language and action. The negative definition of "queerness" as that which is not heteronormative lends itself to a critique of heteronormativity, but when disconnected from organised struggle, such critiques mistake heteronormativity for a problem of bad culture, thus positing the solution as a queer cultural ascendancy that fights straight culture with queer culture. What's lost in this battle between culturally affiliated individuals is the sight of capitalism, colonialism, and imperialism as the systems that lie behind the appearance of heteronormativity and the oppression of queer people.

A 2016 article in *Vice* magazine provocatively titled "Can Straight People Be Queer?" explores the phenomenon of queer cultural ascendancy, pointing out vis-a-vis the growing list of queer celebrities that "for many, [queerness] is a political persuasion as well as a sexual one." Thus, being queer isn't just about sexual or gender fluidity; it's about a politicised opposition to heteronormativity. Interviewing a queer musician who expresses hesitations over the "cultural whitewashing" of queerness, the piece repackages queer cultural politics as the liberal reform of bad ideas. The musician argues that society needs "to be deprogrammed, subverted, or queered, and that involves a process of unlearning and de-conditioning white supremacist, cisnormative, and heteronormative behavior and values."[3]

Topple, a queer media production company founded by a non-binary television writer, takes this fetishization of queer culture to its imperialist extreme: a fantasy of "revolution" summoned by the influx of queers into Hollywood boardrooms and Netflix shows. Topple's corporate manifesto calls on it to start a "revolution" by "lift[ing] up marginalized voices" and advocating for more queers and women of color to be board members, executives, partners, directors, writers, and department heads. To top it off, Topple points to how "Hollywood creates and distributes a collective

3    Dora Mortimer, "Can Straight People Be Queer?" *Vice Magazine*, February 9, 2016.

imagination for this planet" as a justification for why Hollywood must be more diverse, a call that in effect advocates for the queering of imperialism.

To be sure, culture will change over the course of winning queer liberation from colonialism, imperialism, and capitalism. And the project of reforming hegemonic culture through the inclusion of select people from subaltern groups does create political power, but the crucial question is what the class character of that power is in any given circumstance. The politics of Topple's queer inclusivity fights for the class power of middle-class queers whose immediate corporate interests are tethered to the production of media content, a project made possible by the capitalist market's malleability. "Towards an Insurrectionary Transfeminism" by Bash Back! affiliated authors who pen themselves as "some deceptive trannies" points to the contradictions of cultural reform in a capitalist system and resists the reductive view that trans subjectivity is—unlike cis subjectivity—somehow outside of capitalism:

> The trans subject's desires are easily moulded into that which can be profitable to capitalism...That is, trans subjectivity is bound to the conditions of capitalism and disciplinary techniques which have given rise to it...yet the constructedness of the trans subject and the trans body is no more tied to the history of capitalism and domination than the constructedness of woman as an identity and a body...capitalism has an ever-expanding amount of room to incorporate an infinite amount of gendered subjectivities which can be rendered value-creating to capital.

For queer or trans subjectivities to *resist* capitalism, commodification, and appropriation in service of the production of surplus value, those subjectivities must be shaped by and emerge out of struggle *against capitalism*, which is necessarily carried out by classed protagonists.

It's unsurprising, then, that queer cultural producers, academics, and NGOs, whose bread and butter is queer culture and aesthetics, advocate for a politics of reform that posits culture as the cross-class *cause* of gendered and sexual oppression, rather than an expression of ever-shifting relations of power always filled with economic content. Queer ascendancy means that there are more openly out queer and trans bosses today than ever before, but abstracted from capitalist social relations, queerness merely creates a common language between bosses and workers that mystifies the contradictions between capital and labour. Similarly, queer culture abstracted from race and empire treat gender and sex as commensurable across racial and colonial social relations, performing ideological work that merely "queers" the face of Western imperialism.

In 2021, Netflix aired a comedy special by Dave Chapelle, "The Closer," that included transphobic jokes that code the LGBTQ community as white. In response, queer and trans people staged protests outside Netflix offices focused on cultural representation, which led to a group of Netflix staff walking out in support of the demonstrations. B. Pagels-Minor, a former program manager at Netflix who is Black and trans, described in an interview with Al Jazeera their critique of the special as a matter of defending Netflix's reputation. They identified the problem at hand as Netflix not sufficiently representing "the full stories of Black trans lives." Netflix's head of queer editorial content joined the walkout and echoed Pagels-Minor's sentiments, tweeting, "We aren't fighting WITH Netflix. We're fighting FOR Netflix. We all know how great it can be and that it's not there yet." A trans engineer who works for Netflix and who heads the company's trans employee resource group similarly emphasises, in a blog post, that Netflix should promote queer and trans talent and pay them well. These efforts represent and collect together the particular interests of trans consumers, trans bosses, and trans cultural producers.

The trans employee resource group joined the walkout and released a list of demands, focusing heavily on Netflix's content production and calling for Netflix to fund trans talent, hire trans people as managers and bosses, and incorporate content warnings into the platform. The demands end with the statement, "We are employees, but we are members, too. We believe that this Company can and must do better in our quest to entertain the world, and the way forward must include more diverse voices in order to avoid causing more harm. [We look] forward to working with the Company to make this a better, more entertaining place for us all."

While the walkout involved the activity of trans workers *as* workers during the strike wave of October 2021 (although it's not clear how many of the employees involved were managers and bosses), it also figured trans employees of Netflix as part of a cross-class consumer constituency that deserves *representation* by corporations like Netflix, both through the commodities it sells as well as in its boardrooms. Thus, the statement describes trans employees as "members" who are identified with Netflix in a united mission to "entertain the world," equating a better workplace for trans workers as one that is more entertaining for them. Like Topple's "revolution," the statement conflates bad cultural representation and the absence of trans bosses as the central barriers to the interests of a declassed trans group.

Whether or not hiring more trans bosses will improve the lives of trans workers has yet to be widely tested because of the subalternity of trans people at large, but the very assumption that it will hinges on overlooking the objectively exploitative relationship between the bourgeoisie and working class. And given that privileged trans workers—those who are executives, managers, and higher salaried white-collar workers—formed the face of the walkout, it's unsurprising that the demands they published skewed towards their own class interests. Queer culture and cultural interventions, then, have no inherent class content—it depends on which social groups wield these tools and to what end. In the quest to "entertain the world," the better integration of trans consumers, cultural producers, and bosses into Netflix amounts to the queering of capitalism and imperialist cultural production.

If culture is just a terrain of struggle—no more and no less—then it is as much a terrain of struggle for the queer working class as it is for bourgeois queers; as much a terrain of struggle for white queers invested in civil society as subaltern Black, Indigenous, and racialized queers whose liberation depends on the destruction of civil society. Culture, then, cannot resolve the antagonisms rooted in relations of production any more than the lines on a sports field can mandate who will win the game. And yet we cannot dispense with queer culture, subjectivity, and consciousness without ceding anti-imperial, decolonial, and socialist struggles to heteronormativity.

### The queer subaltern

Queer politics in the imperial core are skewed towards the interests of predominantly white middle-class queers who aspire to be part of civil society, but that does not mean that queers are no longer a subaltern population. Rather, it suggests that our potentially revolutionary flames are firewalled in subcultural pockets, private relationships, and cultural enclaves.

According to the 2015 US Transgender Survey (USTS) and 2019 Trans PULSE Survey, trans and non-binary people are far more likely to live in poverty, be unemployed, experience sexual and physical assault, and a whole host of other negative life outcomes. But they are also as or more educated than the general US and Canadian populations, and they are both disproportionately white and disproportionately Indigenous.[4]

Data collected from the 252 Indigenous participants in the Trans PULSE survey similarly finds stark differences in the levels of education of trans and gender-diverse Indigenous peoples as compared to the Indigenous population as a whole. Trans and gender-diverse Indigenous people are nearly twice as likely as Indigenous people as a whole to have post-secondary education.[5] Indigenous participants of the survey are also much

4    The US survey finds that 19.1% of participants have a bachelor's degree, and an
     additional 12.9% have advanced degrees. According to the 2018 US census, 14.7% of
     the general population have bachelor's degrees and 13.1% advanced degrees, which
     is a statistically insignificant difference. The survey uses the same race categories
     that the US census does. The 2018 US census finds that 60.38% of the population
     is white, compared to 81.8% of USTS participants (according to the 2009 census,
     when white Latinx people are included, the number of white people in the general
     US population is 73.1%, still a statistically significant difference from the USTS
     population). While whites are overrepresented in the USTS survey, so are Native
     American and bi or multiracial people. "Hispanic," Black, and Asian people are all
     underrepresented. The Trans PULSE survey finds that 48% of participants have
     college or university degrees and 19% have advanced degrees. The 2016 Canadian
     census finds 54% of Canadians have college, university, or advanced degrees, which
     is a statistically significant difference. Fourteen percent of Trans PULSE participants
     identify as racialized, as compared to 22.27% of the general population, also according
     to the 2016 census, and also statistically significant. Nine percent of Trans PULSE
     participants identify as Indigenous, nearly double the 2016 census figure of 4.9%.
5    81% of Indigenous survey participants have some kind of post-secondary
     education, with 32% having some college or university education, 35% having
     college or university degrees, and 14% having advanced degrees. According to the
     2011 Canadian census, 45.8% of First Nations, Metis, and Inuit people have post-
     secondary education.

more likely to report *not* experiencing racism, with only one in five reporting being "perceived or treated as a person of colour."[6] But despite the higher likelihood of accessing education and not being negatively racialized, Indigenous trans and gender-diverse people seem more likely to have considered suicide in the past year than Indigenous people as a whole, and 80% report experiencing challenges accessing Indigenous ceremony, with only 36% reporting that the challenge they face is a lack of access to Indigenous community.[7] While 55% of Indigenous Trans PULSE participants (90% of which live in cities) report not being connected to Indigenous community, according to one general study of urban Indigenous people from 2010, only 32% of participants report that their community is mostly or exclusively non-Indigenous.[8]

The privileges that mark both Indigenous and non-Indigenous trans and non-binary populations signal that identity is not a pre-existing "thing" that is made visible through cultural or linguistic practices; it is also shaped by access to communities and spaces that are socially coded. It would appear, for example, that middle-class people who have access to universities are more likely to adopt counter-hegemonic modes of gender expression, and/ or that people who long for counter-hegemonic modes of gender expression are more likely to seek out university spaces. But because non-binary and trans gender expression is disruptive to hegemonic gender codes in the vast majority of spaces, having a university degree is no protection against social and economic marginalisation. Relatedly, Trans PULSE survey participants are generally younger than the Canadian population, with the

6    A 2019 survey on race relations finds that 53% of the 340 Indigenous people surveyed report experiencing racism regularly or from time to time, with 44% reporting "very rarely or never." Environics, "Race Relations in Canada Survey 2019," Toronto: The Environics Institute for Survey Research, 2019.

7    41% of Trans PULSE's Indigenous participants considered suicide in the past year. While there is little data on suicidal ideation and attempts in Canada's Indigenous population, a 2017 study on the impact of Residential Schools on suicidal ideation found that roughly 20% of Indigenous people have considered suicide over the course of their lives, with the rates nearing 30% for Indigenous people whose families experienced Residential Schools across two generations.

8    Environics Institute, *Urban Aboriginal Peoples Study* (Toronto: Environics Institute, 2010).

greatest disparity in the over 50 and 25–34 categories, which helps inform the high rates of both education and poverty.[9]

Alongside the perplexing findings on education and poverty, the racial demographics of the studies also point to the dangers of essentializing queerness. The underrepresentation of Black and Asian people in the USTS survey, for example, should not be taken as evidence that Black and Asian people are more heteronormative than whites. It's more likely that the imperial and race power that compresses these communities also mediates access to non-binary and trans cultural expression. If gender power operates differently within communities oppressed by white supremacist imperialism, then we need to be wary of flattening those operations by treating gender identity as commensurable across colonial and imperial relations.

Data on queer and trans people clearly points to the subalternity of our experiences of gender, for which we receive punishment, discipline, marginalisation, and in some groups, elimination. But the dominance of a liberal-reformist politics, championed by the middle class, mystifies the contradiction out of which a subaltern gender politics could emerge: that no matter how many cultural interventions we make, there is no escape from the gender binary that isn't the destruction of Western empire, capitalism, and colonialism.

## Subaltern womanhood

If womanhood is a political category marked by feminizing, racializing, and classed subjugation, then subaltern womanhood is the always-shifting limit against which both masculine and feminine gendered norms are constructed. Because gendered normativity is historically contingent and expands and contracts to include different subjects at different moments—for example, in the assimilation of white, cisgender gay men with disposable incomes into US empire—it is fundamentally insecure. Essentializing ideologies, whether fixated on biological essentialism or identity essentialism, obscure

9    According to 2020 Canadian census data, of the population aged fifteen and above, 6.5% are 15–19 (versus 13% of Trans PULSE participants aged 14–19), 7.7% are 20–24 (versus 22% of Trans PULSE participants), 16.6% are 25–34 (versus 37% of Trans PULSE participants), 23.4% are 35–49 (versus 20% of Trans PULSE participants), and 45.6% are 50+ (versus 9% of Trans PULSE participants).

the insecurity and fluidity of *both* hegemonic gender subjectivities *and* subaltern ones. The threat of being banished to subalternity works so well to
discipline gender because of the very instability of gendered relations, which
queers recognise when they identify the possibility of, for example, pene-
trating the boardrooms of capitalist enterprises.

In 2020, Red Braid's Bread, Roses & Hormones campaign argued that
misgendering is a form of sexual harassment. The campaign outlined how
trans women or trans feminine people are *de*gendered through the feminizing violence of *mis*gendering, which aligns with arguments from "Third
World" and Indigenous feminists who argue that Black and Indigenous
women receive the most abject forms of sexual violence from colonisers.
Black feminist scholar Hortense Spillers argues that "the gendered female
*exists for* the male," which means that women who are closer to hegemonic
power, for example, by virtue of being white and middle class, are gendered
as women insofar as they are claimed and protected by white men as their
property. Spillers contrasts the "gendered female" with the "ungendered
female," or enslaved woman, who is "unprotected" and can be violated by
both white women and men. Because patriarchy insists that hegemonic
womanhood is the only womanhood, subaltern women who are on the
outskirts of this category are degendered and denied the tainted benefits
of patriarchal ownership, while receiving its most excessive violences. In
both Bread, Roses & Hormones' and Spillers's arguments, gendered violence is still *feminizing*, but in its abjecting, degendering forms doesn't just
guard white men's power but also draws a possessive boundary around white,
imperial, cis femininity.

Sexual violence, then, is a useful indicator of subaltern experiences of
womanhood. While one in ten US Trans Survey respondents report having
experienced sexual assault in the past year, respondents who work in illicit
economies are over three times more likely to have experienced sexual
assault in the past year. A 2009 study of women street-level sex workers in
Vancouver's Downtown Eastside neighborhood, roughly half of which were
Indigenous, found that 34% had been raped in the eighteen months preceding the study (the number would surely be higher with the broader category

of "sexual assault"). [10] A 2007 report on homeless people in Toronto found that 20% of homeless women had been raped in the past year (15% of the respondents were Indigenous). [11] Comparatively, the US Trans Survey study cites a National Intimate Partner and Sexual Violence Survey that found that 1.6% of women in America had been raped in the past year.

While rape is always excessive, the incredible disparity that marks some women as preeminently "rapeable" indicates the usefulness of understanding "subaltern womanhood" as a political category that exceeds identity. Not only are subaltern women subjected to profound degrees of gendered violence, but gendered violence is a force that makes women subaltern. In a small 2003 study of women who experienced domestic violence, 38% of participants subsequently ended up homeless. [12] While "economic" reasons, defined as cost of rent, low income, and unemployment in the 2007 Toronto report, are a leading cause of homelessness, women's experiences of class and economy are inextricably gendered. An Indigenous woman being "low income" is as much an operation of colonialism as a working-class woman's poverty is an operation of the sexual division of labour under capitalism.

The binary of trans and cis, developed to make queerness legible and therefore absorbable by imperial civil society, fails to map neatly onto the realities of subaltern womanhood. Queernormativity, in adhering to this static binary, does not seek to do away with violence against subaltern women but to clear a pathway for some subaltern women to ascend closer to hegemonic womanhood, where they would encounter a lower ratio of violence without escaping patriarchal oppression. Similarly, the fight to diversify the bourgeoisie, petite bourgeoisie, and the production of cultural commodities for the benefit of queer and trans consumers, managers, cultural produces, and bosses, massages and expands normative gender expressions through the very institutions that produce them.

10   Kate Shannon et al., "Prevalence and Structural Correlates of Gender Based Violence Among a Prospective Cohort of Female Sex Workers," *BMJ*, August 11, 2009.

11   Street Health, *The Street Health Report 2007* (Toronto: Street Health, 2007).

12   Charlene K. Baker, Sarah L. Cook, and Fran H. Norris, "Domestic Violence and Housing Problems: A Contextual Analysis of Women's Help-seeking, Received Informal Support, and Formal System Response," *Violence Against Women* 9, 7 (2003).

## Feminist unity through multiplicity

In a 2015 article for the materialist feminist journal *Lies*, LaKeyma King critiques the tendency, which developed from the decline of Black liberation struggles of the '60s and '70s, to equate Black patriarchy with anti-racism. While white supremacy enacts gendered violence against both Black men and women, King argues that "the problem is that our brothers think that they understand us because they think feeling powerless because of racism is the same as feeling powerless due to the rapacious nature of sexual and racial violence from which there is no relief, not even at home." She outlines the fraught position of Black women, who face both racism and misogyny in the white supremacist world, as well as misogyny from men within Black radical spaces, and she challenges the conclusion that because white supremacy castrates Black men, there are no meaningful differences between how Black men and women suffer under patriarchal white supremacy.

King's intervention challenges us not to conflate personal experience with political truth. The powerlessness that Black men feel is a real experience, and white men *do* use patriarchal power against Black men to defend their bourgeois and colonial entitlement. But it's one thing for Black men to experience white supremacist powerlessness and another to take it as evidence that there are no politically consequential differences between Black men and women. The consequences of insufficiently nuanced analyses of power are grave: in the case of patriarchal Black nationalism, it undermined Black women's political leadership and remediated white patriarchy for Black men's use against Black women.

In "My Gender is Black," Hari Ziyad highlights how white supremacy genders all Black people without falling into the trap of erasing gendered and sexual differences within Black communities. He argues that his experience of gender as a Black man cannot be conflated with the experiences of Black trans people and women, but at the same time, that it is also incommensurable with the experiences of white people, who have been the authors of gender in the white supremacist, imperial core. Drawing on Hortense Spillers's argument that slavery and its afterlife "degenders" Black people, Ziyad explains that "none of us Black folk can 'conform' to manhood and womanhood as those constructs have been formed, nor can we even 'conform' to queer, trans and non-binary genders that way either—the way that makes the state recognise us as human." His alienation under white supremacy translates to an exhaustion with discussions around pronouns, which are by nature gender reductive. He concludes, "Gender identity under whiteness is a tool, not an end. How do we get to that end, that world in which all of our genders or lack thereof aren't used as the basis for our inhuman treatment?"

If "womanhood" is a political and social category that has an autonomous life from—while remaining implicated in—gendered subjectivities as well as multiple systems of exploitation and domination, then all those who are subjected to womanhood, whether they are cis, trans, non-binary, Indigenous, Black, Asian, or Latinx, have a stake in overthrowing it. Some of us may use "gender identity" as a tool to confront and metabolise the alienation of being a gendered subject in a violently patriarchal world, but like all forms of reduction, thinking of gender outside of class, race, colonialism, and imperialism inevitably deforms our understandings of power and therefore struggle.

Feminist anti-imperial and anti-colonial politics highlight the limitations of liberal identity analytics. If gender is produced historically through misogyny in its colonial, imperial, and bourgeois forms, then only multiple feminisms—decolonial, anti-imperial, and anti-capitalist—can destroy patriarchy. To be a gendered subaltern is to feel as though there is no solution to your gendered subjugation that Canadian or American civil society can produce. The subaltern trans man is the man who is violently shut out from and/or refuses a freedom premised on the exploitation and oppression of women. Subaltern women are women oppressed by colonisation and imperialism, treated as disposable by white men. And subaltern queer people are those who feel like there is no conceivable escape from the violence of the gender binary—that even the enclaves we craft in order to survive only demonstrate that our freedom ultimately necessitates the destruction of the world, including the petty-bourgeois institutions that have made the burgeoning recuperation of some forms of queerness by imperial civil society possible.

*A Separate Star* Section 4

# For the end of world white supremacy

# Introduction
## For the end of world white supremacy

This section outlines Red Braid's approach to anti-racist praxis. We argue that white supremacy is integral to capitalism as a global system that defends the interests of Western nations in the imperial core. That because their state and civil society institutions are integrated into this imperialist system, the mainstream, reformer's approach to anti-racism in the West cannot fight race power as a form of imperial power. Finally, that while working-class whites must fight white supremacy as a condition of their own exploitation, ultimately, race power can only be smashed by the activity of peoples oppressed by imperialism.

White supremacy is produced and maintained through immigration policies that reserve the most insecure, poorly paid, and dangerous jobs for migrants from the Global South; through the gendered violence that women oppressed by colonialism and imperialism face in public and private spaces; through wars and trade pacts that bolster the global power of Euro-American nations; and through the multi-billion dollar equity and diversity industry, which preaches the gospel of a more racially diverse capitalism to corporate executives, government workers, universities, NGOs, and other white-collar workplaces.

Our definition of white supremacy as integral to global capitalism helps us identify the pitfalls of reformist approaches to anti-racism, which Listen Chen outlines in their two contributions to this section: "The Birth of Radical Multiculturalism" and "Sinophobia and the Imperialist Anti-Racism of the Chinese-Canadian Middle Class." Chen's articles critique the "radical multiculturalism" advanced by reformist activists whose radicalism, they argue, is merely advancing the assimilationist multicultural policies adopted by the US and Canada in the latter half of the twentieth century. Chen argues radical multiculturalism is the purview of middle-class people of colour who agitate for better inclusion into the halls of bourgeois power and influence previously reserved for whites only.

The last article in this chapter, "From White Abolition to Working-class Black and Tricontinental Power," is a Red Braid statement that puts forth an alternative to world white supremacy: the abolition of whiteness and a world of multiplicity where many economic, social, and cultural formations thrive in mutual relations to one another and the non-human world.

The statement also critiques class reductionism, a socialist approach to the problem of white supremacy that insists that race power is an effect of capitalism, rather than an integral part of it, that will disappear with the emergence of socialism. Socialist class reductionism overlooks the ways in which colonial, imperial, and race power stratify the proletariat. In practice, it prioritises the short-term economic interests of privileged sectors of the national working class in imperial cores.

Against both radical multiculturalism and Eurocentric class reductionism, Red Braid adopted a stance of white abolitionist multiplicity, which was our fighting strategy for a non-capitalist, non-imperial, and non-colonial world where social-national organisation is multiple. We argued that global liberation and the end of white supremacy requires a total, irreconcilable struggle against the settler colonial, capitalist state, including against all forms of being and belonging premised on white, bourgeois identification. If radical multiculturalism fights for the assimilation of Indigenous, Black, and other racialized people into the middle class and petite bourgeoisie, and class reductionist socialism fights for the expanded belonging of a national aristocracy of labour into civil society, then white abolitionist multiplicity fights for the liberation of the Black and Tricontinental working class, alongside all Indigenous nations, from imperial and colonial oppression. In place of global capitalism, we imagined a world materially based in the actualization and development of multiple, non-alienated economies and political structures in a federation of autonomous states, including sovereign Indigenous nations.

Anti-racist struggle is the responsibility of revolutionary movements and organizations, and what we need are organizations that will develop anti-racist politics by and for Indigenous and working-class Black and racialized people, who themselves will lead the charge to tear down global white supremacy. On Turtle Island, we saw glimpses of such an alternative in the sovereign assertions of Indigenous land defence struggles and the rightful rage of poor Black people setting fire to cities built by their dispossession and protected by racist killer cops. But while we were certain that the subaltern layers of nations and people oppressed by colonialism and imperialism—those whom Frantz Fanon called the "wretched of the earth"—are best positioned to lead the charge against global white supremacy, we were not yet in a position to outline what forms that struggle might take. The needle of our compass pointed us in the direction to go: through a nightmare thicket that only subaltern self-activity can clear, towards a future that is free and multiple.

# The birth of radical multiculturalism

Listen Chen

In Canada, "multiculturalism" is not just an ideology that manages racial difference while preserving whiteness as a category of social power, it is official state policy. In 1963, in response to the increasing influence of Quebecois nationalism after the Quiet Revolution of the 1950s, Prime Minister Lester B. Pearson commissioned a Royal Commission on Bilingualism and Biculturalism. Initially the "bi" referred to Anglo and French cultures and languages, but at the behest of other European diasporas who insisted that their iterations of whiteness be included, Prime Minister Trudeau later declared Canada a "multicultural" nation. In his 1971 speech in Parliament, Trudeau said, "Although there are two official languages, there is no official culture," continuing to provide structural and financial government support to only Anglophone and Francophone languages. Citizenship and Immigration Canada proudly asserts that "Canada was the first country in the world to adopt multiculturalism as an official policy," elaborating that multiculturalism "ensures that all citizens can keep their identities, can take pride in their ancestry and have a sense of belonging."[1]

Canada's feel-good *Multiculturalism Act* of 1988 was preceded by the government's first real multicultural policy reforms. The *Immigration Act* of 1967

1    "Canadian Multiculturalism: An Inclusive Citizenship," Citizenship and
     Immigration Canada website, modified October 2012.

replaced the overtly race-based "preferred countries of origin" categorisation of prospective immigrants with the "points system," which encodes race through global class frameworks. Six years later, working-class migrants were shunted over to temporary foreign worker programs designed to better exploit migrant labour while retaining direct access to permanent residency for migrants with what migration scholar Nandita Sharma calls "middle-class cultural capital," such as fluency in English or French, who are young but not too young, and who have access to money and professional accreditation.[2]

Canada adopted multiculturalism not out of the goodness of its white heart, but in response to shifts in the global capitalist economy that produced new demands for skilled labour and international trade and investment relationships. As critical race theorist Sunera Thobani argues, this shifted approach was also in response to anti-racist and anti-colonial movements in the West and national liberation struggles against colonialism globally. Multiculturalism is an adjustment that preserves the social power of whiteness but with a new organising narrative—one that imagines whiteness as the benevolent centre around which racially othered peoples and cultures are harmoniously oriented in service of a new financialized economy.

Thobani argues:

> Multiculturalism was to prove critical to the rescuing of Euro/
> white cultural supremacy: white subjects were constituted as
> tolerant and respectful of difference and diversity, while non-
> white people were instead constructed as perpetually and
> irremediably monocultural, in need of being taught the virtues
> of tolerance and cosmopolitanism under white supervision.[3]

The United States does not have similar legislative affirmations of multiculturalism, although it went through a concurrent period of immigration reform. The *Immigration and Nationality Act* of 1965 replaced the much more overtly white supremacist "National Origins Formula," designed to preserve

---

2   Nandita Sharma, *Home Economics: Nationalism and the Making of 'Migrant Workers'
    in Canada* (Toronto: University of Toronto Press, 2005).
3   Sunera Thobani, *Exalted Subjects: Studies in the Making of Race and Nation in
    Canada* (Toronto: University of Toronto Press, 2007).

the fantasy of the United States as a white country by limiting the immigration of racialized people. While US politicians on both sides of the political spectrum assured one another that the 1965 *Act* would preserve the demographic breakdown of the country, they were wrong: between 1970 and 2016, eighty-one percent of the growth of the US Asian population came from immigration, facilitated by the *Immigration Act* of 1990, which created a visa category for white collar workers, especially for the needs of tech industries. This increase in Asian immigration has produced a shift in demographic composition as well: whereas Asians were just 0.6 percent of the population in 1960, by 2011 that proportion leapt to five percent.[4]

If the election of Trump as US president represented a white supremacist reaction against multiculturalism and the Barack Obama's presidency, then President Biden's 2021 cabinet, praised for its diversity, represents the triumph of multicultural liberalism against classical white supremacist liberalism. Against Trump's unilateral and brash invocation of the glory days of white rule, Biden adopts a more culturally nuanced approach which seeks to preserve and safeguard the current white supremacist status quo against threats from both the right and the left. Biden's commitment to ensuring that his administration will "look like the country" ultimately reinforces the fantasy that the American state can integrate and include all racial groups, if it is run by the right composition of people.[5]

The era of multiculturalism has coincided with some diversification of income distribution. Brookings reports that in the late 1970s in the US, the middle sixty percent of households on the total income distribution of the country was eighty-four percent white, nine percent Black, five percent Hispanic (the study uses government census data), and two percent "other" (which includes Asian, Indigenous, or mixed race).[6] In 2019, this income group was fifty-nine percent white, twelve percent Black, eighteen percent Hispanic, and ten percent "other." The study notes that the 2019 breakdown

4   Paul Taylor and D'vera Cohn, "A Milestone En Route to a Majority Minority Nation," *Pew Research Centre*, November 7, 2012.
5   Interview with Jake Tapper, CNN, December 3, 2020.
6   Christopher Pulliam, Richard V. Reeves, and Ariel Gelrud Shiro, "The Middle Class is Already Racially Diverse," *Brookings*, October 30, 2020.

is roughly proportionate to the representation of each group in the general population, though the higher the level of income within the middle sixty percent, the more white the demographic.

Critiques of state multiculturalism from the left have emerged alongside multicultural policies, but many of those critiques have merely been incorporated into later iterations of state policy. The settler capitalist state has trouble swallowing up activists and thinkers whose anti-racism is an aspect of their opposition to colonialism, capitalism, and imperialism, but anti-racist radicals whose analysis lacks such a revolutionary thrust end up trapped leading state reforms, and then chasing and denouncing them once again, in effect perfecting the anti-racist language of the state as advocates of *radical multiculturalism.*

Radical multiculturalism, which is the purview of anti-racist reform activists, NGOs, and middle-class progressives, pressures the state to adopt policies that will more successfully integrate racialized populations into jobs as middle-class administrators, and as bourgeois and petit bourgeois entrepreneurs. The Canadian federal government's "Anti-Racism Strategy," which Ottawa funded to the tune of $30 million dollars in 2019, includes a glossary of terms that include "intersectionality," "racialization," and a definition of race as a "social construct."[7] Spurred by spontaneous mass movements that have an anti-colonial and anti-racist character, like the 2020 George Floyd Rebellion or the 2020 Shut Down Canada movement, radical multiculturalism redirects those energies back towards the colonial state, seeking to reform white people out of capitalism.

## The equity and diversity industry

Radical multiculturalism is the grassroots perfection of multiculturalism that never breaks with the fundamental liberal assumption that the representation of racialized people within bourgeois institutions and civil society will end white supremacy. Radical multiculturalism activists position their politics as radical and transformative by critiquing the inadequacy of existing government policy language and then introducing their innovative reforms

7   Government of Canada, "Building a Foundation for Change: Canada's Anti-Racism Strategy 2019–2022," Canada.ca, 2019.

against the foil of what-is. For example, an article by Aida Mariam Davis, CEO of the anti-racist consultancy firm Decolonize Design, critiques the conventional Equity Diversity and Inclusion (EDI—or DEI in the US) approach as assimilative and instead advocates for a framework focused on "Belonging, Dignity and Justice," which she defines as a "mission-critical way of doing business and building teams."[8] Davis's critique of EDI reinforces the progressive bourgeois assumption that diversity is good for business and goes so far as to posit corporations as agents of social change, arguing "the cities and communities that [companies that adopt a Belonging, Dignity and Justice model] do business in benefit from companies taking a stand against dehumanisation and injustice as it impacts employees and public policy."

The growth of radical multiculturalism can be mapped through the growth of the nonprofit sector and rise in activist careers—jobs oriented around "social change" or simply marketed as activist. In the US, the human services and community service nonprofit sectors are worth nearly $350 billion dollars as of 2020.[9] Job-search website Indeed.com lists twenty "activist jobs," assuring millennials that there are careers that "[allow] you to contribute to more social justice or environmental protection."[10] The University of Toronto Mississauga's Career Centre has a brochure on activist careers, which lists as examples social workers, writers, politicians, community outreach workers, and photojournalists.[11] Its "activist spotlight" profiles the university's Indigenous advisor.

The EDI industry, including its more savvy iterations, alongside the growth of the nonprofit industry and the ideology that one can be paid to enact radical social change, operate on the belief that by decentring white people in Canadian and American institutions, we can smoothly and non-violently progress out of the white supremacist, colonial, and imperial social relations that bind us. But because radical multiculturalism is the

8    Aida Mariam Davis, "Diversity, Equity and Inclusion have failed. How About Belonging, Dignity and Justice Instead?" *World Economic Forum*, February 23, 2021.

9    Jon Pratt and Kari Aanestad, "NPQ's Illustrated Nonprofit Economy, 3rd Edition," *Nonprofit Quarterly*, February 24, 2020.

10   "20 Activist Jobs To Help You Choose Yours," Indeed Editorial Team, March 29, 2021.

11   "Careers in Activism: Careers with a Conscience," University of Toronto Mississauga Career Centre, 2018.

promise of class uplift, it only expresses the limited and immediate interests of the racialized, Black, and Indigenous minority most positioned to benefit from policies of diversity and inclusion, narrowly focused on the reforms of middle-class workplaces, welfare state institutions, academia, and NGOs.

Both multicultural policies and radical multiculturalists emphasise the agency of white people in their efforts to diversify the middle class, which is why the anti-racist EDI industry focuses on educating the racism out of white petit bourgeois and bourgeois people. Robin DiAngelo, whose 2018 book *White Fragility* climbed back to the New York Times bestseller list with the outbreak of the George Floyd and Breonna Taylor Rebellion, is a white radical multiculturalist whose career has been built on educating middle-class and bourgeois whites on how to be anti-racist, based on a vision of a post-racial world that is no less capitalist than this one. The middle class and bourgeoisie, whether white or racialized, are the main constituency of radical multiculturalism: whites are the primary audiences of anti-racist workshops run by a new generation of intellectuals who critique white supremacy while remaining loyal to a liberal ideology. In this formulation, the racialized middle class, aspiring middle class, and bourgeois actors are the beneficiaries of the charges to diversify access to bourgeois and petit bourgeois power.

Radical multiculturalism is a strategic dead end for revolutionaries because it can only recognise anti-racist action through a framework of representation and diversity, which by nature breeds suspicion of multi-racial movements. The faith that more racialized bosses and leaders will make imperialist societies less racist assumes that there is something essentially anti-racist within the bodies of racialized people that is unaffected by their class position. But if an essentialized experience is the only bellwether of anti-racist leadership, then no person or group can be authorised to act in strategic defence of another, and any unified mobilisation is suspect. The counter-insurgent narrative of "outside agitators" is a good example of how this suspicion is mobilised by mainstream media and middle-class commentators to dismiss the potential of cross-class, multi-racial movements. During the George Floyd Rebellion, the mayor and police chief of Washington DC blamed "outside agitators" for the property damage and clashes with police that Black Lives Matter protestors engaged in.[12] Seattle Mayor Jenny Durkan specifically blamed "white men" for "co-opting peaceful demonstrations," during the 2020 uprising, preferring to draw a racially coded boundary between inside-outside, while the police chief implied that property damage was caused from people outside the city.[13]

Closely related to the radical multiculturalist suspicion of the idea that working-class whites and racialized people might have shared political interests is its coding of the working class as racist, white, and culturally backwards. Historian Jack Metzgar laments that middle-class professionals frequently assumed that his book on "working-class culture" would include the topic of "white racism," as if the working-class (which is forty percent racialized) is an all-white group.[14] The common but unfounded assumption championed by mainstream media that President Trump's social base was made up of uncultured whites locates racism as a thing of the past, fixed in the present day through the bodies of working-class whites.[15] Sociologist Beverley Skeggs describes poor whites in Britain as inhabiting a "culturally burdensome whiteness" in the context of multiculturalism and the shift from an industrial to finance-oriented economy. Multiculturalists construct white workers as racist, sexist, and trapped in an uncouth past, which justifies limiting anti-racism to reforming the more cosmopolitan-seeming middle class, that group whose role in capitalism is to manage relations between the working class and the bourgeoisie, and whose importance to capitalism has soared with the developments of neoliberalism.

Radical multiculturalism, like state multiculturalism, is fundamentally liberal: it is an expression of the individual freedom to succeed within the

12    Matt Small, "DC Officials Claim 'Outside Agitators' for Disrupting Peaceful Protests," *WTOP News*, August 31, 2020.

13    Danny Westneat, "Don't Buy the 'Outside Agitator' Trope: Arrest Records Suggest Seattle's Riot was More Likely Homegrown," *The Seattle Times*, June 3, 2020.

14    Jack Metzgar, "Racism and the Working Class," *Working-Class Perspectives*, June 15, 2020.

15    Nicholas Carnes and Noam Lupu, "It Time to Bust the Myth: Most Trump Voters Were Not Working Class," *The Washington Post*, June 5, 2017; Thomas Watters, "Dressing the Emperor: The Dangerous Farce of the Petite Bourgeoisie," *Spectre Journal*, January 28, 2021.

capitalist mode of production, against the barrier of white racism, which is itself a product of liberalism. However, radical multiculturalists do not always deliberately or explicitly embrace liberalism. In many cases they employ radical anti-capitalist rhetoric in their championing of the inclusion of racially excluded groups in bourgeois society and institutions, but the "radical" in radical multiculturalism is purely discursive. In a moment where Hallmark publishes Black Lives Matter cards and broadcasts its hiring of Black artists and writers, the contradictions between language and meaning, rhetoric and action, are fundamental to radical multiculturalism but hardly unique to it.

If multiculturalism includes the neoliberal appropriation and neutralisation of the liberatory movements of the 1960s and 1970s, which coincided with new contours of global capital, then radical multiculturalism is the call by activists and progressive middle-class social forces to surpass existing reforms and radically expand racialized and Indigenous peoples' access to middle-class institutions. Lacking a strategy and collective subject capable of overthrowing and replacing white supremacist, cisheteropatriarchal, settler colonial capitalism, the end game of radical multiculturalism is, in practice, the perfection of the gender and race composition of those parts of the middle-class and bourgeois apparatus that are low enough in the power structure to be accessible to reform.

## Radical multiculturalism is "identity politics" severed from insurgent universalism

I critique the grassroots pick-up of hegemonic anti-racism as "radical multiculturalism," rather than "identity politics," because I think the former demystifies the radical-sounding rhetoric that accompanies some currents within anti-racist movements that are, in practice, reformist.

The term "identity politics" is hotly contested, with its liberal defenders and class-reductionist detractors mobilising alternating definitions in order to prove their points. I have come to think of identity politics expansively, as the politicisation of particular experiences that can be captured with the analytic "identity," which serves different ends according to who wields it and in what context. While purveyors of radical multiculturalism adopt rhetoric commonly associated with the phrase identity politics and celebrate the social movements that forged identity politics, I separate these constructs in order to preserve the revolutionary socialist implications we find in the first uses of the term identity politics.

The authors of the phrase identity politics were the Black women socialists and feminists, many of whom were lesbians, who formed the Combahee River Collective (CRC) in the 1970s in order to articulate a politics of Black women's liberation. A lot has been written about the afterlife of the term. Asad Haider celebrates the CRC as socialists in his polemic on identity politics, *Mistaken Identity*, emphasising that the political error underlying today's liberal iteration of identity politics is the excising of socialist politics from it. But the collective's famous statement, while having anti-capitalist sensibilities, is in a way not a particularly socialist text—while the authors engage with class and repeatedly point to the class position of Black women in a way that treats race and class as co-constitutive, their emphasis on the particular content of class position runs contrary to the classical socialist understanding of class as a universal. Haider's celebration suggests that the problem with contemporary identity politics is that its practitioners have forgotten its socialist—which is to say, universal—roots, so what activists of liberal identity politics wield is an inauthentic representation of what the CRC articulated.

Haider's book on liberal anti-racism, while satisfying in many ways, sets up a false dichotomy between the *universal*, which he presents as socialist, class-focused politics, and the *particular*, which he presents as any oppression that has a cross-class character. In "I Am a Woman and a Human," Eve Mitchell, a member of the libertarian socialist organisation Unity and Struggle, offers an alternative critique of contemporary identity politics, arguing that historical circumstances led to it developing a bourgeois character, expressed by the absence of revolution in the US in the sixties, the capitalist appropriation of the liberatory movements of that era, the contemporary absence of class struggle, and the intellectual hegemony of the academy. While I don't disagree, I suggest that it's worth clearly differentiating the bourgeois and petty-bourgeois afterlife of identity politics—identity politics as radical multiculturalism—from its radical origins.

In Red Braid's group reading of the Combahee River Collective's statement, we saw both the particular and universal frames of reference that Mitchell, Haider, and many others grapple with—as if there are two voices speaking through the statement: one that captures the incommensurability of Black women's experiences with those social groups who do not share their class position relative to capitalism, patriarchy, and white supremacy; and one that captures a struggle for freedom that radically bonds together all the world's exploited and oppressed. But while these frames of reference might appear contradictory on the page or in juxtaposition to contemporary practices of identity politics, we think they can be made mutually constitutive *through revolutionary motion*. The reformist practices of identity politics separate and valorise particular atoms of identity, discarding and denying the universal and historical contexts of these subject positions and binding us to a perpetual and powerless present. Revolutionary practices of identity politics tell a different story, contextualising the particular as constituent of the universal, breaking those binds to move into revolutionary practice against our common capitalist, coloniser, and imperialist enemies through a universal classed position that, as the CRC claims, is best expressed through the totalizing and universal struggles of Black women.

At the same time, the CRC text is also part of the legacy of liberal identity politics. The CRC statement is multiple, reflecting different currents within the historical moment that produced it: not just the socialist revolutionary energies, but also a longing for individual freedom. It's the latter energy, threaded through the New Left movements of the 1960s and 1970s more generally, that was accumulated and appropriated by neoliberalism, resulting in the emergence of liberal identity politics and state multiculturalism and the tamping down of revolutionary socialist currents. The movement of history determined which political forms, nascent in the CRC text and the moment that produced it, would gain dominance.

I see the particular and the universal interacting within the CRC statement, which is a reflection of the historical circumstances its authors were writing in: their words reflect their frustrations with the particular exclusion of Black communities from white-dominated socialist movements, of Black women from white-dominated feminist movements, and of women from man-dominated Black socialist movements in the 1960s and '70s. The CRC statement was a statement of militants in liberation movements that did not allow them to fight for their total liberation, not of a particular organisation with a complete program. As such it is a responsive, reflective, visionary, and also an incomplete offering of what should be.

Liberal individualism has become the dominant form of identity politics today not because such particularism is especially authentic or inauthentic to the CRC statement, but because of the intervention of historical forces that have made use of some of the politics expressed by the collective and discarded others. It should come as no surprise that decades of neoliberal assault on working class, racialized, Black, and Indigenous people have materially eroded the institutions necessary to practise and sustain socialist revolutionary politics.

Radical multiculturalism is the one-sided afterlife of the CRC's dialectical understanding of identity politics. But the statement itself offers an important intervention into a one-sided understanding of the universal by capturing the interplay of the particular experiences of Black women with a vision of radically universal freedom. When they write, "If Black women were free, it would mean that everyone else would have to be free since our freedom would necessitate the destruction of all systems of oppression," they are not presenting a narrow, static, fixed definition of identity, but a vision of universal liberation that challenges the white and male coded legacies of socialist Eurocentrism which imagines that the freedom of a white, industrial proletariat in Europe will pave the way for global liberation. Against a universalism based on abstract rights or presumptions of sameness, the CRC forwards what philosopher Massimiliano Tomba calls "insurgent universalism"—a universal struggle for freedom premised on a multiplicity of particular struggles that mutually reinforce one another. Whereas Eurocentric universalism draws on the legacy of the French Revolution and its emphasis on the "universal rights of man," insurgent universalism draws on the legacy of the Haitian Revolution, which bestowed citizenship to all those who fought for Haitian freedom, irrespective of their skin colour.

The CRC's assertion that the social relations that oppress Black women can only be overthrown through Black women's self-activity recognises that oppression is not essential but created within and through *relations*. The unit of truth here is a dialectical one: it is the multiplicity captured in a relation, rather than the one-ness captured in a static, ahistorical understanding of identity. If the unique class position Black women occupy is composed of multiple social relations, then the freedom of the Black woman is bound to the freedom of those who are on the other side of those social relations. What the CRC presents is not a zero-sum game where Black women winning freedom means a loss of prestige for Black men and white workers, but a vision where the freedom of Black women would break open the possibilities of freedom for social groups who benefit from their exploitation and oppression.

## Radical multiculturalism or insurgent universalism

In working to recover the socialist revolutionary thread in the CRC, we come up against the activists of radical multiculturalism who insist that we can reform white supremacy out of capitalism and imperialism on a national level. The problem here is not just the limitations of representation and declaration that tend to accompany identity politics when it is divorced from insurgent universalism, but the colonial and imperial state's constant adjustments and accommodations, which appropriate and neutralise anti-racist resistance.

A 2018 TED Talk by Janet Stovall, a Black corporate inclusion speaker, captures the politics of radical multiculturalism: "Imagine a workplace where people of all colours and races are able to climb every rung of the corporate ladder—and where the lessons we learn about diversity at work actually transform the things we do, think and say outside the office. How do we get there?" Facing a crowd of predominantly white people, she connects her efforts to diversify her private liberal arts college with diversifying corporate boardrooms, concluding that "business can dismantle racism" and that racial diversity is good for business.

Reducing white supremacy to individual biases and inclusion or representation in bourgeois institutions overlooks how such institutions reproduce hegemonic forms of capitalist, colonial, and imperial power. Additionally, Stovall imagines white supremacy as autonomous from exploitative social relations. Even if every white boss and middle manager were replaced with racialized counterparts, a great bulk of the working class would remain racialized, with the most precarious work reserved for women of colour barred from inclusion in imperial nation states.

More insidiously, to argue that the stage of anti-racist action is individual agency also insists that white supremacy is a national rather than international system. Even if countries like the United States and Canada *could* close the income gaps between various racialized groups and institute expansive reforms that would correct against the over-representation of white people in positions of power, that would leave the imperial domination of the US empire and its partners over the Global South untouched.

Radical multiculturalism bears two problems: first, it contorts the goal of liberation by representing only the partial class interests of people who are oppressed by imperialism and colonialism but hopeful about belonging to civil society; second, in theorising oppressed social positions as fixed, ahistorical identities that can be represented and included in various institutions, it fails to grasp the historical and material character of race. Thus, even critiques of multiculturalism as being too liberal can rebound against those limitations. An article on the blog *Everyday Feminism* titled "First it was All About Diversity, Then Inclusion. Here's Why Neither of Those are Enough," argues that inclusivity is insufficient without "reparations," understood as giving marginalised people "money, resources, and power" by centring them in "platforms, companies, and organisations."[16] In other words, the radical multiculturalist cure for the inadequacy of liberal inclusion is deeper liberal inclusion.

The claim that the more Black, Indigenous, and other racialized people wield middle-class and bourgeois power, the less racist society as a whole will become, is tethered to a reformist anti-racist politics, whether or not it is accompanied by radical rhetoric. But at the same time, while multiculturalist adjustments have material consequences that benefit some racialized people and are not merely ideological dressing on a fixed economic base, it is a gross overstatement to suggest that racialized people have become so

16   Ayesha Sharma, "First it was All About Diversity, Then Inclusion. Here's Why Neither of Those are Enough," Everydayfeminism.com, July 16, 2018.

integrated into the middle class that they are no longer oppressed as nations and communities through colonialism and imperialism.

Radical multiculturalism competes for a piece of the imperial pie that is stolen from the wealth of Indigenous nations globally and from a global working class that is predominantly racialized and located outside of the imperial core. As such, it trades a vision of liberation for the short-term and limited gains of inclusion in settler-colonial, imperial society. Insurgent universalism instead locates liberation from white supremacy and capitalism outside that society, insisting that freedom can only be won through a revolutionary struggle where the particular leads to the universal, and the smashing of any oppressive or exploitative social relation is an advancement not just for one unique social group, but for humanity as a multiple whole.

We are finding that the most powerful movements of the twenty-first century in the US and Canada are primarily anti-colonial and anti-imperial. From Indigenous sovereignty battles, united across many nations under the slogan "Land Back," to the George Floyd Rebellion, it is not the so-called "universal" struggles of white working men that are most actively disrupting Canada and the United States. The spontaneity of these movements smash the limits of reformist anti-racism: the Wet'suwet'en-led movement to oppose Coastal GasLink's fracked gas pipeline raised the slogan "Reconciliation is Dead" and the explosive street energy of the George Floyd Rebellion made the imperative that "Black Lives Matter" real through attacks on police and property, rather than through rhetorical appeals to whites in power.

But for these spontaneous, subaltern paroxysms to break society apart so that we can create something new and lasting in its place, what we need are institutions that can organise and buoy the leadership of subaltern Indigenous, Black, Latinx, and Asian fighters. For subaltern institutions to lead an ineluctable attack on the colonial and imperial state and its sprawling civil society—one that anticipates and resists any and all efforts to accommodate, assimilate, and appropriate revolutionary movement—we need to develop a working-class anti-racism capable of synthesising class antagonisms within the diasporic nations of peoples oppressed by imperialism.

# Sinophobia and the Imperialist Anti-Racism of the Chinese-Canadian Middle Class

Listen Chen

In March 2021 I went to a "Stop anti-Asian hate" rally in Coquitlam, a suburban city near Vancouver. It was one of many actions that cropped up in response to the 2021 Atlanta spa shootings, which drew attention to the pronounced spike in anti-Asian hate that had already been facilitated by COVID-19 and the US-Sino trade war. The organisers took a predictably nationalist approach, festooning the event in Canadian flags and leading the crowd to chant, "We build this nation together!" When I began handing out leaflets arguing that anti-Asian misogyny is an expression of Canadian imperialism, the organisers told me I was "distracting from our message against anti-Asian racism," and then harassed me as I continued to distribute leaflets.

The Chinese-Canadian middle class has been a vocal criticiser of contemporary yellow peril, but only inasmuch as anti-Chinese racism disturbs their desire to access forms of property and power historically reserved for whites only. Far from ending yellow peril, the Chinese petit bourgeois diaspora's partial assimilation into Canadian citizenship has legitimised Canada's contemporary sinophobia and bolstered Canadian imperialism, locally in the form of increased racist attacks against Chinese communities, and internationally in the form of the escalating cold war with China. The jingoist embrace of Canadian nationalism by some Chinese-Canadians demonstrates the fraught prospects of relying on racialized middle-class power as a brake on white supremacy.

The supposed threat China poses to US global hegemony has reinvigorated a new cold war and mobilised the countries of the US-led imperial bloc to the defence of the liberal world order. In British Columbia, sinophobia is richly textured and multifaceted, tapping into centuries of white imperial anxieties. Like a virus ever producing new, more contagious variants, western Canadian sinophobia knows no narrative bounds. From conspiracy theories about Chinese people "distorting" the real estate market, to laundering "dirty" money and fueling the opioid crisis, to the COVID-era pedestrian classic, spreading disease, sinophobia in western Canada is ever-diversifying methods of scapegoating China and Chinese people.

The challenge of combating sinophobia offers a useful case study of the limits of radical multiculturalism, which reduces racism to individual hate crimes or aggression. As I argue in the previous chapter, radical multiculturalism takes as fundamental the hypothesis that the entrance of racialized people into the middle class and bourgeoisie will result in a less racist society. As such, it relies on a narrow definition of racism fixated on individual actors and recipients of prejudice and discrimination. While sinophobia certainly encompasses grassroots violence against Chinese people, which has surged exponentially in the past few years, it cannot be reduced to individual victimhood. Sinophobia's component parts play out on national and international stages, involving trade deals, sanctions, diplomacy, military manoeuvres in the South China Sea, immigration policy, and the ideological defence of the US empire. Radical multiculturalism has no means of combating the imperialist roots of sinophobia because it cannot grasp the structural operation of racism within global capitalism and contests between nation states.

## Yellow peril and the western Canadian housing crisis

In Vancouver, Canada property prices have been steadily rising since the early 2000s, with the temporary exception of the 2008–2009 financial crisis. Local pundits, journalists, and politicians have rushed in to explain the "housing crisis" (defined by the affordability of detached homes), with many relying on the dog-whistle of "foreign investors" to scapegoat Chinese people for driving up the price of real estate.

This is nothing new—there was a similar sinophobic reaction to the hot property market of the late 1980s. But today's sinophobic scapegoating aligns with the US-led imperialist bloc's attempts to contain the competition China poses. While the conspiracy theory that rich Chinese people caused the housing crisis was primarily popularised by the BC New Democratic Party—Canada's nominally social democratic electoral party—and in particular, Premier David Eby, middle-class Chinese-Canadians have also hopped on the sinophobic bandwagon in an attempt to gain admission to halls of Canadian power classically reserved for whites only.

Urban planner Andy Yan lent early corroboration to the scapegoating of Chinese people for Metro Vancouver's housing crisis and has subsequently built his career on blaming "foreign capital," "foreign buyers," and "satellite families" for ruining the prospects of home ownership for more established settlers. A profile on Yan by sinophobic journalist Terry Glavin describes Yan as coming out of "proud working class ranks," taking care to highlight that Yan's great-grandfather had to pay a head tax to enter Canada.[1] Glavin's celebration of Yan indicates that there is a possible collaboration to be made between the Chinese-Canadian petite bourgeoisie and white Canada, premised on a mutual defence of Canadian property interests.

In tethering their interests to the "muticulturalizing" of Canadian property ownership, Yan and other racialized middle-class actors are effectively rallying for a more inclusive Canadianness—an expansion of whiteness and white race power that would include bourgeois and petit bourgeois Chinese Canadians. As whites who cannot pay the rising price of a detached home

---

1    Terry Glavin, "Andy Yan, the analyst Who Exposed Vancouver's Real Estate Disaster," *MacLean's*, February 14, 2018.

resent their loss of social prestige, Chinese Canadians like Yan bemoan the loss of their full entry into Canadian citizenship, blaming the figure of the rich mainland Chinese speculator for their incomplete assimilation into Canadian nationhood. But because Chinese-Canadians are still, in the eyes of white Canada, seen as essentially *Chinese* and therefore alien, Yan's pursuit of whiteness is a farce, and his move to defend Canadian property interests is, in the end, a defence of whiteness.

One of the outcomes of the lobbying of Yan, Eby, and pundits like Glavin was the Greater Vancouver foreign-buyer tax, a fifteen percent tax implemented against non-resident purchasers of real estate by the BC government in late 2016. While prices dropped momentarily, the BC Real Estate Association notes that they rebounded within a year—indicating that the tax was not successful in making real estate more affordable.[2] The tax does seem to have decreased the proportion of BC real estate transactions that involve foreign buyers—whereas there was a high of $400 million dollars of transactions with a foreign buyer in June 2017 (roughly three percent of all transactions), by October 2019 the number had dropped to $135 million, or 1.87 percent of all transactions.[3] Defenders of the tax, like Andy Yan, argue that it was never intended to slow buying but to "capture value for the BC taxpayer."[4] Yet even by that standard, finance professor Andrey Pavlov argues that the tax has created negative revenue.[5]

The primary function of taxing foreign buyers has not been a pragmatic lever to improve the access of locals to property markets, it has been an ideological defence of Canadian property as belonging to Canadians, who are coded as white by default. Like any policy that targets non-citizens, the tax is just one tool in Canada's arsenal of diplomatic, economic, and ideological warfare. And on other fronts of Canadian imperialism, the

2    BCREA, "Foreign Buyer's Tax: Impact on Housing Market," *Connections: Advocacy News from the British Columbia Real Estate Association*, July 2017.

3    Steve Saretsky, "Foreign Buying Activity in BC Drops to $135M in October," SteveSaretsky.com, November 22, 2019.

4    Chuck Chiang, Biv, and WI Staff, "Foreign Home Buyers Have Nearly Vanished From Metro Market," *Western Investor*, April 1, 2021.

5    Stephanie Hughes, "National Foreign Buyer Tax May Have Unintended Consequences: Experts," *BNN Bloomberg*, December 18, 2020.

Chinese-Canadian petite bourgeoisie is no less eager to demonstrate its embrace of Canadian nationalism.

## Yellow peril and the rise of China

In October 2019 a group of pro-bourgeois democracy Chinese diasporic groups published "CanSave," an open letter calling on the Canadian state to "take a much stronger and tougher approach when dealing with China." The letter refers to the "barbarism" of the Chinese Communist Party (CCP) and demands the suspension of Chinese student visa applications, the launch of an investigation by Canadian Security Intelligence Service (CSIS) of Chinese student groups in all post-secondary institutions, the reduction of trade with China, and sanctions against Hong Kong and Chinese officials. It mobilises jingoist cold war tropes that conflate the CCP with Chinese people, characterising Chinese students as "an integral part of CCP's propaganda machine" and claiming that any trade with China means "surrendering the control of our economy to them."

At a Hong Kong solidarity rally organised by signatories of the letter shortly after it was released, groups reiterated demands that Canada mobilise state power to discipline China. Fenella Sung with Canadian Friends of Hong Kong described how the Chinese Communist Party's "sharp claws have overreached into our land" and described the screening of the trailer of a Chinese state-produced film in a secondary school in Richmond as "brainwashing." Yellow peril discourse would exist without the enthusiastic consent of these middle-class Chinese-Canadian forces, but the active participation of people with an ostensibly shared racialization with mainland Chinese people usefully shelters sinophobic Canadian nationalism from the charge of racism.

In mid-2021, one of the groups who endorsed the CanSave letter, Alliance Canada Hong Kong (ACHK), released a report titled "In Plain Sight: Beijing's Unrestricted Network of Foreign Influence in Canada." The report makes sensational claims about Chinese "interference" in Canada's pristine democracy, using as evidence newspaper articles, reports from Western institutions (including defence agencies like CSIS and think tanks funded by defence agencies like the Australian Strategic Policy Institute), an online

Chinese-Canadian forum, and two anonymous interviews with Chinese professionals. The Alliance Canada Hong Kong report represents the interests of an increasingly right-wing Chinese diaspora who march to the war drums of anti-China US hawks and Western intelligence agencies. The report's rhetoric is evocative of the demagoguery of US politicians across the spectrum, from William Barr to Anthony Blinken, mobilising the same talking points as the FBI in an attempt to pose as a defence of Canadian sovereignty while claiming the inherent anti-racism of Western values.

While solidarity activists defend Hong Kong by portraying Canada as similarly vulnerable to China's "claws," Alliance Canada Hong Kong takes a more aggressive and militaristic approach. "In Plain Sight" calls for a "public registry of individuals, organisations, and representatives who are actively acting on behalf of foreign states ... paired with investigative and enforcement powers to ensure foreign actors are registered appropriately." This demand is not unprecedented. In 2018, the US Department of Justice launched their China Initiative, which aims to "apply the Foreign Agents Registration Act to unregistered agents seeking to advance China's political agenda, bringing enforcement actions when appropriate."[6] These recommendations spur Canada to follow in the footsteps of the US, which has ramped up its targeting of Chinese nationals for charges of economic espionage, grant fraud, theft of trade secrets, and conspiracy.[7] In sum, the ACHK report seeks to develop new state tools to defend bourgeois Canadian interests against China.

Without a shred of irony, the report claims its recommendations—which call for the broad expansion of state surveillance and enforcement powers—come through an "anti-racist and anti-oppressive lens." Such rhetorical manoeuvres, which excise Canadian sovereignty and the colonial, imperial, bourgeois state from the realm of racism and oppression, are made

6   "Information About the Department of Justice's China Initiative and a Compilation of China-Related Prosecutions Since 2018," *The United States Department of Justice*, May 5, 2021.

7   Andrew Kim, "Prosecuting Chinese 'Spies:' An Empirical Analysis of the Economic Espionage Act," *Committee of 100*, May 2017; Yangyang Cheng, "The US Is Building Walls Around Science, and We're All Poorer for It," *VICE*, December 3, 2021.

possible only by the anti-racism of multiculturalism. The same speakers who mobilise intensely racist Canadian chauvinism to stereotype mainland Chinese people as CCP drones have no problem speaking out against the overt racism that liberals no longer tolerate, like COVID-19 related hate crimes. The difference between the racist hate crime and anti-Chinese Canadian nationalism is that the hate crime commits the cardinal sin of failing to distinguish between the good, democracy-loving Chinese from the bad, authoritarian, drone-like Chinese. Multiculturalism provides an ideological cover that shrouds the contradiction between the immediate interests of middle-class Chinese people who aspire to full Canadian citizenship and belonging, and the interests of working-class Chinese people all over the world.

## The class characters of the Chinese diaspora

The active participation of the petit bourgeois Chinese diaspora in ramping up imperialist aggression and anti-Chinese Canadian nationalism demonstrates the need for a working-class anti-racism premised on internationalism, anti-imperialism, anti-capitalism, and anti-colonialism. The poor Chinese migrant worker with active connections to mainland China has as little to gain from the US and Canada's stake in the trade war with China as the mainland Chinese worker. The position of the Chinese petite bourgeoisie is less clear. While petit bourgeois class interests always compete against monopoly capital, the Chinese petite bourgeoisie in particular has demonstrated much more opposition against Chinese capitalists than against Canadian capitalists. This suggests something else is at play: the aspirations of this racialized petite bourgeoisie to gain entrance to white Canada by demonstrating fealty to white property interests, which unites them with the Canadian bourgeoisie against China. The lability of the multi-racial petite bourgeoisie opens up the possibility for them to side with working-class interests, but whether or not that opportunity develops depends on the development and power of a working-class anti-racist movement.

Most Chinese people in Canada are not members or aspiring members of the petite bourgeoisie. The most recent data on racialization and poverty comes from the 2006 census, which found that while Chinese people make up just 3.89 percent of the general population of Canada, they constitute nearly one in four of the people living below the poverty line. In Vancouver, over half of poor racialized people speak a Chinese language as their mother tongue. Across Canada, ninety percent of racialized people living in poverty were born outside of Canada, with forty-two percent having immigrated in the five years preceding the census.[8] While a minority of privileged Chinese diaspora rally to weaponize Canada's colonial border in defence of their entrepreneurial position within Western imperialism, the greater mass of working-class Chinese people remain absent from public discourse.

In the United States, income inequality is greater amongst Asians than any other racial group. There are obvious methodological problems with measuring "Asians" as a homogenous group, as Chinese and Japanese people are less likely to be poor than, for example, Hmong people. Nevertheless, according to a 2018 Pew Research Centre study that measured income inequality within categories of whites, Black people, Asians, and Hispanic people of all races between 1970 and 2016, the income inequality gap amongst Asians doubled.[9]

Between 1970 and 2016, eighty-one percent of the growth of the US Asian population came, in part, from two major changes in immigration legislation: the 1965 *Immigration and Nationality Act*, which replaced the "National Origins Formula" that was designed to preserve the United States as a white country by limiting the immigration of racialized people; and the *Immigration Act* of 1990, which increased white-collar immigrants. By 2016, the majority of Asian adults living in the US were born outside of the US (seventy-eight percent, compared to just forty-five percent in 1970). If Asian immigrants are entering either as refugees, or as white-collar workers under the H-1B visa program, then that would help account for the massive increase in income inequality within the "Asian" census group.

8    Canada National Council of Welfare, "Poverty Profile: Special Edition. Report: A Snapshot of Racialized Poverty in Canada," Government of Canada Publications, January 2012.

9    Rakesh Kochhar and Anthony Cilluffo, "Income Inequality in the U.S. Is Rising Most Rapidly Among Asians," *Pew Research Centre*, July 12, 2018.

The perplexing economic data on Asian and Chinese populations points to the necessity of understanding imperialism as both cultural and economic. That Asian earners in the United States now have incomes that surpass white wage earners cannot be taken as evidence that Asians no longer experience white supremacy. But it does beg the question of the material basis for yellow peril. As always, the racism directed at Chinese migrants and the diaspora within the US and Canada are reflections of national anxieties. Unlike, for example, the white supremacist narrative that Black and Indigenous people are "backwards," occupying a position irrevocably outside of modernity and behind the progress of Europe, white supremacy has constructed East Asians as competing, illiberal civilizations. Anti-Chinese racism has been a reflection of the imperialist anxieties of Canada, taken up by white settlers anxious to claim Indigenous lands as the natural possessions of white people. In this context, the prevalence of Chinese people in middle-class jobs is not particularly contradictory, especially because their representation has been shaped by immigration policies overtly designed to encourage the immigration of certain classes of workers and entrepreneurs.

While there is a material basis for the Chinese petite bourgeoisie to actively help construct a Canadian nationalism fit to represent imperialist interests in an era of multiculturalism, the same cannot be said of the Chinese working class, who constitute a tremendous portion of the global proletariat. The globalisation of Chinese labour dates back to the Opium Wars, in which Western powers forced China to reduce its restrictions on emigration, prompting the explosion of the "coolie" trade. It is difficult to estimate the number of Chinese overseas contract workers today, but in 2017 and 2018 the Ministry of Commerce reported that 500,000 contract workers were dispatched each year, with the total number of overseas workers reaching nearly 1 million in 2018. Since 2013, the construction industry has accounted for over forty percent of these overseas jobs. While there is no direct correlation between Belt and Road Initiative (BRI) projects and an increase in China's labour exports, the number of overseas workers has been steadily growing since 2000 and has been relatively stable since the launching of BRI. The top destinations for Chinese workers are BRI partner countries like Singapore, Japan, Algeria, Malaysia, Saudi Arabia, Pakistan, Algeria, and

Laos. In 2019, roughly 180,000 Chinese workers were stationed throughout Africa, down from the all-time high of 250,000 in 2015.[10]

Not only does the fate of global capitalism rest heavily on the workers' movement in China, but the export of Chinese workers to other parts of the world imbues that workers' movement with an international character. The Chinese working classes, whether diasporic, located in China or working overseas, have nothing to gain from identifying with *any* national bourgeoisie, unlike the Chinese Canadian lawyers and urban planners pining for detached homes and a piece of the Canadian imperialist pie.

## Conclusion: For an internationalist and revolutionary defeatist anti-racism

The solution to the crisis of housing insecurity and homelessness for workers in Canada is the end of the commodification of Indigenous land, which means the end of land ownership and property. The solution to the threat against all life on earth posed by a new cold war is the defeat of Canadian and US imperialism. While it is true that working-class people as a whole can make this happen, Chinese workers are specially positioned to block and help smother Canadian chauvinism. While the white working class inherits the baggage of the promise of whiteness, the same cannot be said of poor Chinese people, who have no reason to believe that owning Canadian property is their birthright, particularly when they are recent migrants. But this race dynamic is deeply classed. The Chinese petite bourgeoisie's buy-in to Canadian civil society suggests that who can take part in the Canadian settler colonial and imperial project is historically contingent and by no means fixed to whites-only.

The stark inability of the Chinese petite bourgeoisie to mount any alternative to Canadian chauvinism that captures the interests of Chinese workers offers useful insights into the price of admission to centres of white power. The uncritical celebration of Canada's genocidal bourgeois democracy, to

---

10   Aaron Halegua and Xiahui Ban, "Labour Protections for Overseas Chinese Workers: Legal Framework and Judicial Practice," *The Chinese Journal of Comparative Law* 8, 2 (2020); "Number of Chinese workers in Africa from 2009 to 2019," *Statista*, January 2021.

which a section of the Chinese diaspora turned in order to express solidarity with the Hong Kong movement of 2019–2020, is an endorsement of its anti-Black, anti-Indigenous, and anti-migrant foundations. And the embrace of tax policies designed to curb competitions between different groups of real estate consumers interprets the housing crisis as a crisis of unfulfilled property ownership, rather than a crisis of the death and displacement of Indigenous and working-class people.

The Chinese petite bourgeoisie's longing to be embraced by white Canada, which is nothing more than a desire to wield imperial power, has a precedent in the entrance of ethnic white people, like the Irish, into whiteness. But unlike Irish, Germans, Poles, and other non-Anglo whites, Chinese people continue to be racialized as Chinese and typecast as either communist proxies or pro-bourgeois democratic champions of Western values. For the Chinese Canadian who aspires to be accepted into whiteness, nothing stands more clearly in their way than China's economic rise and the growing influence of the Chinese bourgeoisie. The contradiction between serving imperial interests and yet being barred entrance into whiteness finds its most naked expression in the confused attempt of the Chinese Canadian middle class to stand against anti-Chinese racism while defending, if not pushing for an expansion of, Canada's imperial power globally.

The tragedy of the Chinese-Canadian middle class is that despite their best efforts to champion Canadian chauvinism, their agency is still limited and compressed by white race power. Whatever aspects of Chineseness are unassimilable into white hegemony (a barbaric disinterest in bourgeois democracy, for example) must be shed in order for middle-class Chinese Canadians to find a place in Canada's multicultural system of national belonging. Like a moon trapped in the gravitational field of a planet, so long as the imperialist Chinese diaspora tether their interests to "Canada," they will never be free. Only an internationalist, anti-imperial, anti-colonial, and anti-capitalist movement that locates the end of white supremacy in the leadership of the racialized working class can exceed the corrupt promise of a more inclusive white nationhood.

# From white abolition to working-class Black and tricontinental power

Red Braid

The class character of radical multiculturalism is petit bourgeois because it is oriented towards the race and gender diversification of the middle class and bourgeoisie. Class reductive socialism is a politics of the aristocracy of labour because it is oriented towards those upper tiers of the working class that are invested in their inclusion in hegemonic civil society, including in their colonial and imperial property interests over Indigenous nations, Black people, and racialized people figured outside the bounds of national belonging. So what is white abolitionist multiplicity and who are the actors who can fight and end the totalizing structures and social processes of white supremacy?

Our theory of white abolitionist multiplicity analyses race power, envisions a revolutionary world without white supremacy, and proposes a strategic vision for how we can get there, because the work of multiplicity asks and does different things for whites than for racialized people and Indigenous people.

Only the agency and protagonism of Indigenous nations can overthrow colonialism, and only the agency and protagonism of the racialized working class of the Global South and its diaspora can overthrow imperialism. An anti-capitalist movement that lacks the participation of those oppressed by colonialism and imperialism risks leaving national oppression and exploitation intact.

Working-class whites must fight white supremacy to free themselves from the bonds of capitalism, because white supremacy encourages their identification with the white bourgeoisie of imperial nation states at the expense of the global working class. Only through revolutionary struggle and fighting for class interests on an international basis can white workers come to identify their destiny with the global working class.

## Class struggle and why it's not "okay to be white"

White workers are "white" because they experience whiteness as a social benefit in a white supremacist society, but their experience is different from that of the white middle class and bourgeoisie. For white workers, whiteness is like a balloon filled with the helium of a lifetime of entitled social expectations; the balloon is large, but the actual benefits it provides are as thin as its skin.

The whiteness of white workers has a different currency than the whiteness of the middle class and capitalists because of their exploited relationship to social processes of production. W. E. B. Du Bois, in his study of the reorganisation of white supremacy in the US South after the end of chattel slavery, wrote that for the poor white, whiteness was characterised by the *ambition* to be white—to be an owner of slaves. "It fed the vanity" of the poor white to participate in the policing, hunting, and punishment of enslaved Black people, Du Bois explains, "because it associated him with the masters."

Racism is the experience of feeling white by identifying others as not-white, and for white workers, their investment in whiteness is an investment in their own exploitation and alienation as junior, exploited partners of white bosses. White workers can be homeless, living in deep poverty and social marginalisation, and yet continue to cling to their whiteness by experiencing their material condition as an inappropriate oppression, a betrayal of the property ownership and social centrality they believe themselves entitled to as whites. But the poverty of the white worker is an inevitable consequence of capitalist exploitation, and to feel it as a racial betrayal means to identify not as a worker but a white person. Overcoming whiteness, then, means feeling and acting as *workers* who are part of an international social group defined by a shared class position relative to the bourgeoisie, rather than as *white people* defined by a shared social position relative to all racialized people.

## The problem with socialist class reductionism

Identity politics took root in the left as a reaction against economistic, class reductionist politics that were dominant particularly in white-majority socialist organisations and movements in North America and Europe during the postwar period. Class reductionist socialism treats race, gender, sexual orientation, and other experiences of the processes of capitalist production and reproduction as secondary (or worse, irrelevant) to class, which it misidentifies as existing only at the point of capitalist production, which is coded as white, male, industrial, and wage-earning.

But class and race have dialectical and co-constitutive relationships to one another. As cultural studies theorist Stuart Hall wrote, "race is a modality through which class is lived"—so race and class identities are *both* formed through class struggles. These include struggles over race because class struggles take place against the ways that class is experienced, not against abstractions. Radical multiculturalism treats race as an ideological problem that can be solved by perfecting the ideas and practices of middle-class and bourgeois elites, and socialist class reductionism treats race as a secondary, inevitable feature of capitalist rule that a universal class struggle will automatically disrupt. Both these approaches implicitly treat race and class as independent of one another, whether discursively or through action.

At a strategic level, class reductionism collapses the interests of racialized workers into a broader working class coded as white by limiting class struggle to those bread-and-butter issues that affect "all workers," meaning racialized workers *as well as* white workers. For a class reductionist, if a particular issue does not also affect white workers (which often implicitly means white *men* workers) then it is a fringe, special interest issue—not a unifying class issue around which it is possible to form a coalition. While few socialists would say so as directly today, the class reductionist idea remains that we'll get rid of racism "after the revolution."

For example, in January 2020, prominent democratic socialist Bernie Sanders said that white workers embrace racism because of their economic desperation. After Sanders said that white racism is explained by white disillusionment in the political establishment, the *New York Times* reporter asked him, "That explains the appeal of racism?" Sanders dug in:

> Yeah. People are, in many cases in this country, working longer hours for low wages. You are aware of the fact that in an unprecedented way, life expectancy has actually gone down in America because of diseases of despair. People have lost hope, and they are drinking. They're doing drugs. They're committing suicide. And when that condition arises, whether it was the 1930s in Germany [or today in the US] then people are susceptible to the blame game…Trump didn't invent demagoguery. It's an age-old weapon. You take a minority and you demonise that minority and you blame that minority. And you take the despair and the anger and the frustration that people are feeling, and you say: "That's the cause of your problem."

Sanders misrepresents Trump's base as poor whites rather than the white petite bourgeoisie in order to argue that his social democratic redistributive agenda could win this make-believe group away from Trump's embrace. To see race as a *material* rather than purely *ideological* motivator in US society would expose Sanders's "political revolution" as inadequate to the task of fighting the totality of bourgeois, settler colonial, white supremacist rule. Even imagining he is correct that poor whites were won over en masse by Trump's demagoguery, Sanders implies that race is a static weapon on hand for use by capitalists and bourgeois politicians to divide the working class, rather than part of how workers understand themselves within national contexts, crafting hierarchies based on who they consider part of their community of interests.

## Class reductionism is colonial and imperial

In settler colonial contexts, class reductionism commits a worse error. By equating Indigenous struggle with class struggle, class reductionist socialism ignores the unique relationships Indigenous peoples have to both capital and land. Indigenous nations are confronted by capitalism, and therefore the entirety of Canadian and US settler society, as an external, invading force that arrives in gunships, helicopters, tanks and SUVs to occupy and plunder their lands. This settler colonial capitalism has treated Indigenous peoples in Canada and the US as obstacles to colonial land theft, not as a potential workforce to be proletarianized and absorbed into a regular circuit of capitalist production as wage labourers. This does not mean that Indigenous people do not work wage labour jobs, but that Indigenous people defend and enact land relations as non-capitalist modes of production, despite, underneath, and alongside capitalist production.

The premise held by class reductionist socialists, which is also elaborated in some of Karl Marx's writings (though at a historical moment when the development of productive forces was a barrier to the survival of billions of people globally), is that socialist revolution must be led by workers at the industrial point of production. This is a racist, sexist, Eurocentric fantasy, which misidentifies the struggle for justice as "progress"—a linear version of history that mechanically pairs the rate of production with the level of development of any given society. Class reductionist socialism excludes Indigenous peoples from the process of making revolution and proposes a settler colonial *socialist* society to replace the settler colonial capitalist society we are fighting against.

Class reductionist socialism fails to fight racism *and* capitalism because it imagines white workers as passive dupes of the ruling class, rather than active agents in maintaining white supremacy and settler colonialism. Although settler colonial capitalism benefits capitalists, and its civil society is dominated and organised by the middle class, some groups of white working-class settlers have at times been vanguard activists for settler colonialism and white supremacy in Canada. But at other times, other groups of white working-class settlers have fought principled struggles arm in arm with racialized workers of the world, and in defence of Indigenous sovereignty. Historically, the political commitment of white workers for or against empire has often been a matter of the specific social class strata they belong to within the working class. *Subaltern* white workers are more likely to betray empire, while those of the *aristocracy of labour* are more likely to be imperial loyalists.

## Class reductionism centres the aristocracy of labour

The term "aristocracy of labour" refers to the privileged subgroup of the working class, particularly in imperialist countries, that enjoys a greater share of wealth stolen through imperialist and colonial war and occupation. In 1916, Russian revolutionary leader Vladimir Lenin wrote:

> Because monopoly yields superprofits, i.e., a surplus of profits over and above the capitalist profits that are normal and customary all over the world, the capitalists can devote a part (and not a small one, at that!) of these superprofits to bribe their own workers, to create something like an alliance...between the workers of the given nation and their capitalists, against the other countries.

This "economic bribe" of the "upper strata" of workers works to produce racial, national, and material differences within the working class. The bribery that forms the subgroup of privileged workers is not delivered as a benevolent gift of the capitalists downwards, but is formed through the priorities set by that self-selecting group of workers who move towards civil society belonging by excluding others: concretely, by using their greater influence in production and distribution in the heart of empire to further their own narrow interests, identified by social rubrics like whiteness and masculinity, and by corporate and legal measures like membership within particular collective agreements, rather than an attunement or commitment to the interests of the world working class.

In western Canada, as settler colonial domination was consolidated, it was British workers, understanding themselves as partners and citizens of empire, who rallied for the exclusion of Chinese and South Asian workers from their industries and the country itself. All over Canada, predominantly white resource workers and their labour unions have allied with logging and mining corporations to invade and steal from Indigenous lands. In the prairie provinces, white workers threatened Black migrants during the Great Migration with lynching, swearing to block any "Black spots" from tarnishing the white west. Settler colonialism's promised benefit of white workers' ownership of Indigenous lands and imperialism's promise of relatively high wages and preferential hiring, both abutted by a white supremacist border, have profoundly shaped white workers' participation and self-identification with the project of Canadian nation-building.

The tendency to overlook how this upper tier of mostly white workers identify with their colonial and imperial nations is class reductionist, because it substitutes a concrete analysis of how race and nation constitute class identities and practices with a hyperbolically optimistic and historically unfounded determinism, promising that when that magic day arrives and revolution comes, white workers will lead in the interests of all. In the case of the social democratic variety of class reductionism exemplified by Bernie Sanders, race is figured as an ideological distraction that the right wing of the bourgeoisie uses to obscure the leftist-appearing but no less imperialist myth that white and racialized workers in the US have shared national interests.

Our solution is *neither* an anti-racist reformism that uses racialized individuals as building blocks to perfect colonial, imperial, and bourgeois society nor a racist class-reductionism that treats class as primary and all other points of oppression and exploitation as secondary. What we need in place of both these partial understandings are anti-racist working-class institutions that, through the motions of collective struggle, tether the particular class appearances of race and nation to the universal of global class processes— allowing us to chart and combat the divisive forces of white nationalism and identity, and feel and encourage the unifying force of anti-white supremacist multiplicity.

## The leadership of the global subaltern is a brake on fascism

Understood as part of an international social group, white workers who are part of that privileged group, the aristocracy of labour, represent just a tiny splinter in the body of the world's working class, and a more substantial but still minority part of the working class inside imperialist countries. Like the petite bourgeoisie, privileged workers get more space in civil society and attention from social democrat and class reductionist socialists than subaltern, socially excluded workers who constitute the majority of the working class. While we do not write off privileged workers in imperial nations, we recognise that the divisions of relative privilege in the working class constitute material and political differences that must be attended to by fighting in the interests of the oppressed, which means we cannot afford to wait for privileged workers to be won over to the side of the global subaltern to take action. Subaltern working-class action might not have the participation or support of the group that presents itself as the majority of the working class in the imperial core, and the self-activity of the subaltern may be dismissed by class reductionist socialists or social democrats as "ultra-left" for daring to step past the limits on action and political imagination set by the aristocracy of labour. But what might appear as a fringe action to privileged workers can be a vital, life-or-death action with the widespread support and participation of the subaltern.

The struggle of the global subaltern is not particular or narrow; subaltern struggle is an inroad to mass class struggle that includes even the interests of those upper tier white workers. This premise is becoming less abstract and more real as the social position of this upper tier of workers becomes even more insecure than the increasingly precarious position of the middle class. Resource industry workers may invest themselves politically and through a white settler identity in the theft of Indigenous peoples' lands, but when they are seasonally laid off, injured, or aged-out, their $100,000 annual paycheque is suddenly gone, and they find themselves scrounging to survive. The gap between their social entitlements as white, privileged workers and this new reality of poverty can result in their turn towards racism, white nationalism, and fascism. But this is a problem of political struggle because these disappointed workers can also turn to the cause of the global subaltern, if only that politics is ready, available, and relevant to them.

The material incentives that produce whiteness means that rational persuasion is not enough to divest white workers of their race consciousness and identification. That these benefits are doled out within an exploitative and alienating system that happily discards workers as soon as they are unable to contribute to the production of capitalist value—white or not—does not mean that white supremacy is purely a problem of consciousness. Radical, anti-racist transformation in the white working class can only be brought about through direct, revolutionary confrontations with class exploitation, because nothing short of revolution, including the everyday revolutionary processes of survival and political struggle, can offer white workers something better than the psychological and material wages of whiteness, and nothing short of revolutionary struggle can unify the world's working class against capital.

## The liberation of racialized people from white supremacy

If the task of white workers is to overcome their whiteness so that they feel and act like workers rather than feeling and acting like white people, then the task of racialized working-class people is to lead their own, autonomous charge against white race power and white hegemony, in the broader world as well as in social movements and radical organisations. Indigenous and racialized peoples' oppression under white supremacy cannot be collapsed into class struggle because there are times when working-class people of colour and poor Indigenous people need to ally with other classes in their nations in order to fight against racist, colonial, and imperialist assault. These fields of anti-capitalist, anti-colonial, and anti-imperialist struggle certainly overlap—because global capitalism is reliant on colonial and imperial processes—but each also demands distinct strategies and alliances.

The hierarchies that white supremacy enforces within racialized and Indigenous people's communities and nations and between nations complicates anti-racist struggle, particularly as national structures of white supremacy, such as elected governments, slowly approach a racial diversity reflective of the general population of Canada and the United States. Racially and nationally oppressed people are not immune to absorbing racist and bourgeois values, and the shifting nature of white supremacy and the state's embrace of multiculturalism offer structural opportunities for the assimilation of racialized elites into white-led ruling class structures. The ascension of certain petit-bourgeois and bourgeois racialized groups does not make them white, but it does consolidate and legitimise anti-Black, anti-Indigenous, and anti-migrant race power. We see the rising prominence of petit-bourgeois and bourgeois Chinese Canadian nationalists as an example of racialized people colluding with the racist, colonial, and imperial state for their corporate benefit.

One of the dangers of white supremacist hierarchies and their historical contingency is that proximity to centres of race power can be bought, however precariously, by participating in the racist exclusion of working-class people of colour, or through the ascension of elites into civil society and, in some cases, the capitalist class. Our solution to this phenomenon is to understand and fight white supremacy as a totality that consists of both a material foundation and an ideological, or cultural, life.

## Culture as a terrain of struggle

We see culture through a class lens: as a theatre of struggle through which people come to terms with the contradictions of any given society and become aware of themselves as political, class actors, consciously or unconsciously. Culture is a politicising force that has no inherent quality, because the content of its force depends on the situation at hand. Culture in the context of imperialism, capitalism, and colonialism is a fraught terrain, but nonetheless a terrain where we must fight, particularly because it is through the realm of culture—including the culture of the oppressed—that imperialism cultivates consent amongst its subjects.

If radical multiculturalism seeks to reform white hegemonic culture by diversifying middle-class institutions, then revolutionary anti-racism seeks to abolish whiteness itself through anti-capitalist, anti-imperial, and anti-colonial struggle. We are not rallying for the progressive defeat of the conservatives in the bourgeois culture wars, but another alternative: the emergence of forms of cultural expression that, in their particularity, insist on the freedom of the world's global working class, Indigenous nations, and peoples oppressed by imperialism. If, as Edward Said argues, imperialism *is* culture, then cultural reforms cannot break imperialist stricture except when woven through politicised, revolutionary struggle.

If culture helps reconcile the contradictions of any society, then hegemonic cultures do so by mystifying and sublimating them. It is difficult to see past this present imperialist hellscape towards an anti-imperialist culture, but we know that it must be fought for through international struggle. We see revolutionary culture as practises of subaltern people being together and expressing themselves and their messy social being in ways that emerge through collective struggle, that expose and propel the fundamental, violent contradictions of society toward social resolution.

## Indigenous liberation is decolonisation

Indigenous sovereignty cannot be reconciled with or integrated into Canada. Under the banner of reconciliation, the colonial state attempts to subdue Indigenous anger and resistance, treating Indigenous peoples as one of many satellites of cultural diversity orbiting in service of a white, settler colonial centre. Canada celebrates Indigenous cultural practices when they can be sold as commodities, but when Indigenous people assert national cultures through sovereign home and land defence struggles, which defend the material basis of those cultures, Canada sends the RCMP's "lethal overwatch" snipers.

Behind the feel-good, liberal veneer of reconciliation, the housing, opioid, and climate crises rage on, disproportionately killing Indigenous communities. And while the settler middle class, politicians, and bourgeoisie pride themselves on mastering territory acknowledgements, social workers barge into Indigenous homes to kidnap and incarcerate children in the foster system; cops criminalise and imprison Indigenous youth and adults; bylaw officers steal the belongings of unhoused, low-income Indigenous people; supportive housing operators lock in isolation those who have made it indoors; resource extraction corporations invade Indigenous territories without consent; landlords evict Indigenous tenants onto the streets; and Canadians, acting as perfect embodiments of the state, contribute to the extermination of Indigenous people through the murder and rape of Indigenous women, girls, and Two-Spirit people.

Canada wants to kill the sovereign Indian and make a racialized Indigenous-Canadian. But Canada will fail, because Indigenous practices of political and national sovereignty pre-exist Canada and will be stronger still when Canada is gone. The truth of decolonisation is that for Indigenous nations to survive on sovereign terms, Canada must be destroyed.

## In defence of sovereign and autonomous struggle

Autonomy is organised self-activity that seeks to sever, rather than reform, the particular social relations that oppress and exploit each group within the global subaltern, and sovereignty is the assertion of nationhoods oppressed by colonialism. In asserting that only the sovereign activity of Indigenous people will end colonialism, and that only racialized people, through their own self-activity, can end white supremacy, we are arguing that no other actors can substitute themselves in these struggles, which consist of creating and defending forms of self-organisation that can countermand the disorganisation of colonial and imperial oppression. Recognising the revolutionary value of self-activity means supporting and creating space for the sovereign struggles of Indigenous nations and autonomous struggles of racialized people within decolonial and socialist organisations and movements.

However, there are cases where the need for unity with whites complicates autonomous anti-racist and sovereign anti-colonial struggles and organisational forms. For example, in Red Braid's primary social base of street communities in and around metropolitan centres in British Columbia, Indigenous and racialized poor people are often pressed into unity with poor whites in order to survive the compressing attacks of powerful, external forces like cops, bylaw officers, social workers, and business owners. Sometimes, the self-activity of Indigenous and racialized low-income people is about leading the charge against common enemies on the basis that an attack on kin and comrades is an attack against the self. While there are limitations to this self-activity, in that it produces a subjectivity that is more conscious of the common experience of poverty rather than the particular experience of, for example, settler colonialism and imperialism, it is also an expression of autonomous resistance. For low-income subaltern Indigenous, Black, Latinx, and Asian people in mixed, white-racialized communities to become leaders, they need to exercise autonomy *both* from middle-class civil society *as well as* subaltern whites. But in racially and nationally mixed subaltern communities where whites outnumber Indigenous, Black, Latinx, and Asian people, the former can appear more immediately necessary than the latter.

Autonomy is not a dogma, and what constitutes self-activity and how that self-activity can be nurtured, socialised, and developed is historically contingent. We insist that the participation of Black, Indigenous, and racialized leaders in broader struggles be recognised as inalienably part of those struggles, without ignoring the ways in which white subaltern people can exercise and sustain white hegemony. Self-activity can be mixed up with and made fraught by hegemonic influences even while straining towards liberation. Through the self-movement of fighting for the interests of the communities Indigenous and racialized people imagine themselves belonging to, they actualize the particular as part of, rather than external to, the universal. As our movement develops, so will the institutions and forms of organisation we need to sustain it.

Respecting autonomous struggle also means defending the rights of workers, peasants, and Indigenous people in the Global South to engage in their own, organic struggles against capitalism, imperialism, and colonialism. We oppose the wars of imperialist nations—trade, diplomatic, or military—because they interfere with the self-activity of oppressed and exploited peoples within nations on the receiving end of imperialist aggression. When the US and Canada attack China, we oppose it, not in celebration of China's government, but in defence of the working class and nationally oppressed peoples in China, whose struggles for freedom would be interrupted by imperialist war and meddling.

## White abolitionist multiplicity as a revolutionary praxis

Our fundamental political commitment is to global revolution: the unequivocal end of capitalism, colonialism, and imperialism. And we believe that only the self-activity of the global working class and Indigenous peoples can achieve this goal. Radical multiculturalism and class reductionism, despite the frequency with which they are cited as "radical" or "revolutionary," are fundamentally limited to reformism because their theoretical content can only be put into motion by, on the one hand, individuals who are part of, or aspire to be part of, the middle class and bourgeoisie in the West, or on the other, a national, privileged working class coded as white. The strategies these ideologies promote—and class interests they represent—fail to challenge, and thereby offer a leftist cover for, the ongoing hegemony of white supremacist and imperialist capitalism.

Political struggle is truth-making. Against the narrow visions of radical multiculturalism and class reductionism, we fight for a politics that can capture the imagination and long-term interests of a global, subaltern majority capable of wielding the power necessary to actualize revolution. That imperialism has equalised the precarity, poverty, and alienation of masses of people around the world—across the designations of core and periphery, or Global North and Global South—is an objective truth, but it is not yet a *political* truth that is felt, understood, and acted upon collectively. Revolutionaries today must fight to develop a praxis that can make true the political reality that in order for humanity to survive, we must wage a global war against capitalism—including its destructive co-systems of colonialism, white supremacy, and imperialism.

A world free from whiteness is a world where Indigenous and working-class people have smashed capitalism to liberate their spirits and unleash new panoramas of human activity and creativity, founded on many non-alienated economies and cultures. Our movement is against the totalizing force of capitalism and against the totalizing socialist vision of a global, unitary proletariat. For those oppressed by colonialism and imperialism, the struggle through and against particular experiences and oppressions will break open an insurgent universe and carve out a path of many paths, towards a future that is multiple.

*A Separate Star* Section 5

# Imperialism and the legacy of revolutionary defeatism

# Introduction
## Imperialism and the legacy of revolutionary defeatism

In, "On the Class Character of the State in China," Listen Chen rejects the dominant "bogeyman" narrative about the rise of China as competitor to US global hegemony, as well as the narrative that is more marginal but significant in socialist circles that heralds China as socialist alternative. Against both of these simplifying stories, Chen argues that the Communist Party of China's (CCP) embrace of market levers for development does not tell the whole story of China. They point to China's long march of revolution as unfinished—not ending in socialism, but not entirely overturned by capitalist reaction either. The self-activity of workers and peasants in China, which includes militant strikes and protests that defy Western narratives of Chinese quiescence, occur within a "socialist superstructure" that, despite erosion by decades of pro-capitalist reform by CCP leaders, still plays a serious role in governance and class struggles in China. Whether the revolution can find its feet once again depends not on the sage advice of socialists in the belly of the imperialist beast, but on workers' self-activity.

The point that Chen makes about Western socialist opinions about China is germane to the theme of this section overall. Rather than thinking of the struggle for decolonial socialism in Canada and the US as a national struggle, with a constituency of what Bernie Sanders repeatedly calls the "working families" of "America," Chen's framing challenges revolutionaries to think strategically about building the power of the global subaltern.

This ambitious imagining is inspired by the strategy adopted by the revolutionary anti-war and anti-imperialist section of the Second Socialist International at the outset of the First World War. They called themselves the "Zimmerwald Left" in reference to the conference they held in Zimmerwald, Switzerland to consolidate their left wing of the International. They polemicized against the politics then-dominant in the biggest socialist party member of the International, the Social Democratic Party of Germany, which adopted a confused policy encapsulated under the slogan "revolutionary defencism." According to the right wing of the German social democrats, Russian Tsarism was a bigger threat to the workers of the world than the war, so they justified voting to fund Germany's entry into war, "defending the motherland" in order to protect their working-class party's power to make revolution afterwards.

Against the revolutionary defencists, the Zimmerwald Left instead proposed the slogan of "revolutionary defeatism." The premise is simple: in times of war or other conflict between one national capitalist class and another, the job of revolutionaries in each country is, above all, to work for the defeat of their own capitalist nation and government. For socialists who happen to live and struggle inside imperialist countries, the duty is greater: to also offer "mutual aid" to revolutionaries in the country under attack. The program of the Zimmerwald Left was proven out in practice with the victory of the Russian Revolution over Tsarism, in large part won through revolutionary opposition to the war. Meanwhile, revolutionary defencism failed, with the German social democrats splitting and its revolutionary former members facing execution by members of the vigilante force that would go on to become the shock troops of fascism.

The second chapter in this section, "Canadian Imperialism and Revolutionary Defeatism," is a statement from Red Braid that seeks to put the strategy of the Zimmerwald Left into practice in the context of twenty-first century national contests and wars, including the cold war between the US bloc of powers and China.

# On the class character of the state in China

## Against US imperialism, and for a return to the Chinese revolutionary process

Listen Chen

Unlike the imperial nations of the West like the US and Canada, China is new to capitalism and came to it through a process of socialist revolution. Socialists have long debated the character of the Chinese state, the extent to which a native capitalist class has emerged, and the tenability of instituting socialism through state-led reforms. In this chapter, I analyse social relations in China and beyond with an emphasis on a strategic horizon for anti-colonial socialists based in the West. While I conclude that China is capitalist with emerging imperialist social relations, I leave the question of how to return the socialist revolutionary process to the Chinese workers movement. I identify Chinese capitalism not as an end point of Chinese history, but as a product of incomplete social revolutionary processes. My hope is that by rooting an analysis of China from within a lineage of Chinese socialism and with attention to historical processes, that I can carve out

290 A Separate Star

a strategy for supporting anti-capitalist, anti-colonial, and anti-imperialist movements within China. Central to this vision for a global struggle for the Chinese working class is committed opposition to the US-led imperialist bloc, which is crucial given the developing war on China.

I have been informed in my thinking by mid-twentieth century socialist thinkers C. L. R. James and Raya Dunayevskaya's analysis of Stalinism as "state capitalism." They argue that the development of capitalism in the post-revolutionary Soviet Union was a counter-revolution that gave rise to a new bureaucratic-capitalist class. In China's case, the social base of the Communist Party when it took power in 1949 were peasants, not workers, which in the context of a socialist revolution in a severely underdeveloped economy gave rise to a voluntaristic dynamic which emphasised the will of party cadre in carrying out revolution over the self-activity of peasants and workers—a dynamic that continues to haunt the party today. Nonetheless, James and Dunayevskaya's analysis of state capitalism can help us make sense of China's capitalist turn and the distinct way in which socialist superstructures have been reshaped by the imperatives of capitalism, suppressing class struggle and transforming the class character of the Chinese Communist Party (CCP) and government, which together I refer to as the Chinese state, away from representing the interests of peasant and working classes and towards representing the autonomous interests of capitalist production.

James and Dunayevskaya split from the Trotskyist movement in the late 1940s, partly over their analysis of Russia as state capitalist, which broke sharply from Trotsky's analysis of Russia as a "degenerated workers' state" with an overstuffed bureaucracy at its head. Trotsky argued that the Russian Revolution could be righted with a *political* revolution that would change the political leadership of the country, rather than a *social* revolution that would overturn existing social relations. When news broke about the scandalous Hitler-Stalin pact of 1939, Trotsky vigorously argued within the Fourth International that communists must offer an "unconditional defence" of the workers' revolution in property forms in the USSR—regardless of the catastrophic behaviour of the bureaucratic caste that had taken charge over the administration of those property forms.

The James and Dunayevskaya group, known through their pseudonyms as the Johnson-Forest Tendency, argued to the contrary that this bureaucratic caste had exceeded a managerial role and was ruling on behalf of capitalist power. They argued in their 1950 "State Capitalism and World Revolution" position paper that state capitalism must be overturned not *within* the property forms that had been turned against Russian workers by a bureaucratic ruling class, but by Russian workers and all the workers of Europe in a social revolution. While historically these two positions were treated as irreconcilable, I want to suggest that in China's case, there may be a mix of property forms, with some worth defending and others, including capitalist social relations, to combat. What this means for decolonial socialists in the West is that elements of the Chinese Revolution should be defended from bourgeois recuperation (including a US-backed regime change), which would serve both national and international capitalist interests, whereas other elements of Chinese social relations, such as the colonial domination of national minorities profiled as separatists, should be overthrown.

While the Chinese state appears more capable than Western counterparts of managing the contradictions of capitalism, Chinese capitalism differs ideologically and historically from established bourgeois economic modes of production. China does not fit the bill of a neoliberal state that mobilises public resources in order to support the production of value by private corporations. Instead, the Chinese state makes use of a socialist superstructure in order to facilitate the law of value and defend the interests of a capitalist ruling class.

## Capitalist base, socialist superstructure, and the law of value

The metaphor of base and superstructure comes from Marx's preface to *A Contribution to the Critique of Political Economy* and conceives of the mode of production of any given society in terms of an economic base—how production is organised—and the social and ideological social forms that arise to serve that base—laws, the state, culture or ideology, and so on. Marxists have at times relied on a simple cause-and-effect interpretation of this metaphor—as if the economic base determines superstructure along a one-way path—which leads to class reductionist assumptions that see all social phenomena as emerging from the exploitation of workers. In China, the socialist revolution eradicated a feudal, landowning class, as well as the national bourgeoisie, overthrowing a feudal and semi-colonial economic base. Redistribution of land coincided with new forms of land governance that have shifted throughout China's post-revolutionary history: first, peasant households were given privatised land seized from landowners, then people's communes took over collectivised land in the late '50s, then production teams and villages took over ownership and production in the '60s, before a "household responsibility system" (HRS) was instituted in 1980, which introduced some rudimentary market mechanisms, allowing farmers to sell their surplus produce on the market after fulfilling government quotas.

In 2007, China introduced a new property law that, for the first time, introduced private property rights that, leftist critics argued, disproportionately benefited urban homeowners. Chinese leftists argued that the law strayed too far from China's socialist roots by instituting legal protection of private property and that it effectively disenfranchised peasants, who were posed to suffer from land grabs propelled by property developers seeking to capitalise on developing rural land, and by corrupt local governments who rely on revenue from these exchanges (rural land is all owned by village collectives). In seeking to defend socialist property forms from their gradual conversion into forms that serve capital, Chinese leftists were also revealing China's hybrid superstructure, which retains socialist forms won through revolution, like, until recently, the absence of private property rights.

The Chinese economy is subservient to and organised by the capitalist law of value, which mandates that the value of any given product or commodity is equal to the socially necessary labour time required to produce it. Chinese socialism, like Soviet socialism, has depended upon utilising the law of value to create a surplus that can then drive the development of productive forces as a way to overcome profound economic underdevelopment and mass poverty. Che Guevera, when he was the head of revolutionary Cuba's national bank, argued that while the law of value was necessarily present in poor socialist nations striving to transition to communism, socialists should work towards *undermining* and then *abolishing* the law of value, emphasising the use of central planning to do so. In a 1965 letter commonly titled "Socialism and man in Cuba," Che cautions that "the help of the dull instruments left to us by capitalism (the commodity as the economic cell, profitability, individual material interest as a lever, etc.) can lead into a blind alley. When you wind up there after having travelled a long distance with many crossroads, it is hard to figure out just where you took the wrong turn."

In the long distance crossed since 1949, the CCP has relied upon and even sharpened the instruments of capitalism, but there nevertheless remain socialist superstructures worth defending and capable of undermining the law of value. Yet these socialist superstructural forms, on their own, have to be filled with the content of class struggle in order to serve socialist purposes. While the ownership of rural land by village collectives, for example, is easily co-opted into the service of capitalist production by corrupt officials and property developers, peasant struggle is a break on that co-optation that could mobilise socialist property forms to undermine capitalism.

The Chinese government's socialist ideology and one-party system equip it to respond swiftly and nimbly to the crises and vacillations of capital. To anti-capitalist critics of China, this is just a nefarious feature of China's unique history that helps maintain global capitalism. David Harvey, for example, points out that China resuscitated global capitalism following the 2008–2009 financial crisis by investing in a massive public works program, involving huge purchases of raw materials from other nations, that funded infrastructure projects to create jobs within China. As a result, China's net job loss in 2009 was three million, as opposed to the US's fourteen million. For Harvey, China represents a capitalist alternative to the bourgeois, neo-liberal capitalism of the West, too attached to liberal free market ideology and hamstrung by partisan politics to use public funds to create jobs in the wake of the financial crisis. US politicians also seem to be sensing the need to "catch up" with China's efficient approach to mitigating capitalist crises, as within a few months of taking office in 2021, the Biden administration introduced a massive infrastructure plan, pointing to competition with China as part of its rationale.

To socialist defenders of China, China's ability to manage crises like COVID-19 and the 2008–2009 financial meltdown are proof that the state represents working-class interests, or at the very least does *not* represent capitalist class interests and can, through technocratic methods, bring China closer to socialism. Samir Amin's influential "China 2013" article, for example, expresses a cautious optimism about China—a sense that while China is not socialist, it is also not capitalist. Amin argues that China is sovereign from global capitalism because "China remains outside of contemporary financial globalisation." This is also the sentiment of many of China's Marxist New Left thinkers (not to be mistaken as the New Left movement of the '60s and '70s in the US), who advocate against neoliberal policies and in support of broadly Keynesian ones—policies that mobilise public resources to soften or counteract the negative aspects of capitalism or the market economy.

Amin's emphasis on the ambiguity of the nature of the Chinese economy also implies an ambiguity of class relations. Fellow world-system theory thinker Paul Sweezy similarly saw China as a transitional, "two-way street"–a class society that *could* develop toward capitalism or socialism, but has stalled in its pursuit of the latter. In his critique of Sweezy's analysis of post-revolutionary class relations, which favourably contrasted Mao's China with the Soviet Union, scholar Yiching Wu argues that "the 'two-way street' formula implies that the central determiner of socialism is correct political and ideological leadership."[1] Sweezy, Wu continues, invests too much faith in the role of voluntarism in post-revolutionary transitional societies at the expense of attending to class struggle, which is determined by relations of production that have a material, objective character. Today, anti-imperialist defenders of China, the CCP, and some of China's Marxist New Left thinkers sidestep the question of class struggle in favour of such a voluntarist view, emphasising the transitional nature of China's society and investing varying degrees of faith in the power of the party to provide correct ideological leadership that will move China towards, rather than away from, socialism.

From a decolonial socialist perspective, the class character of the Chinese state—which is the question underlying the problem of whether the party is developing socialism or maintaining capitalist relations of production—is a matter of revolutionary strategy. Firstly, revolutionaries located in Canada and the United States must see our fundamental responsibility and primary

1    Yiching Wu, "Rethinking 'Capitalist Restoration' in China," *Monthly Review* 57, 6 (November 2005): 44–63.

strategic space of operation as the defeat of Canada and the US in all wars, inter-imperial or otherwise. But we also have to ask if China, which broke from a subordinated, semi-colonial global position through a socialist revolution in 1949, today represents the Chinese working class. If it does not, we must still defend China from reactionary imperialist attack while also supporting and encouraging the self-activity of workers in China, including their struggles against the state.

While I argue that the character of the Chinese state is capitalist and therefore necessarily imperial, China's unfolding capitalist counter-revolution and newly embarked upon imperialist course cannot be analysed independently of global power relations, which, in all measures, continue to be dominated by a US-led bloc of imperialist powers. China's willingness to fund development in the Global South and "Five no" approach to foreign diplomacy may indeed represent a superior alternative to the neoliberal deathtraps of Western institutions like the World Bank and the International Monetary Fund (IMF) from the perspectives of ruling classes in poor nations.[2] However, debating which forms of capitalist development are least harmful is hardly the purview of revolutionaries, and the advantages China can offer in terms of economic development are also reflections of how cautiously China must navigate its capitalist expansion in the shadow of the increasingly hawkish, war-mongering West.

The peculiarity of Chinese state capitalism—its reliance on a socialist superstructure—suggests that unlike in the case of long-established imperialist nations of the West, China's working class may be able to defeat capitalism through a combination of political *and* social revolution, given that the capitalist counter-revolution has not achieved the total transformation of property forms. For example, the working class might wage

2    See Xi Jinping's opening speech at the 2018 Forum on China-Africa Cooperation, in which he pledged that Beijing would adhere to the Five Nos: "No interference in African countries' pursuit of development paths that fit their national conditions; no interference in African countries' internal affairs; no imposition of our will on African countries; no attachment of political strings to assistance to Africa; and no seeking of selfish political gains in investment and financing cooperation with Africa." "Full text of Chinese President Xi Jinping's speech at opening ceremony of 2018 FOCAC Beijing Summit," *Xinhuanet*, September 3, 2018.

a political revolution for hegemony within the Communist Party, as part of a broader undertaking of social revolution against the capitalist class's footholds in China. Whether or not nationally oppressed groups could wage their struggle through the party or another organisational apparatus would depend upon the extent to which Chinese workers recognise their interests in an internationalist and anti-colonial socialist movement. But these are questions for the Chinese working class and nationally oppressed peoples within Chinese borders to take up. In the West, where our sight-lines should always be set on the defeat of our own imperialist states, China's turn towards capitalism means that we must, while opposing all imperialist war and regime-change, simultaneously devote mutual aid and support to those social forces fighting against the exploitation and oppression of the Chinese state.

## Chinese state capitalism and class struggle

The danger of fixating on the juridical absence of private land ownership in China is that it isolates individual structures or policies from the total-ity of China's mode of production, as well as its class relations. Thus, while agricultural land cannot be privately owned, the state has adopted market incentives in order to manage the threat of food scarcity (China has very little arable land) while facilitating GDP growth through urbanisation and industrialisation. In Chongqing, for example, the central state piloted a "land ticket" program that allows rural residents to commodify the use rights to their land. In a 2015 interview, the mayor of Chongqing, Huang Qifan, out-lines how the system ostensibly benefits both farmers and developers by providing a market for them: "If we can give farmers who have left rural areas a "land ticket" for their property that can be auctioned in land exchanges and urban developers can only get the land by buying the ticket, a market-ori-ented system will be established."[3]

Yiching Wu argues that the institution of market reforms in China expanded the ruling class's power despite its inchoate character, thus laying the groundwork for the class's economic and political consolidation as one

3    Jia Huajie, "Chongqing Mayor Says Rural Land Reform Pilot Has Been Just the Ticket," *Caixin*, September 17, 2015.

devoted to the interests of capital. "Market mechanisms," he suggests, "are introduced to bring about some controlled (and controllable) openings in social life, to shield the ruling elite from the popular dissatisfaction by depoliticising socioeconomic decision-making through commodification of large areas of social life, and to buy time in relation to both global capitalist competition and growing domestic discontent."[4] The development of a land ticket system is one such example of a depoliticising market mechanism that, through commodifying rural land use, offers concessions to rural migrants who have migrated to urban centres out of economic necessity, while introducing new arenas of profit-making for commercial developers and political-power-making for village elites. As such, we should read it as an act of bourgeois class-consolidation.

Market reforms were not the conspiracy of a handful of capitalist roaders in the party, but rather products of the weakness and disorganisation of China's subaltern classes following the failure of the Cultural Revolution to enact structural changes that would limit the power of the CCP bureaucracy. Wu describes marketization as a "passive strategy" for the self-preservation of the ruling class; marketization institutes changes in political and economic power that transform a bureaucratic ruling class into a capitalist one. Unsurprisingly, China's capitalist turn has also resulted in the changed composition of the party, which permitted capitalists to join in 2001. By 2011, over ninety percent of the richest 1,000 people in China were party members.[5]

China's abstention from global finance, which Amin relies on in his ambiguity-centred view of China, is shifting too. Between 2014 and late 2020, the volume of foreign-purchased Chinese bonds and stocks rose exponentially, from less than .5 trillion RMB (about $150 billion US dollars) to nearly 3.5 trillion, fueled by China's economic resilience to the disruption of COVID-19, while foreign holdings of domestic RMB assets rose from $669 billion US dollars in December 2018 to $1.16 trillion in September 2020.[6] Significantly, China announced in 2020 that it would begin to allow

4   Wu, "Rethinking 'Capitalist Restoration' in China."
5   "China's Rich Lists Riddled with Communist Party Members," *Forbes*, September 14, 2011.
6   Sofia Horta e Costa and Enda Curran, "China's Epic Battle with Capital Flows is More Intense Than Ever," *Bloomberg*, April 6, 2021.

full foreign ownership of more financial services companies, from secur-
ities and mutual fund firms to insurance and futures-trading firms, which
led to Bloomberg Intelligence predicting that even having a small stake in
China's financial services industry, worth $54 trillion US dollars, could lead
to annual profits of more than $9 billion by 2030.[7]

The optimistic thesis that China is in transition and therefore technocratic fixes can either widen or narrow the possibility of socialism discharges
the role of working-class self-activity from the pursuit of socialism. The
party's constitution, amended at the 19th Party Congress in 2017, states that
"a certain amount of class struggle will continue," but that class struggle is
"no longer the principal contradiction" in China.[8] In place of class struggle
as the engine of socialism, the party substitutes itself and the development
of productive forces, naming "economic development" as the "central task"
of the party. As such, anything that threatens economic development is
figured as a threat to socialism and national unity. Thus the constitution
chillingly points to the necessity of reforming "those elements and areas
within the relations of production and the superstructure that are unsuited
to the development of the productive forces."

Market reforms and the development of capitalism in China depended
upon the political weakness of workers and peasants and further entrenched
their alienation and disenfranchisement, currently justified under the banner
of apolitically raising living standards and combating poverty. The market
reforms begun by Deng Xiaoping in the late 1970s, known in China under
the banner of "Reform and Opening-up," resulted in the dismantling of the
Iron Rice Bowl, which deprived a generation of industrial workers who previously enjoyed life-long job security, healthcare, and housing. For coastal,
export-oriented industries to develop, an internal migrant workforce had
to be created as part of a process of accumulation. China now has a population of nearly 300 million migrant workers—double the amount there
were in 2009—who flock to urban areas in search of work, are barred from

7   "China's Finance World Opens Up to Foreigners, Sort Of," *Washington Post,*
    June 2, 2021.
8   Communist Party of China, "Constitution of the Communist Party of China
    (Revised and adopted at the 19th National Congress of the Communist Party of
    China on October 24, 2017)," Xinhuanet.com.

accessing social services and live in cramped and substandard housing, and are often forced to leave their children behind. By characterising such horrors as a matter of uneven economic development rather than a social relation between migrant workers and China's growing middle and bourgeois classes, the party justifies the very cause of such social relations as their solution.

The party's increasing centralization of state power and emphasis on itself as the protagonist of revolution are counter-revolutionary tendencies that can be traced back throughout its history. Today, as in the post-revolutionary era, the counterweight to the party's tendency to centralise power has been the autonomous organisation of workers and peasants, actualized in fleeting moments quickly crushed like the 1967 Shanghai Commune. If class struggle is the engine of socialism, then the party's embrace of capitalist development and GDP-growth represents a hard severing from its revolutionary history and the victory of a counter-revolutionary bureaucratic elite that towers above workers, asserting itself as the authority and agent of liberation through centralization and repression.

## Chinese imperialism and the Belt and Road Initiative

The Belt and Road Initiative (BRI) was announced by Xi Jinping in 2013 shortly after his election as president by the National People's Congress and described as a contemporary "silk road" that would facilitate trade and development between China and surrounding regions through land and maritime routes. In a 2017 article, Erebus Wong, Lau Kin Chi, Sit Tsui, and Wen Tiejun describe the BRI and Asian Infrastructure Investment Bank, launched to facilitate the BRI financially, as "an ambitious spatial expansion of Chinese state capitalism, driven by an excess of industrial production capacity, as well as by emerging financial capital interests."[9] While the Party insists the BRI represents China's commitment to "peaceful development" and a non-interventionist approach to investment and development, which distinguishes it from the West, this ideological dressing helps China pursue its national interests as a contender to Western power.

9   Erebus Wong, Lau Kin Chi, Sit Tsui and Wen Tiejun, "One Belt, One Road: China's Strategy for a New Global Financial Order," *Monthly Review* 68, 8 (January 2017).

With the rise of international trade conglomerates, pacts, and organisations, soft power, alongside the more traditional dyad of hard (military)
and economic (trade) power, plays a central role in the administration of
global capitalism. Out of these three, soft power is the hardest to measure
objectively, but refers broadly to ideological, cultural, institutional, and
multilateral influence. In the case of imperialist exploits, soft power consists of the influence nation states have in multilateral institutions and trade
agreements, which allow imperialist countries to broker deals with the
national bourgeoisies of other countries to mutual but usually not proportionate benefit. The US in particular continues to ride on the windfall of
World War II, which placed it at the helm of every international body created in the post-war period, like the United Nations, the IMF, the World
Bank, as well as the Inter-American Development Bank, the US Agency for
International Development (USAID), the Export-Import Bank of the US,
and the World Trade Organization, founded a few decades later. Uruguayan
anti-capitalist Eduardo Galeano sums up the character of all these institutions when he writes, about the IMF in particular, that it was "born in the
United States, headquartered in the United States, and at the service of
the United States."[10] These soft power institutions develop infrastructure
and other aid for formerly colonised countries in the service of the economic, hard, and soft power interests of the particular bloc of countries
that lead them.

US-authored, post-war multilateral treaties and international rules and
regulations of trade, investment, and finance will not serve the interests
of China when competing for markets against these instruments of US
hegemony. The formation of these international bodies, agreements, and
laws internationalised property rights and helped shape a global capitalism
dominated by the US, which used aid and loans to defend its security and
expand its military presence all over the globe. China has been trying to
develop alternate centres of global trade and law, like the $100 billion New
Development Bank, founded with Brazil, Russia, and India in 2014; the
$100 billion Asian Infrastructure Investment Bank; and, most notably, the

10  Eduardo Galeano, *Open Veins of Latin America: Five Centuries of the Pillage of a
Continent* (New York: Monthly Review Press, 1997), 221.

China Development Bank, which has committed $250 billion to Xi's Belt and Road initiative.

Though Western hysteria over "Chinese influence" is certainly dispro-portionate and motivated by racist yellow peril, China does represent a threat to Western dominance, particularly in the context of increasing weaknesses in US power, domestically as well as in its global hegemony, evidenced in no small part by the Taliban's catastrophic defeat of the US occupation of Afghanistan. In direct response to Chinese competition, the US has increased military excursions into Chinese waters and consolidated a multilateral anti-Chinese bloc that flexes its muscles through aggressive actions like the 2018 detainment of Huawei CFO Meng Wanzhou and rallying roughly a dozen nations to block Huawei from their 5G networks.[11] Economic initiatives like the G7's BRI rival, the "Build Back Better World" initiative, and Biden's massive infrastructure investment plan similarly seek to out-compete China. These military, diplomatic, and economic actions escalate soft and economic power tensions with China and prepare the West for war.

Today over 100 countries have signed up for BRI partnerships with China, with roughly 2,600 projects amounting to US$3.7 trillion underway. Western attention to Chinese investment in countries in Africa glides over the less novel activities of Western nations, but while as of 2015 China still invests far less in African mining sectors than the classic colonial players, Chinese investment in Africa has undoubtedly skyrocketed over the past twenty years. Investment in mining increased from US$13 to $35 billion between 2010 and 2015, though still trailing behind the US ($65 billion), UK ($58 bil-lion), and France ($54 billion).[12] Between 2003 and 2019, Chinese foreign direct investment increased from US$75 million to $2.7 billion, and China is now the largest bilateral trading partner and creditor for countries in the African continent (though the World Bank is still the continent's largest single creditor, and overall banks as bondholders are the largest creditors of

11  Ralph Jennings, "Year of Unusually High US Activity Noted in South China Sea," *Voice of America*, April 3, 2021.

12  Andy Higginbottom, "A Self-Enriching Pact: Imperialism and the Global South," *Journal of Global Faultlines* 5, 1–2 (2018): 49–57.

all).[13] Outside of BRI infrastructure development, privately owned Chinese firms are spread out across sectors of the economy, from fishing to manufacturing to services to construction to resource extraction, with natural resources forming the bulk of African exports to China.[14]

Alongside economic investments, China has also been pursuing its national interests by investing in its soft power in Africa. The number of international students from African countries in China rose from less than 1,800 in 2003 to over 60,000 in 2016, second only to France, and China upped its investment in fellowships significantly at the 2018 Forum on China-Africa Cooperation as part of a broader commitment to offer training to African officials, academics, journalists, and engineers.[15] StarTimes, the only private Chinese media corporation authorised by the Ministry of Commerce to engage in foreign radio and TV industries and described by the ministry as a "Cultural Exports Key Enterprise," expanded to Africa roughly ten years ago and is now present in thirty African countries with ten million subscribers.[16]

Some academics have thoughtfully challenged the reductionistic debt-trap narrative peddled by Western China hawks, suggesting that the impact of China's BRI projects and foreign investments are the product of multiple social forces: local workers, local elites, various levels of Chinese government, Chinese state-owned enterprises (SOEs), private Chinese firms, and Chinese migrant workers and managers. But these various actors are also embedded in global relations of forces, and the differences between how "Chinese capital" and "private capital" behave in Africa point to the constraints of China's relative lack of soft power, which it must cope with by offering concessions to African states that are, at times, unprofitable, but hardly outside of capitalist production. Unlike Western nations, China does

13    China Africa Research Initiative, "Data: Chinese Investment in Africa," Johns Hopkins School of Advanced International Studies; Kevin Acker, "Africa's biggest official lender: China or the World Bank?" *The Africa Report*, June 1, 2021.

14    Yun Sun, "Xi and the 6th Forum on China-Africa Cooperation: Major Commitments, but with Questions," *Brookings*, December 7, 2015.

15    "China-Africa in Numbers: Education Exchange," *CGTN*, September 2, 2018.

16    Arve Ofstad, Elling Tjønneland, "Zambia's looming debt crisis—is China to blame?" *CMI Insight* 1 (2019).

not have the IMF at its disposal to force adjustments to local economies that would produce windfall profits for its constituents.

Ching-Kwan Lee's ethnographic research in the copper and construction industries in Zambia investigates differences between "Chinese capital" and "private capital," concluding that the latter is more vulnerable to "politicisation," expressed in the capacity of Chinese state-owned enterprises (SOE) to sacrifice profit in pursuit of political goals. Lee gives multiple examples of this trade-off. In the wake of the 2008 financial meltdown, which resulted in the plummeting of copper prices, thirty percent of the Zambian mining workforce lost their jobs. Whereas two massive foreign-owned mines made significant layoffs, the Chinese state-owned mine made none. And in 2011, the Chinese state-owned mine was the only foreign mining firm that did not oppose the doubling of a mining royalty tax.

Lee suggests that Chinese state-owned mining enterprises are interested in stable, long-term copper production in order to meet China's need for copper, while foreign multinationals are less attentive to the use-value of copper, preferring to make profits from short-term fluctuations in price. She also argues that the concessional loans that Chinese banks offer are given out to foster political ties and produce overseas markets for Chinese firms. While Chinese loans have a higher interest rate and shorter repayment terms than World Bank loans, they have lower interest rates than private banks. Still, the bounds of these concessions are set by the market; a study by Rhodium Group found that China's leverage in renegotiation loan terms depend on loaning nations' access to other sources of credit.[17]

The question unaddressed in New Left critiques of BRI, as in their critiques of domestic state policy, is whether or not the Chinese Communist Party is capable of controlling the contradictions of capital. And even more decisive than the will of the party, how will Africa's workers and peasants confront capitalist development for development's sake, funded by foreign nations and brokered by local elites? For the BRI to pursue a common global good, or in Xi's and the CCP constitution's words, a "Community of Common Destiny for Mankind," there must be no class conflicts or

17   Agatha Kratz, Allen Feng, and Logan Wright, "New Data on the 'Debt Trap' Question," *Rhodium Group*, April 29, 2019.

contradictions within receiving nations or between the classes of those nations and classes in China. The ruling classes of various poor nations come to stand in for the will of those nations as a whole.

## Chinese colonialism: From socialist multiculturalism to settler colonialism

The Belt and Road Initiative exemplifies what Marxist geographer David Harvey calls a "spatial fix"—a geographic solution to problems of capitalist accumulation that, in China's case, exports excess capital beyond national borders in order to maintain economic growth. China's expanding political and economic influence abroad has coincided with repressive enforcement of national unity domestically. Movements asserting regional autonomy and sovereignty have triggered particularly violent state backlash, from the protests in Xinjiang's capital Ürümqi in 2009 to the 2019 anti-extradition movement in Hong Kong. While the spectre of ethnic or national separatism (or merely separateness) has been newly reanimated by nationalist and global ambitions under Xi Jinping's reign, recent CCP policies on national minorities represent only the latest iteration of a long and divergent history of the party's approach to what socialists call "the national question."

While early CCP members advocated for a Soviet-style federalist model that secured the sovereignty of national minorities (or minzu in Mandarin), for most of its history the CCP has instead relied on a policy of regional autonomy, which I call socialist multiculturalism. China's capitalist turn, however, has threatened the socialist multicultural model, enflaming latent colonial tensions and promoting the development of full-blown settler colonialism in frontier regions like Tibet and Xinjiang. While the socialist multiculturalist model set the stage for the possibility of colonial social relations, Mao's critique of Han chauvinism has been forgotten, with the party instead pursuing a hegemonic vision of national unity that depends on national minorities assimilating into Han culture and embracing economic development from above.

The early federalists and defenders of self-determination within the CCP were historically inspired by and associated with the Soviets. For example, the *Manifesto of the Second National Congress* of the CCP, adopted a year after its founding in 1922, advocated for a "federated republic," imagining the unification of "China proper" as well as the liberation of frontier regions Mongolia, Tibet, and Xinjiang as separate republics. But the party's strongest support for self-determination appears in a resolution passed at the First All-China Congress of Soviets, held in the Jiangxi Soviet Republic in 1931, a resolution that went further than Bolshevik policy did at the time. The Jiangxi resolution stated that national minorities "shall have the right to determine for themselves whether they wish to leave the Chinese Soviet Republic and create their own independent state, or whether they wish to join the Union of Soviet Republics, or form an autonomous area inside the Chinese Soviet Republic."

As the Chinese communists turned away from Soviet influence, they also dialled back their support for self-determination. Once Mao ascended to leadership in 1935, and in response to Japan's imperialist occupation and war against China, the CCP reverted to an emphasis on regional autonomy in its definition of self-determination. Mao located this turn in the need to fight Japan, arguing at the 1934 Second National Congress that the difference between the CCP and the Soviet national policy was the necessity for the CCP to fold oppressed minorities into the revolution against imperialism and the Guomindang. But while Mao pointed to the common enemies of Chinese masses and national minorities, which the 1931 Jiangxi resolution does as well, his conclusion is different: that a common struggle requires a unity premised on the assumption of equality, rather than a multiplicity premised on self-determination.

Recognising the danger of the Japanese and Guomindang winning over national minorities, the CCP tried to appeal to minorities without offering a form of self-determination that included the right of secession. In 1936, the CCP issued a statement to the Muslim Hui people promising religious freedom, the abolition of taxes, improved living standards, and the development of education and Hui culture, proposing an independent Hui army to fight the Japanese. Shortly after, the party's Central Committee solidified a policy towards national minorities that became the cornerstone of the CCP's approach after liberation. They argued that national minorities should "manage their own internal affairs" and that the government should respect their religions, cultures, and languages and "assist them in improving their economic conditions of life." This policy was affirmed after the founding of the People's Republic and most recently enshrined in the 1984 "Law on Regional Ethnic Autonomy," which provides national minorities with certain affirmative action-like benefits and exemptions and the right to practise their cultures and receive education in their native language.

Mao's only written mention of Han chauvinism, "Criticise Han Chauvinism," was circulated to the Central Committee of the CCP in 1953. The brief directive identifies Han chauvinism as reactionary, bourgeois, and existing "almost everywhere," including within the Party. He writes that "it will be very dangerous if we fail now to give timely education and resolutely overcome Han chauvinism in the Party and among the people." But Mao's solution is the rectification of Han cadre and people through education and propaganda, as he sees Han chauvinism as a deviation from the nationality policy of the Central Committee rather than a product of social processes and relations. Contrast that with Mao's support for Black freedom struggle in the US, in which he argued in 1963 that "national struggle is a matter of class struggle." The subtext is that Han chauvinism is a reactionary hangover from prior to the revolution that can simply be educated away.

Just as the seeds of Chinese capitalism lay in the tension among a bureaucratic ruling class and workers and peasants without direct democratic control of the means of production, so did the seeds of Chinese settler colonialism lay in the limitations of regional autonomy. While national minorities took part in the Chinese Revolution and cannot be excised from it, it is also clear that the demands of national unity set predominantly by Hans, who make up ninety percent of the general population, have always formed the limit of the right to regional autonomy for national minorities. The spectre of separatism, always present, has taken on new urgency with China's capitalist turn, promoting the emergence of a new Han chauvinism that reacts against socialist multiculturalism and an organised crackdown on minorities profiled as separatists, like Uyghurs and Tibetans.

## National unity, capitalist development, and the spectre of separatism

The Chinese state's fear that Turkic Muslims within its borders will seek independence date back to the 1950s, when cadres in Xinjiang, which was majority Uyghur at the time, were primarily leaders from the short-lived, Soviet-backed East Turkestan Republic and had close ties to the Soviet Union. Some of these leaders called for a Soviet-style federated republic of Xinjiang while others wanted outright independence, and during the anti-rightist campaigns of the late 1950s, over 1,500 Turkic nationalists were expelled from the party or reeducated. The party's current "People's War on Terror" and campaign to expose Uyghur Party members accused of being "two-faced" under the banner of fighting separatism and religious extremism are part of a longer party legacy of failing to recognise the necessity of national minorities' right to self-determination.

China's market reforms lay the groundwork to define national unity in terms of economic development, positing separatism as a grave threat to the needs of capitalism as well as the ideological cohesion of the nation. In this colonial vision, national minorities must embrace both Han culture and economic development at once, for their good and the good of the nation. Thus, the party constitution's mention of pursuing economic development as its central task goes hand in hand with the repression of national minorities on the basis that their desires for self-determination threaten that project. A 2019 white paper on Xinjiang outlines the assimilatory and economic imperatives of the party's vision of national unity:

> Having a stronger sense of identity with Chinese culture is essential to the prosperity and development of ethnic cultures in Xinjiang ... For the ethnic cultures in Xinjiang to prosper and develop they must keep pace with the times, be open and inclusive, engage in exchange and integration with other ethnic cultures in China and mutual learning with other ethnic cultures throughout the world, and play their role in fostering a shared spiritual home for all China's ethnic groups.[18]

The idea that national minorities must embrace whatever the central government doles out to them for their own good is a colonial farce. In their analysis of the March 2008 uprisings in Lhasa, a group of progressive

18  "Historical Matters Concerning Xinjiang," *Xinhua*, July 21, 2019.

Chinese lawyers argue that the state's aggressive policy of modernisation has not benefited ordinary Tibetans; it instead exacerbated inequality and introduced Han and Hui settlers to the region, who are the primary beneficiaries of the government's economic policies and the main property owners. Critiquing the central government's treatment of Tibetans, they write that in the 1980s and '90s, "economic development and the marketization and modernization of all social life in Tibetan areas became the core thinking for resolving problems in Tibetan areas." [19]

The promotion of settler colonial policies compelled by market reforms has sparked not only uprisings by Tibetans and Uyghurs, but a reactionary rise in Han chauvinism and nationalism amongst the Han majority. Right-wing ideas about dismantling the regional autonomy system in order to assimilate national minorities were once quite obscure but have become more mainstream since 2008, with many liberal democrats who formerly advocated for more autonomy for national minorities reversing their positions in response to the Ürümqi uprising of 2009 and calling for a US-style "melting pot" system more compatible with liberalism and the free market. Hu Angang and Hu Lianhe's proposed reforms at the party's Tibet and Xinjiang Work Forum in 2010, oriented around maintaining national unity and combating ethnic separatism, are exemplary of this right-wing tendency. Using a slogan of "ethnic contact, exchange, and blending," they called for the eradication of special legal rights for minorities, increased economic integration between frontier regions and the rest of China, the promotion of nationalism, and the promotion of immigration and assimilation of minorities through inter-marriage and Mandarin education. [20]

The *minzu* intelligentsia and party elites were critical of Hu and Hu's reforms in a number of forums held in 2012, characterising them as nothing short of fascistic, forced assimilation. But since then, Xi Jinping's ideology of the "Chinese dream of national rejuvenation," increase of party control over the governance of national minorities, and People's War on Terror have,

19  Gongmeng Law Research Centre, "An Investigative Report into the Social and Economic Causes of the 3.14 Incident in Tibetan Areas," 2009.
20  James Leibold, "Ethnic Policy in China: Is Reform Inevitable?" *Policy Studies* 28 (2013).

while maintaining official state ideology emphasising the harmony of China's multicultural nation, retreated from a socialist multiculturalist ethos. It is impossible to isolate these policies from the party's central goal of promoting economic development. Thus, the party's claim that it will "balance commonality and diversity, and expand common ground and the convergence of interests" figures those convergence of interests exclusively through the lens of a hegemonic national unity and the pursuit of capitalist development.[21]

China's capitalist adventure has set it upon the path of imperialism and exacerbated colonial contradictions between the Han-run state and national minorities stereotypes as Muslim extremists or separatists. But from the very beginning of the Chinese Communist movement, revolutionaries have advocated for a federated system, for at least one moment in the early '30s going beyond official Soviet policy in their calls to respect self-determination as encompassing the right to full independence. As such, today's Xinjiang policies represent the triumph of a capitalist counter-revolution now stewarded by a right-wing, misogynistic Han nationalist force within the CCP. Ending Chinese colonialism is not a matter of championing the interventions of Western imperialism states, but reviving a nascent, Chinese politics of multiplicity that, while a minority force in the party's history, is intrinsic to the Chinese Revolution.

## Revolutionary defeatism and global class struggle

With the outbreak of the first inter-imperialist world war, the left wing of the Second Socialist International championed the strategy of "revolutionary defeatism"—that in times of war, revolutionary socialists must work first for the defeat of the imperialist country where they live and organise. Revolutionary defeatism was forwarded against a right wing, socialist embrace of so-called "revolutionary defencism," exemplified by the mainstream of the German Social Democratic Party, which reversed its anti-war stance as World War I became imminent, arguing that German capitalism was superior to Russian Tsarist despotism. The West's warmongering efforts against China have produced similarly reactionary politics amongst

---

21   Xi Jinping, "Secure a Decisive Victory in Building a Moderately Prosperous Society," *Xinhua*, October 18, 2017.

the Western left, as even liberals and leftists who are critical of Western imperialism fall trap to a defencist position in their support for, or refusal to disrupt and critique, the West's diplomatic, economic, and ideological war on China.

But revolutionary defeatists in the West have at times bent the stick too far in the other direction, hesitating from critiquing, if not going so far as celebrating the rulers of those states that are attacked by empire, thus mistaking defeatism for a total politics rather than a strategy. Defences of or celebrations of these states under the banner of revolutionary defeatism fail to register the necessity to develop the forces of revolution *globally*, just as contemporary defencism fails to register that imperialist wars are a theatre for revolutionary development, for sharpening both objective conditions and subjective forces against our primary enemies.

The character of the Chinese state, then, influences how we must organise our revolutionary defeatism because it locates those international revolutionary forces that can use our support in pursuit of a global revolution against capitalism, including a Chinese working class spread over the globe whose interests exceed the party's container of "national unity." China is a new capitalist nation and has only recently entered the arena of global capitalism as an aspiring hegemonic power in its own right. If the restoration of capitalism and the development of colonialism and imperialism are products of post-revolutionary class tensions and contradictions, then only class struggle can revive China's revolution and foil the imperial aspirations and colonial power of the Chinese state.

The lessons of China's capitalist counter-revolution are the lessons of its revolution as well: that in a transitional, post-revolutionary context a voluntarist party that substitutes its cadre for workers and peasants sets the stage for a bureaucratic elite who can rapidly transform into a new capitalist class without any popular, socialist breaks on their power. The centrality of the self-activity of the working class in actualizing socialism demands forms of organisation that are capable of resisting bureaucratic institutionalisation and of exercising direct control over social and economic life, including the means of production. To call for a return to the Chinese revolutionary process, then, has repercussions in struggles against capitalism elsewhere, as the triumph of China's counter-revolution points to the decisiveness of a working class capable of adopting autonomous organisational forms. It also points to the possible continuities of a working-class project of socialist liberation and the sovereignty of Indigenous peoples and other oppressed nationalities from the violent structures of the nation-state form, without which the CCP could have no claim to representing either workers or national minorities within China.

Analysing China as capitalist and therefore colonial and imperial does not mean supporting Western imperialism. But it does mean supporting the resistance of China's working class against Chinese capitalism, as well as the resistance of Uyghurs and other nationally oppressed minorities against Chinese colonialism, and finally, the resistance of workers and peasants in Africa against Chinese imperialism. In the case of the Uyghur struggle, we face the challenge of providing alternative solidarities to the Western spy agencies that are eager to pose as saviours in order to advance imperialist interests. Only by bridging anti-colonial, anti-imperial, and anti-capitalist movements globally can we topple Western imperialism and help create room for the return of China's revolutionary process.

# Canadian imperialism and revolutionary defeatism

Red Braid

"Imperialism is piracy transplanted from the seas to dry land; piracy reorganised, consolidated and adapted to the aim of exploiting the natural and human resources of our peoples. The imperialist phenomenon has been a historical necessity, a consequence of the impetus given by the productive forces and of the transformations of the means of production in the general context of humanity."—Amilcar Cabral, in his speech to the first conference of the Tricontinental of the Peoples of Asia, Africa, and Latin America held in January, 1966, Havana Cuba.

Imperialism is the irregular, loud, recurring beat in the pulse in the circuit of capitalist production; the violent energy that reaches out to grab and pull resources in; the elastic that fires consumer goods out beyond the usual markets to sell those things that cannot be sold at home. We use the term "circuit" because the model of capitalist production is a loop where a capitalist invests money into property, raw materials, machinery, and labour power into manufacturing goods, which are then sold. The profits from this sale are re-invested back into production. When the always-growing demands of this circuit of production come up against a competitor, a fight ensues, and the strongest wins. When the demands of these competitors—as a whole group—come up against the borders of the country they call home, a fight ensues, and the government wages a border war to take resources from within the borders of weaker nations and to dominate the markets of weaker peoples.

Imperialism is "overripe" capitalism—it is the expansion of the compass of capital outside of its local circuit because of the godly rule of accumulation that trumps the sovereignty of non-capitalist economies and regions. Imperialism is an inevitability in our historical moment, when massive monopolies war to absorb each other—and the US-dominant world is dying—but a world without capitalism cannot yet be born. Imperialism makes capital global, and it pushes rival capitalists into contest and eventually war with each other over rivalrous control over militarily and economically weaker countries and regions. Canada, despite its small population, is a powerful imperialist country with its own distinct imperialist interests as well as its own alliances of opportunity with the US, Britain, and Europe.

## Imperial identities

British imperialists founded the Canadian nation state as a home branch of their empire. In the years after Confederation, white settlers fought to establish the west as a "white man's country" where whites were entitled to property carved out of Indigenous lands, and Asian, African, African-American, and Caribbean peoples were not welcome. White settlers—including Anglophone workers—identified with British imperialism: in 1907 they carried the Union Jack and sang "Rule Britannia" while smashing windows along Pender Street in Vancouver's Chinatown. Although formal multiculturalism has modified the original Anglo-singularity of Canadianness, the imperial roots of Canadian belonging have remained. Imperialism's double helix is imperial culture operating in the hearts and minds of the Canadian working class and imperial power operating as Canada's "foreign policy," competing with and going to war against Canadian capitalists' competitors. Imperial culture in the working class is what Russian revolutionary Vladimir Lenin referred to as the "aristocracy of labour": that section of the global working class who receive "a certain benefit" through imperialist policy, specifically, "the higher wages that could be paid to workers out of capitalists' superprofits." The aristocracy of labour became bloated in Canada during the postwar boom, as labour unions made deals with capital in exchange for higher wages and standards of living for their members.

## The beginning of the end of the US world order

Since the labour peace years ended with neoliberal austerity and anti-union attacks, and especially since the Great Recession of 2007, this aristocracy of labour has campaigned for Canadian imperial power, motivated by a racist nostalgia for the good ol' days of post-war prosperity. To recover the financial security of the postwar years, some private-sector unionists have argued for increased imperial exploitation of tar sands to retrench imperialist theft from Indigenous nations, and professionals and public-sector unionists (represented in the NDP provincial government in British Columbia) have called for a trade war with China to continue the status quo of Canada's beneficiary position in a US-dominated global economy.

Since the fall of the USSR in the 1990s, imperial power has mostly been expressed in trade agreements that facilitate the internationalisation of capital. Although US wars have continued to define global power, they have been wars and occupations of domination—the accoutrements of the new "free trade" world administered by spaces of economic, political, and military inter-imperialist collaboration, like the World Trade Organization, International Monetary Fund, United Nations, and NATO. But the years of cooperation between imperialist powers seem to be ending alongside the end of the US's post-1991 rule as the world's only superpower. In this power shift, China is not merely a place; it is an idea that threatens the Anglo-American liberal world order.

The 2007 world recession may have been the turning point in the US's unchallenged global hegemony. While the US lost 14 million jobs in 2007, China lost nearly 30 million. But by 2010, the US had not recovered any of those lost jobs, while China had recovered all but 3 million. The economic policies of China have proved better suited to managing crisis and collapse, whereas the Anglo-American models of state capital management have not. The sort of welfare-state concessions to white workers that ruled the US and Canada in the 1950s and '60s came out of a time of boom and sharing in imperialist superprofits. In the depression of the 1930s and the recession of 2007, the Anglo-US model of capitalist state management refused a bail-out to the unemployed. But China quickly intervened to stop a depression. In this context, and in a time of unpredictability and crisis, the prospect of China's growth against American crisis increases the prospects of Chinese challenge to Anglo-American hegemony.

Such an unstable shift in global power was also a global dynamic in the lead-up to World War I at the beginning of the twentieth century. The Socialist International collapsed at the outset of war in August 1914 precisely because many of the anti-capitalist parties supported their own countries and governments in the war. This tied these parties to the interests of their national capitalist classes and aligned their political goals with that of empire. The first casualty of this turn was the end of the Second International organi-sation of socialist parties. Contact between member parties was broken off, and instead, working class people met each other across fields of battle in the trenches of the First World War.

## Revisiting the World War I anti-imperialist position of "revolutionary defeatism"

The opportunity of inter-imperialist war is for radical anti-imperialists and anti-capitalists to strengthen their connections with each other, across lines of national difference, and to break their nationalist ties to their own ruling classes and end their toxic allegiances to their national-imperial cultures. In September 1915, forty-two delegates from eleven countries met in the first international conference of socialist currents opposed to World War I, held September 5–8, 1915 in Zimmerwald, Switzerland. The resulting *Zimmerwald Manifesto* helped inspire a mass movement of antiwar and socialist activists across the warring countries of Europe.

The basic idea of Zimmerwald was revolutionary defeatism: "a paral-lel struggle by the workers of each country against their own imperialism, as their primary and most immediate enemy." This principle united work-ers against war with an eye to toppling capitalist-imperialist power in each of their countries. Vladimir Lenin, one of the authors of the *Zimmerwald*

*Manifesto* and a leader in the Russian socialist movement, argued, "The opponents of the [revolutionary defeatism] slogan are simply afraid of themselves when they refuse to recognise the very obvious fact of the inseparable link between revolutionary agitation against the government and helping bring about its defeat."

As organisers in renter and homeless communities, we have experienced the counter power present in these spaces that communities carve out, apart from state governance and dominating civil society. In Red Braid's political strategy document, we discuss these counter-power spaces as examples of potential "dual power," which "refers to a revolutionary moment when self-organized peoples exercise control in a site within a country where capitalists or the settler colonial state still has power overall."[1] Tenant and unhoused community struggles are places where we can develop non-capitalist and non-colonial property forms independent of the rule of Canada's coloninal government and capitalist economy, based on the use of and relations with land because they do not rely on a static, authoritative, and bounded property regime under the hegemony of Canadian settler law.

At the height of nationalist war hysteria in 1915, Karl Liebknecht, a leader of the German Social Democratic Party's left wing, which embraced a revolutionary defeatist strategy against Germany's involvement in World War One, argued, "Every people's main enemy is in their own country!" He said, "is in," because he was referring to the capitalist class. In our case, as Canada goes to war in Africa, the Caribbean, and the Middle East, and increases trade wars and stokes yellow peril panic against China, we see that our main enemy is in this country, including those who compose the state. Revolutionary defeatism means that we are working for the defeat of Canada in all cases—and that we must develop ties and alliances with workers in China so that we can support them in their fight against their state, which is their primary enemy.

---

1     Red Braid, " Global crisis and revolutionary possibility: Red Braid's political strategy," in the last section of this book, "The living character of Red Braid's organisational documents."

*A Separate Star* Section 6

# The living character of Red Braid's organisational documents

# Introduction
## The living character of Red Braid's organisational documents

Throughout our years organising together, Red Braid's organisational documents have been revisited, reevaluated, and rewritten many times. When we were meeting as the Social Housing Alliance, our basis of unity and structure documents were few and mostly implied through practice. It was through talking about the inadequacy of our political documents—that what they said did not match up with the political direction we found ourselves moving—that we pushed out of single-issue campaign work and into a more thoroughgoing politics. Then, as we gained practise talking about political ideas, our formal agreements started to take on an aspirational and ambitious tone; our thinking reached out ahead of us, anticipating the ideas we would need in the next, coming period of struggle. Social Housing Alliance leapt into Alliance Against Displacement, which leapt again into Red Braid.

Through this collective work, thinking became an action alongside others, as indispensable to Red Braid's organisational life as the actions of meeting in communities, marching in the streets, and occupying abandoned buildings. Working out an accountable division of labour around thinking work challenged our conceptions of collective leadership, which is reflected in the individually authored articles in *A Separate Star*. These individually authored chapters are no less the product of Red Braid's collective work, but they have not been subjected to the group reading, discussion, editing, and writing-by-committee that we used to draft our organisational documents, or those group statements included throughout this book. Formal Red Braid documents have been read out loud in meetings, often over and over again, in order to ensure they represented the ambitions not just sensed by a particular writer, but by the group as a whole.

But because these organisational documents both stood on our group's collective experiences and anticipated struggles ahead, trying to form the structures and political agreements that we thought we'd need to prepare for what was ahead, they are necessarily imperfect and impermanent. They are documents that lived so long as Red Braid lived and, like all living things, moved. Red Braid's dissolution has stopped our future work on these organisational documents, but they still are not really *finished*. We hope they can be of use to others who strike out on these same winding, braided paths on which we have thought hard while walking.

The first document in this section is Red Braid's founding document: our basis of unity. Here we set out our basic political agreements and shared understandings. We say that we see the totalizing political and economic systems of colonialism, capitalism, and imperialism as interdependent, that a fight against any one of these systems is incomplete without a fight against them all, and that a victorious revolution against these "braided" systems of power will be characterised by a braided leadership of revolutionary protagonists: Indigenous people against colonialism, the subaltern working class against capitalism, and oppressed nations—including those racialized workers in the diaspora—against imperialism.

The second document is Red Braid's organisational strategy, which we used to carry out this braided struggle. This strategy was particular to our historical time and place, which was characterised by the rise of the middle class and the disorganisation of subaltern groups, but the methods, we hope, are applicable elsewhere. In a word, this is a strategy of building social bases for our revolutionary organisation—bases where communities kept us accountable by testing and making relevant our politics for their everyday needs.

The third and final document in this section is the most technical, but the most revealing of how our group actually operated. "Democratic Protocols and Processes of Red Braid Alliance for Decolonial Socialism" explains the organisational stopgaps and checks and balances we used to balance the broad political ambitions of our group (to overthrow the whole system of power as it exists) with the real lives and needs of subaltern people. This is in fact not a technical problem but the one that made the difference between a revolutionary group that was a group of thinkers hived-off from society and one that mattered to the people whose destinies we claimed to represent.

# Who we are and what we want
## Red Braid's basis of unity

Red Braid

Red Braid Alliance is a revolutionary organization dedicated to building the sovereign power of Indigenous peoples and the autonomous power of the working class—in all their multiplicity. We are active primarily on lands occupied by British Columbia, Canada.

We practice and advocate for a strategic unity between Indigenous peoples fighting for sovereignty through dismantling colonialism, the national struggles of peoples around the world against imperialism, and the working class for worlds without capitalism.

We test our politics through practices of politicizing community survival struggles, political education, protest, and direct action.

We prepare to take power away from capitalists and colonizers by increasing the autonomous power of communities where we are, as part of the insurgent working-class and Indigenous peoples' movements of the world.

While our communities may rely on the scarce resources offered by the state as a matter of survival, we fight to abolish police and prisons and for community control over social wage institutions. Through our struggles we create autonomous supports and transformative justice that help us heal, care for ourselves, and build the power to collectively strike at the roots of our shared trauma, alienation, and despair.

We fight for multiple worlds where production serves the needs of our communities, and where the free, full, creative development of each person is the responsibility of all.

## Our vision: Indigenous and working-class people unite!
*Our struggle*

Colonialism, capitalism, and imperialism are destroying our communities and the nonhuman world. These three processes confront our communities differently, but each depends on the other for the sustenance of the global capitalist system.

Colonialism attacks Indigenous economies, land relations, and ways of being in an ongoing, genocidal war waged by occupying nation-states and settler civil societies, including those closest to us—Canada and the USA.

The global machinery of capitalist production, exploiting and alienating workers in Canada and around the world, is fed by imperialism, including colonial land theft, producing unprecedented luxury and scarcity, unprecedented comfort and environmental destruction, and unprecedented free choice and desperate need.

Imperialism is the arm that reaches around the world, smashing through national boundaries to steal land wealth and labour power and impose commodities markets with the violence of military invasion and extortionist treaties and trade agreements while enforcing a white supremacist border around Euro-America. Our struggle must, therefore, be global: we fight this triumvirate all at once or not at all.

*Decolonial revolution*

Indigenous revolution against colonialism is our full national assertion of sovereignty. As Indigenous nations exercise distinct cultural and economic practices, we refuse colonial governments and economies. As urban Indigenous people who have been displaced from our traditional territories, we exercise land relations and stewardship by healing, building, and defending our communities, homes, and spaces against colonial forces that seek to assimilate or annihilate us. From our strategic position at choke points in the flows of global capital, our blockades and disruptions are practices of Indigenous ways of being and relating that work to dismantle the settler colonial country of Canada.

Our decolonial socialism is the practice and defence of Indigenous nationhood as separate centres of gravity, politically independent from settler colonial nation states, taking back sovereign Indigenous land and being.

### Socialist revolution

Working-class revolution against capitalism is workers seizing community control over the production and distribution of the things we need and desire, guaranteeing the wellbeing of our communities internationally. To produce for the needs of the many and the wellbeing of the biosphere instead of for the profits of the few, we wage our working-class struggle wherever the pressures of survival and competition bear down on us, from our workplaces to our homes to community sites like tent cities.

Our decolonial socialism depends on autonomous working-class fights that undermine state and capitalist power, developing the independent power needed to overthrow the economic and political system of capitalism.

### Anti-imperialist revolution

National revolution against imperialism is the defence of the sovereignty and organic political processes of the countries of the Global South against domination, exploitation, invasion, and military occupation by the armies and trade syndicates of the Global North. Red Braid seeks alliances with the Indigenous, peasant, and working-class protagonists of national liberation globally, but when the struggle for national liberation presses the poor into coalition with an oppressed nation's bourgeoisie, we support that whole national struggle for the defeat of imperialism.

Our decolonial socialism joins with the Global South for the defeat, in battle or trade war, of Euro-American national power in any imperialist conflict.

### Our alliance

Indigenous peoples, the working class, and nations fighting imperialist aggression are the protagonists in our braided struggles against colonialism, capitalism, and imperialism. We believe that only through a principled alliance between Indigenous peoples and the international working class can we overcome our powerful enemies to realize a better world for future generations. Beyond colonialism, capitalism, and imperialism, working-class and Indigenous peoples will continue our cooperation through principles of consent and relationality, to rebuild multiple worlds where our full, creative selves and communities can flourish.

## White abolitionist multiplicity

Both Indigenous and working-class communities hold within them tremendous multiplicity. Indigenous nations are diverse in economic structures, cultures, languages, and worldviews. Working-class communities vary along lines of culture, race, nation, gender, and sexual orientation. White supremacy is a global structure of power created and reproduced through colonial and imperial conquest that will end only when racialized people free ourselves from colonial and imperial bonds. Whiteness also corrupts the humanity of white people by enticing us into a system of power where our racialized relationships with others are characterised either by our dominating violence or our patronizing deference and deferral.

While we reject the flattening universals of Western, European epistemologies—including socialist ones—we believe that the vast majority of humanity shares interests that only a strategic alliance against the white supremacist, colonial, capitalist, imperial apocalypse looming on our horizon could make real. In this struggle, our multiplicity is our strength. We organize to create a world that can hold the multiplicity of our differences and nurture reciprocal relations with the nonhuman world.

## Decolonial feminism

Feminism is not included alongside the "braided" struggles against colonialism, capitalism, and imperialism because we see gender power as a wire within each cable, and as the intimate power that completes the circuitry between them. Gender power encompasses the patriarchal and colonial processes that code, sculpt, and police us into a gender binary.

Colonialism attempts to eradicate myriad Indigenous gender relations, which pre-exist Anglo-European invasion, and replace them with a system that mirrors the patriarchy that was instrumental in developing capitalism in Europe. Gendered violence against Indigenous people is always colonial: the murder and disappearance of Indigenous women is fundamental to settler colonialism's drive for domination, and police violence and mass incarceration are the Indian wars of the everyday, attacking Indigenous men, women, and Two-Spirit people in distinctly gendered ways.

Settler colonial capitalism also kills and exploits non-Indigenous women. Working-class women are gendered to perform over and above their class exploitation in the waged workplace: their emotional, sexual, and domestic labour are also exploited through unwaged social reproduction work in the nuclear family. While the professional middle class has integrated white women into its lower rungs, the rule of the public-private gender divide continues to defer power to men. Men, including working-class men, express their gender power through the abuse, sexual harassment, and assault of women and those of us outside the gender binary or compulsory heterosexuality in the male-dominated public and in the nuclear family home.

Imperialism steers gender power, including its refusals, into national containers that involve people oppressed by patriarchy in a defence and elaboration of the settler and imperial nation state. Canada ensures that there is room for white feminism and queer assimilationist politics that seek to carve out a space for us in the project of imperialist nation-building.

Against colonial and capitalist patriarchal hegemony, we fight for women, trans, Two-Spirit, and gender non-conforming people to thrive in a world that honours multiple genders and kinship relations.

### Organization: From non-tendency to new tendency

Our organization does not ascribe to any single revolutionary lineage. We think of Red Braid as an inheritor of all revolutionary anti-colonial, anti-capitalist, and anti-imperialist experiences and projects of the past, including struggles for Indigenous sovereignty, national liberation from imperialism and colonialism, and a wide range of socialist, communist, anarchist, and feminist experiments. We strive to approach our history with openness and curiosity, always seeking to learn from the victories and advances and mistakes and failures of comrades and fighters, past and present.

We need organizations that build the power of movements by analyzing our experiences, creating and recalling histories, and coordinating self-defence actions within and towards the thinking-fighting-thinking work of developing and testing revolutionary decolonial socialist theory. Red Braid is one such organization.

We also need international networks that link groups and movements that are connected through shared commitments to essential political principles of fighting to end capitalism, colonialism, and imperialism and building sovereign Indigenous nationhoods and working-class community power.

Neither Red Braid nor these informal revolutionary networks can be bound by a single political dogma, but neither can we be satisfied with an eclectic "non-tendency" solution, which can bury and mask important differences of politics and strategy. The task of twenty-first century decolonial socialism is to draw together, through our process of struggle and in communication with multiple pasts and in anticipation of many futures, a new political tendency.

To survive together in a time when reform is impossible, and to build revolutionary movements powerful enough to overthrow colonialism, capitalism, and imperialism, we need a revolutionary politics that provides relevant power to our everyday struggles, explains our suffering, and answers our dreams and desires. The power we build together will enable us to transcend the local conditions of individualized survival, seeding and sprouting the forms of our global revolutionary tomorrows.

# Global crisis and revolutionary possibility
## Red Braid's political strategy

Red Braid

> "It's not a question of 'when the revolution is going to be':
> the revolution is going on every day, every minute, because
> the new is always struggling against the old for dominance."
> —Huey Newton, 1971.

Before we do anything, we always need to have a concrete analysis of our concrete situation. That principle is not to privilege thought over action. We know that thought *is* an action. And we know that every tiny and important gesture we make in our lives is sparked first by thought—by the electrical impulse of decision that flashes from our heads or hearts along the columns of nerves to our fingertips or feet. We move by the activity of thought, which sums up our knowledge and experience and creates the foundations for action; thought places the stone stable enough to leap from, over the rushing water of the dangerous world around us.

Marx, in discussing his philosophical method, explains: "The concrete is concrete because it is a synthesis of many determinations, thus a unity of the diverse." The "many determinations" Marx refers to are the multiple forces that create our specific moment and position in history, which in our case includes the objective forces of grand global imperial power since World War II; the economic forces of class restructuring in the globalization movement; the political forces of local governments embracing austerity and legal forces of Supreme Court judges deciding to displace tent cities; and the subjective forces of our own capacity organizationally; and, individually, our determination and the danger of discouragement.

Marx continues: "In *thinking*," the process through which a person reckons with this synthesis of many determinations, "[the concrete] therefore appears as a process of summing-up, as a result, not as a starting point, *although it is the real starting point, and thus also the starting point of perception and conception.*" Marx is saying that only after "summing up" these "many determinations" to better understand who we are in the world and in the flow—or circular movements—of history, can we then begin to analyze the problems that face us and to act to change the world.

For an organization, the communication between collective thought and action mobilizes a complicated series of events. We think, and then act; we reflect on the experiences and lessons of those actions, which again is thought; we find occasion to write about and think more deeply and more together, to decide, and then act collectively again. There is more to it, too. Our activity as members of an organization is carried out and measured in community spaces amongst those we experience as our social base—who we are accountable and responsible to—and against those we consider the enemies of our social base and therefore our enemies. The responses of our friends and our enemies must also be counted, measured, and considered as we decide what to do next.

The terms of our considerations, our principles that we weigh our experiences against and the goals that we chart our progress against, are laid out in our basis of unity. Again: thought. But while our political principles are secure (not unthinkable or eternal because we must assess them as well), our political strategy and tactics must always be reflexive and dependent upon, one, the objective conditions that face us as obstacles put in place by history and by our enemies, and two, the subjective conditions of our own leadership development and the limitations and strengths of our collective power.

This political strategy comes out of our reflections on our experiences of our initial years of collective struggle and our initial strategy, where we decided to organize along two roads of anti-capitalist and anti-colonial struggle, and where we decided to focus strategically on building social bases in communities outside the imperial metropole of Vancouver. We do not think this strategy is particular to the conditions in western Canada; we believe that this strategy speaks to an emergent political tendency of revolutionary struggle in subaltern spaces throughout the world.

## Part 1: Summing up
*Part 1a. Inter-imperialist rivalry*

1.  The end of the second decade of the new century is shockingly similar to the world at the beginning of last century: the old empires suddenly *feel old*. Fault lines of power between nation states are creaking as new powers are straining to fill the space they find themselves suddenly and already occupying. China's Belt and Road Initiative has a double character in this dynamic. On one hand it heralds the arrival of a new power eager to challenge US hegemony in Asia and Africa, and even eastern Europe. This new power hurls baubles and promises to the colonized, as President Xi swears that the Chinese dawn will be different than the American twilight. But if the Chinese state's attacks on the power of workers at home—to whom Xi denies political citizenship and the right to organize independent unions—are any sign, then the more appropriate slogan may be "meet the new boss, same as the old boss."

2.  But on the other hand, China's challenge to US hegemony deals an important challenge to the revolutionary left and anti-imperialists in the West. Anti-imperialists in Canada and the US have become accustomed to a unipolar world where opposing imperialism means supporting the struggles of oppressed nations for self-determination. But the US-China dynamic recalls the challenge met by revolutionaries in Europe at the opening of the First World War, when the armies of one bloc of imperialist countries squared off against the armies of another. The lesson of the Second International's response to World War I should be, in the words

of the Zimmerwald Left and later the Third International: revolutionary defeatism. The primary tasks of revolutionaries in inter-imperialist war must be to work, in collaboration with revolutionaries globally, for the defeat of the mother country—our own country first and foremost—and to never to fall in line in support of our own government and armies against foreign enemies.

3. Inter-imperialist war was, 100 years ago, premised on an old-style imperial power, feeding national capitalist demands within the imperialist country itself. The role of armies in times of so-called "peace" was to orchestrate the corporate theft of land and life from colonized nations, to speed stolen wealth back to the metropole, to process it into manufactured goods, and then sell those goods back into the international market. War was the open, military contest between imperialist and inchoate imperialist powers for control over that mass theft.

4. Inter-imperialist contest today—not yet and hopefully never to be open war—is a new-style imperial power. Capitalist power is still concentrated in imperialist countries, but in a financialized global network of cities where office towers and "financial services" are the marker of influence rather than the presence of factories and mills. The presence of the machinery of production itself is a symbol of poverty and underdevelopment, whether in rural and impoverished areas and special economic zones within the imperial nation, or in colonized and formerly colonized countries. The imperialist contest today is for control over distribution channels and hubs, technological and administrative networks, the centrality of banking and currency exchange, and majority ownership over the companies that organize the theft of land. This economic dynamic alone should have pushed the nation state into the shadows of a globalized finance capital, where corporate boardrooms that are transnational and multinational would be the stars.

## Part 1b. White nationalism

5. But imperialist nationalism has proven resilient and particularly toxic when threatened. White nationalism is resurgent. It has not been the

contradictions of the economy that has given rise to white nationalism: not "financialization" and the offshoring and deunionizing and deskilling and technologizing of white men's industrial jobs. Racism was present, but played a secondary role in the anti-globalization movement. White nationalism is surging against two threats: global climate catastrophe and its resulting mass displacement crisis, which has produced the largest refugee and international movement of people from poor, Black and brown nations into the imperial metropoles of Europe and North America; and the decline of Euro-American global hegemony.

6. In and around global financial cities in North America, these global political and economic dynamics are hardening lines of civic citizenship. A civil society—those who feel they are part of the hegemonic order and play the social and cultural role of state actors—is re-forming amidst immense wealth in the metropole, and amidst increasing insecurity in the suburbs and smaller towns. In both cases this civil society is recasting belonging through exclusion: the exclusion of the poor and especially the homeless, Indigenous people in the in-between spaces, Black and South Asian youth, racialized and migrant working-class communities, trans and gender non-conforming workers, employed or not, and people who are too young and too old. Those of us excluded from civil society are the subaltern, and our numbers are swelling.

*Part 1c. The long retreat is still not over*

7. This social and historical crisis also arrives during the continued, long retreat of the revolutionary left that began in the 1970s with the end of the postwar decades of national liberation and anti-colonial movements and the New Left. This period marked the beginning of the neoliberal era, which championed, in the words of Margaret Thatcher, "individual responsibility," and was premised on the belief that "there is no alternative" to capitalism.

8. Since around 2010, a series of rebellions in Canada and the United States have indicated that the retreat may be coming to an end: Occupy, Idle No More, Black Lives Matter, and the democratic socialist movement,

all should be read as hopeful signs that young people are not settling for the "no alternative" thesis. But these spontaneous energies have not crystallized into a cohesive revolutionary politics, into organizational forms independent from a bourgeois political apparatus or with sustained and deep social bases. The retreat may be slowed, but it has not turned into an advance, nor are we yet holding independent ground.

9.  The challenges and opportunities of global capitalist crisis have made virtues of our retreat, which has driven declarative and practiced politics into separate islands. A crevasse separates speaking and acting so completely that it is possible for one person or group to utter one position while holding another in practice without feeling any contradiction or hypocrisy. Declarative politics have been perfected by professional thought producers who receive pay in exchange for developing innovative slogans and thought frameworks. For our movements, declarative politics have dovetailed with the hyper-individualism of neoliberalism and a retreat into pure idealist politics that make a point of refusing the really existing world and its struggles as hopelessly contaminated by practice. Practical politics are, meanwhile, contaminated by pragmatism. Lacking infrastructure and institutions that we can mobilize to make revolutionary politics relevant in the lives of people in survival struggle, community organizers capitulate to bourgeois institutions like social service organizations, NGOs, and legal and political reform projects directly or indirectly connected to bourgeois political parties and institutions.

10. Indigenous reformers in Canada have taken advantage of the one space that multiculturalism is expanding rather than contracting: what Canada calls Indigenous "rights." In 2018 the Trudeau Liberals reopened the legal and political rights framework that was started with the 1969 White Paper in order to wipe out distinct Indigenous status and, more importantly, to convert reserve lands into fee simple private property. "Rights" is the framework that threatens to assimilate Indigenous difference—which is based on Indigenous, non-capitalist, national land relations, apart from Canada's private property regimes—into a racialized position within Canadian multiculturalism, and a legal-administrative position within

a legislative division of power as a "fourth" level of governance, similar to municipalities. Rights are the opposite of decolonization, but aspiring Indigenous politicians and investors argue that this is no time to be idealistic, that sovereignty is unrealistic, and that it is time to settle for rights and self-government within Canada.

11. Left practice, meanwhile, emphasizes investing in elections where, some leftists assert, they can "move the Overton Window" to normalize a sanitized and defanged version of "socialism" in public discourse. The opportunity this project seizes is for revolutionary intellectuals; the underlying premise is that the "marketplace of ideas" is an important space of transformation, and that, lacking a mass movement of workers, the best that intellectuals can do is take their space as protagonists of reform.

12. There is a contradiction between the objective possibilities of our historical moment and the subjective powers and political vision of mainstream left and Indigenous leaderships. Feeling the effects of global economic and political crisis, and without a socialist, decolonial politics at hand, fascist currents are rising in the cultural and ideological spaces of middle-class communities, and working-class people are influenced by this movement. Our responsibility is historic. If we cannot rebuild a revolutionary, decolonized socialist politics, then we are facing a future of, in a historically modified version of Rosa Luxemburg's warning, fascism.

## Part 2: Subaltern revolutionary subjects and our theory of power

13. Our goal is not to win arguments against the mainstream, respectable, and reasonable leadership of progressive forces in Canada and the United States. Our goal is to build relationships that allow us to be part of community experiences of political contradictions and tensions—to make revolutionary politics relevant at a moment when the truth is that there is no practical reform possible that will make a real difference in poor and oppressed peoples' lives. Our goal is to build institutions of struggle that are independent of bourgeois and settler colonial state power, grounded instead in the democratic self-activity of working-class and

Indigenous communities. Our goal is to rebuild a decolonial socialism through practices of revolutionary struggle.

14. White nationalists are acting as though their nation-state form is vulnerable. A nationalist reaction—from the left through protectionist border controls and a redistribution-based social democratic agenda, and the right through white nationalism and anti-migrant racism—is the first manifestation of this vulnerability.

15. To imagine a future without Canada or the United States we must broach the subject of dissolving Canada. Now is the time to work through imagining a post-revolutionary social form. The contemporary nation state model is unimaginable without its colonial dominations. A revolutionary union of intercommunal spaces could be a post-revolutionary model premised on dissolving the colonial nation states of the Americas as the starting point of imagining.

*Part 2a. Base building*

16. In our organizing, then, it makes sense to adopt a similar form: not depending on nation-state forms, but seeking points of identity, unity, and collaboration through similar politics and struggles regardless of nation state. A "base building" tendency has begun to emerge in North America; it is not completely or clearly defined, but the spirit of base building is somewhere we feel at home, and finding and working with comrades outside of our region who share our basic political tendency is absolutely necessary political work.

17. "Base building" as an organizing strategy has some competing and overlapping definitions. We do not see base building as simply "community organizing" in the model defined by Saul Alinsky's "non-communist left" of the 1960s, where organizers seek to mobilize oppressed communities as a constituency to advocate for reforms on issues that affect them. Alinskyism plays at self-activity by creating avenues for oppressed peoples' self-expression but only within the theatres created and controlled by the organizer. The politics and theory of the organizing is controlled

by the organizer, who would better be called the puppet master of the reform effort.

18. We also do not see base building as the "serve the people" model practiced by some groups influenced by Maoist traditions, where the needs of communities are met through the direct provision of services by organizers. Serve the people projects refer to a dialectical model where the revolutionary organization is in touch with and responsive to their base communities, but the political theatre is one-way: activists can introduce and test their political slogans in the communities but the interpretation and organization of those slogans into action is a power held exclusively by the organizers. Serve the people undermines the dialectical moment of self-activity, where the possibility of politics is realized through the creation or revelation of the political core of community life.

19. Our social base building strategy politicizes the existing survival struggles of subaltern people. We do not bring services to poor people, particularly because we have to confront the influence of social workers in low-income communities, who arrive bearing gifts and represent the corrosive power of the state. Our contribution to survival struggles of the subaltern is political: we offer organizational infrastructure, experience in coordinating and managing meetings, and analytic lenses that sharpen contradictions and build the collective power of the community in struggle.

20. The purpose of Red Braid is to be the spinning transmission belt between the suffering, needs, rage, and dreams of these subaltern communities in struggle and revolutionary politics. Our organizational structure is set up to support this purpose: members are the sovereign body that direct the organization overall, with decision-making and coordination delegated to the Coordinating Committee for the overall work of the group, and to specific campaign leaders and organizers to carry out the work of the group in corroboration with these communities.

21. Our structure becomes complicated at the point of contact with communities. We conceive of our relationships with communities, exercised

through campaigns, to be our dialectical point of contact with our social base. We have contact with our, what we term, "tangible" social base through meetings, discussions, and mobilizations, and discuss and analyze the meanings of these experiences and relationships in order to divine the feelings of what we see as the "conceptual" social base overall. We approach and interact with our tangible social base as the expression of the most developed, political consciousness of the social base as a whole, assuming that those who become active and assume leadership positions in their community are those who represent the fighting edge of the social group as a whole.

22. A "declassed" membership, driven primarily by identity with political ideals, by default would exclude Indigenous and working-class people who join the movement through recognition of their group interest. While we may develop close relationships with people in the social base, because our campaigns are connected to and influence the conditions of peoples' survival, it would be a mistake to make a structural assumption that our members are benevolent. So long as the enfranchised member is only an outside organizer who approaches the community as supporter, any accountability over Red Braid's interactions in communities depends on voluntary recognition and transmission of the character of our relationships.

23. The conclusion of our social base organizational strategy is, therefore, to fight to draw the majority membership of Red Braid from the Indigenous and working-class subaltern communities that are the engine and actuality of revolutionary struggle.

24. Building social bases does require organization, and our social bases strengthen and root our organizational infrastructure. But the organization is not an end to itself. Organizationally, we tie our political future to the self-activity of the subaltern. Our destiny and power are identical. Our organization is alive in the crashing waves of a dialectical tide between the concrete analysis and the concrete situation that we experience in struggle. Our commitment is to building a militant,

autonomous organization as servant of the struggle, not as a fetish unto itself.

*Part 2b. The subaltern and the aristocracy of labour*

25. Who are we wanting to build bases with? The short answer is "Indigenous and working-class communities." But this has to be more clearly defined. In short, we believe revolutionary political possibility begins at the point where our people feel socially, politically, economically excluded from bourgeois, settler colonial, imperialist society. Revolutionary transformation begins with flipping exclusion into its opposite: from misery, isolation, humiliation, and dangerous poverty into shared, positive expressions where each of us feels we are part of international groups and experience the power of collective action that transforms the real conditions of being for ourselves and our communities.

26. Indigenous peoples are those who have relations to land and nation that precede, and continue to exist separate from, the settler colonial nation states of Canada and the United States. Some Indigenous people, particularly some Indigenous intellectuals and politicians, are investing in forms of inclusion in settler colonial society and power. But their potential or experienced inclusion does not represent possibility for most Indigenous peoples, who remain radically excluded. Our people are the unrepresented and excluded, subaltern Indigenous people who have been displaced from their home territories and forced to live in poverty in cities and towns, and who live in impoverishment and without basic infrastructure in rotting and inadequate housing on reserves. There is a political point of division between Indigenous peoples who aspire to be part of Canadian civil society through assimilation, and the subaltern, who are positioned as protagonists of a revolutionary struggle for sovereignty.

27. Working-class people are those who are forced to work, selling their labour power to capitalists in exchange for wages and in order to survive. Whether or not working-class people are working jobs at a given

moment in the day or in their lives is unimportant because it does not change their class position. If you can't or won't work, then you are punished with horrible poverty and, in the worst case, homelessness—which is a form of collective punishment used against working-class and Indigenous people.

28. The consciousness of many members of the working class in Canada is corrupted by imperialist and settler colonial power. This partial, imperial consciousness is not an ideological problem alone but is rooted in the real material benefit that some workers, particularly white workers, receive as a portion of the super profits that capitalists harvest from Canada's imperialist adventures globally and especially from Indigenous peoples on territories regularly occupied by Canada.

29. The working class is divided by social role, race, gender, and by imperialist identity. The social role of some workers is administrative; they administer bourgeois and colonial power through discipline, education, and social services. These people are not really part of the working class; they are petty bourgeois or middle class. Race, gender, and imperialist identity is accumulated by workers themselves regardless of their social role; the feeling a white worker has that they are part of Canadian civil society is an imperialist identity that usually coincides with making high enough wages that they live the lives of the middle class and not of the average worker in the world. This section of the working class is what revolutionaries historically have called the "aristocracy of labour." We refer to this group as "privileged workers," and understand that, even though these workers objectively share interests with the rest of the workers of the world, their consciousness is tied to the wellbeing of the imperialist and settler colonial nation state.

30. We are not trying to organize with the middle class or privileged workers, and we are not catering to their consciousness. This means we are not, at this point, a "mass movement" organization that measures success by the size of mass demonstrations or the support of mass institutions like trade unions and churches. We do not automatically dismiss these mass

organizations as inevitably counter revolutionary like we do state and bourgeois institutions like Business Improvement Associations, social work agencies, and police, but so long as the overall working-class retreat continues, mass politics will be limited to reforms within the limits of civil society, which are premised on the exclusion of national, racial, gender, and subaltern others. In this context, we are not afraid to oppose majority opinion or to stand out as too radical. We see our political role as fighting against both reactionary right-wing politics and against the conciliations and compromises of social democrats and assimilationists that sell out the actual needs and lives of the subaltern.

31. While privileged workers have a material basis for their existence as a wing of the working class globally, its membership is sustained and expressed ideologically. The main questions that divide privileged workers from the subaltern working class are property ownership, which indicates attitudes towards Indigenous sovereignty, and nationalism, which indicates attitudes towards racialized migrants and the international structures of class.

32. The subaltern working class includes the unwaged, unemployed, and underemployed, the young, elderly, refugee, homeless, and criminalized, as well as illicit and sex workers, and some social reproduction workers. At the point of production (the workplace), the subaltern are to be found where low wage, precarious work intersects with oppressive race and gender power. Some rural and producer workers, many migrant workers—especially temporary foreign workers—many day labourers, and many private-sector service workers who rely on this work long term are also subaltern. There is no sure, categorial way to identify and organize subaltern workers because of the powerful influence of imperialist ideology in Canadian and US society. The way to find the working-class subaltern is through outreach, education, and collective action that must be militant, clear, and uncompromising.

33. The need to call out clearly in order to identify and collaborate with subaltern groups is, if nothing else, the reason electoral tactics are not

appropriate to our time. Electoral tactics appeal to civil society: amongst the working class, an electoral orientation emphasises privileged workers who harbour imperialist and settler colonial consciousness and desires to win inclusion in the project of making and being Canada.

34. The potential power of the working class is in seizing the value and productive power that we create, and which is stolen from us by capitalists. Workers' power is necessarily aggressive—it must seize what is rightly ours from bosses. Outside the point of production, it is possible for workers to take space and defend their communities, but this is limited to protest and resistance activity. The strategic locus of worker power is at the point of production. If we do not mount attacks on capitalist power at the point of production—working *past* labour unions where they exist, not waiting for or trying to reform them—then we will never find our hand on this lever of power.

35. The potential power of Indigenous peoples is in defending, keeping, and building sovereign Indigenous economies and societies. Indigenous power is necessarily defensive—it must stop the settler colonial and imperial theft of lands and life that has been underway for hundreds of years but remains incomplete. Indigenous power is qualitatively different from working-class power because while working-class power exists in contradiction and must emerge from its *potential* form in the capitalist process of production, Indigenous power already exists, and has to be exercised and increased. Colonial power is repressive and violent against Indigenous peoples because Canada represses the existing power of Indigenous nations. So Indigenous blockades and national defence campaigns are not protests, they are elements of war. Indigenous refusal of colonial power is, in our current climate, the clearest expression of the organic existence and resurgence of Indigenous nationhood.

*Part 2c. Dual power*

36. Our revolutionary group seeks to develop bases of activity with Indigenous and subaltern working-class people. By politicizing survival struggles of these social bases, we can explode the possibilities of dual

power into autonomous spaces and moments where our people can develop a deeper revolutionary consciousness.

37. "Dual power" refers to a revolutionary moment when self-organized peoples exercise control in a site within a country where capitalists or the settler colonial state still has power overall. In the weeks before the Russian Revolution, workers in Saint Petersburg controlled most of the factories and the infrastructure of daily life in the city through their workers' councils, called Soviets. Workers in Winnipeg managed a similar feat through the "strike committee" that decided which parts of the economy functioned and which did not during the General Strike of 1919. These experiences of workers' dual power control over production, economy, and social life operated precariously and temporarily within the cauldron of bourgeois and colonial state power overall. In Russia this tense equilibrium broke in favour of the Soviets, which swung their power from factories and cities to toppling the state completely in the October Revolution. In Winnipeg, the bourgeois, colonial government of Canada restored its monopoly over the use of force by crushing the secondary power of workers through the force of guns wielded by the North-West Mounted Police and special constables.

38. Dual power is also a term used to discuss Mao's "base area" and Che Guevara's "foco": the rural and mountainous territories controlled by guerilla armies. These too were outside the control of the bourgeois, colonial nation state, though the force that held the state at bay was the guerrilla army rather than mass control over factories and worker self-organization.

39. The autonomous spaces of our community survival struggles are not characterized by the dual power of the self-organization of a mass and militant group of subaltern people who have taken control over productive forces, the economy, or the infrastructure of everyday life. And they are also not strictly bordered and defined territories controlled by armed guerilla armies. Our dual power is not realized: we are not in a pre-revolutionary moment, but the potential of our dual power is a force

that we can sense, and which is the motor for a revolutionary politics and consciousness.

40. Our dual power space is defined by two political features: one, the exercise of a collective power by a subaltern group—a group that expresses a positive inversion of their exclusion from civil society with possibilities of dual power; and two, the expressed and practiced connection of that collective power and group identity to others, including internationally.

41. One example is the tent city, which we defined as a people's autonomous space only when communities exercised political direction over the space and determined—always in contest with police—access to the space. A potential dual power site is not only a protest site, although protest and opposition to the dominant order is part of its characteristic. It is also an organic survival space that affords subaltern people a means of survival in adverse conditions.

42. In our experience, with the capacity we have had available to us, we have been able to defend dual power territories, though we have not managed to develop self-governing practices of economy, education, or social supports beyond those that exist organically.

43. Our organizing goal should be to *always expand the political terrain* influenced by our revolutionary project. Although territory always matters, the more important terrain is cultural and ideological, expressed through the self-organization of subaltern communities for freedom and power. We must prioritize education work and the sharpening of autonomous organizational skills and revolutionary class and decolonial consciousness amongst people in our social base projects.

44. We cannot call dual power spaces into being at will; the opening of these possibilities requires political preparation, the existence of a social base, and the analysis, identification, and elaboration of political crises. It requires us to move on opportunities where the radical social exclusion experienced by our subaltern communities can be turned on its head into expressions and possibilities of political power.

45. There is a danger in such a strategy of turning localism into a virtue, and it is the internationalist aspect that presses back against that force. Rather than embracing, strengthening, and reforming the nation state, subaltern struggle identifies with other peoples in struggle rather than with the nation state; the activity of being in struggle is the human thread that connects us across imperial borders.

46. Our strategic formula is: Social base building + dual power = revolutionary transformation.

47. Building a decolonial socialism with subaltern Indigenous and working-class communities should be the basis for a new political tendency.

# Democratic protocols and processes

Red Braid

## Member agreements

Red Braid Alliance is a social revolutionary organization. The purpose of our organization, and of the work of our members in our campaigns and organizational spaces, is to intervene with revolutionary politics in the class and decolonial struggles that appear, for the most part, as depoliticized everyday life. But these everyday spaces and processes *are* the definitive spaces of politics: of domination, of accommodation and reform, and of revolutionary possibility.

Politics, according to Stuart Hall, is "the level which condenses all other levels of practice [economic, social, ideological, legal, and so on] and secures their functioning in a particular system of power." Through political action and analysis, we identify how systems of power—colonialism, white supremacy, imperialism, cis supremacy, capitalism—move and reproduce in space and time, so that we can disrupt and destroy them. Wherever there is conflict and contradiction, we see the urgency of critical and practical politics, so all of our protocols and processes are grounded in our political work and analysis.

We strive to balance the practice of creating a new world out of the throes of a violent one, recognizing that individual will and agency mean very little outside of the context of collective struggle. Our group is accountable to more than just its members, because we exist to advance the power and revolutionary consciousness of Indigenous and working-class people. This means that our expectations of one another take place within the context of a broader political project. Below are the practices we strive towards to build and safeguard a culture of accountability, trust, and respect that supports our political goals and work.

## We take ownership over the direction of the organization

As a social revolutionary organization, we exist to make a new world. We see ourselves not as sovereign individuals volunteering our time to an external project, but as social and historical beings who are ourselves transformed in the critical practice of transforming the world. Though our levels of commitment, capacity, and energy may vary, it is nobody's job to lead the organization for us. While we recognize that we have varying degrees, roles, and styles of leadership within the organization, we reflect critically on the ways we shape the group. Our group is more than the sum of its parts, and each of us feels responsible for and committed to bringing political contributions forward.

## We treat one another with kindness and good faith

We trust our mutual commitments to our basis of unity, and work to recognize the best impulses and interests in one another's actions. We vocalize our disagreements with intent and care, recognizing the importance of creating spaces where debate builds trust, rather than removes it. We value and listen to hesitations that arise amongst members and think critically about why they exist, working to develop countering opinions rooted in thought out analyses. Where a breakdown of trust is impacting the group, we address that breakdown politically, in order to identify the differences, disagreements, or discomforts causing the distrust. When debates or disagreements are tense, we aim to resolve them in person, rather than online.

## We are accountable for our behaviors and self-reflexive when given feedback or criticism

We all have flaws and blind spots that others are better able to recognize than we are, and so we trust others to hold us accountable when we've behaved harmfully or in ways that disrupt our work and hinder our ability to trust one another. Some harmful behaviors emerge from using systemic power; some emerge from the trauma of suffering from systemic power; some are patterns of behavior rather than a single harmful action. When we feel harmed by other members, we work to phrase those criticisms clearly, concretely, and politically, to best enable others to cultivate their self-reflexivity.

## We support one another emotionally, while recognizing one another's boundaries and the group's accountability to a broader political project

There is no clear line that separates the *emotional* from the *political* within our beings. The work of transforming the world has a deeply emotional nature, which, as much as it energizes us, can at times be draining. Many of us are coping with traumas that result from the violent systems that Red Braid seeks to destroy: colonialism, white supremacy, patriarchy, capitalism, and cis supremacy. We support one another, emotionally and politically, so that we can participate in the group's work in the ways we need and want to, including when that means stepping back. We ask for help if we need it and reach out to our comrades when we feel saddled by doubts and pessimism, so that we can explore the political basis of our feelings. We recognize one another's boundaries and limitations around emotional support. We aspire to collectively share the work of caring for one another and ourselves.

## Base building through campaign work

Red Braid's relations of community accountability are cultivated through direct (though informal) democratic (and dialectical) exchange in the form of social revolutionary political activism. Our organization is dedicated to building the power of the social bases we fight alongside, and we hold ourselves accountable to those social bases. Our power comes from the credibility and trust we build with these communities through the actions we engage in. We operate on an informal level of accountability to members of our social base, and continually work to increase mutual trust and build stronger connections to them while working with them to develop and build upon their political analyses. Community campaigns that engage our social base is the work that holds Red Braid accountable.

Red Braid theorizes our social base in two ways: as "conceptual" and "tangible." The tangible social base are those who are involved in Red Braid campaigns carried out at community levels. We analyze the feedback, critiques, and participation that we have with our tangible social base as information about the feelings, ideas, and desires of the communities that they come from—the broader, conceptual social base. For example, people who show up to Stop Demovictions Burnaby meetings are the campaign's tangible social base, and we interpret the contributions those community members make in these meetings and their reactions to our ideas as important information about the consciousness of the broader, conceptual social base. Base building is key to our political project. We aim to politicize the struggles of the subaltern by offering infrastructure, analytic lenses, and support as individuals continue to develop consciousness through action and study.

We work to shift the conceptual social base into the tangible social base. While we value and encourage the leadership development of the tangible social base, we do not restrict our engagement with the social base overall just to those who show up. We publish and distribute leaflets, newsletters, newspapers, and posters throughout the social base in order to draw more people out of passive engagement with our work and into tangible, direct activity. And we organize protest actions and public meetings in order to activate the conceptual social base and to expand the tangible social base so that the quality and range of information we get from communities expands.

### Freedom of discussion and unity in action

Our organization exists to spur on and express the revolutionary movements of working-class and Indigenous peoples. This means that our practice of democracy is rooted in our social bases. We understand and analyze the movement of our social bases as a starting point to discuss and decide what to do. Three principles that guide this process are curiosity, openness, and relevance.

## Curiosity

*Organizational curiosity* is the regular and organic interaction of our members with the communities involved in struggle, and a thoughtful, not predetermined, organizational discussion and investigation about the meanings of difficulties and feelings that we encounter in struggle.

Our curiosity leads us to draw into our group organic leaders from struggles and prioritize building a democratic process around their participation and leadership.

## Openness

If information flows only one way, then we would be guilty of using community struggles to build our organization, rather than the other way around. Our disagreements and decisions must be considered as of vital interest to the communities involved in the actual movements that we are oriented towards.

This places a *double burden of openness* on us: first, to fight the urge to be conspiratorial and secretive and to make our political discussions open and vulnerable to those outside our group; and second, to translate and make accessible the political differences and decisions that we make so that these communities can understand and register their agreement or disagreement with these ideas.

Our openness leads us to regularly publish and distribute materials in community spaces.

## Relevance

Finally, all this discussion and analysis is only commentary unless we can convert it back into action, and particularly to increase the power of the actual movement with the political tools we are able to add: organizational infrastructure and skills, political analysis and consciousness raising, and militant activist support in moments of conflict with police and other

350 A Separate Star

antagonistic forces. But this presents a different set of challenges than the rule of curiosity and openness needed for good analysis and decision making is designed to address. To be effective revolutionary political actors and especially as fighters when we face our enemies, we must be coldly calculating and ruthlessly disciplined—acting as a single unit that does not expose our disagreements or vulnerabilities.

*Making revolutionary politics relevant* to the actual movements in struggle requires unity in action: a strategic agreement to hold our differences and suspend them until we are out of danger. However, this unity in action must not be exaggerated into a virtue or a permanent exception. It does *not* mean that when we are criticized by opponents or enemies that we must double down and defend the organization at all costs. Completely the opposite. Moments of disagreement and critique, including from outside, are opportunities to deepen our understanding and analysis, not moments to harden and hide and sink disagreements below the surface of the group where they will fester and rot. Unity in action must be restricted to moments of open confrontation with our enemies when discussion would be a distraction from the pressing tasks at hand.

# References

This is a partial list of the critical articles, books, and other sources we used in thinking through the ideas in this book. While these sources are not noted specifically throughout the text, we tried to name the thinker we were in-conversation with in the body of the text. Sources that we used for empirical data are cited in footnotes throughout the chapters and are not included here.

Amin, Samir. "China 2013." *Monthly Review*, March 1, 2013.

Anderson, Perry. "The Antinomies of Antonio Gramsci." *New Left Review* 1, 100 (November 1976–January 1977): 5–78.

Azcarate, Manuel. "What is Eurocommunism." In *Eurocommunism*, edited by G. R. Urban. London: Maurice Temple Smith, 1978. Marxists' Internet Archive. https://www.marxists.org/reference/subject/philosophy/works/it/eurocommunism.htm.

Baroque Fray, and Tegan Eanelli, eds. *Queer Ultraviolence: Bash Back! Anthology*. San Francisco: Ardent Press, 2011.

Boggs, Carl, and David Plotke, eds. *The Politics of Eurocommunism: Socialism in Transition*. Boston: South End Press, 1980.

Brophy, David. "The 1957–58 Xinjiang Committee Plenum and the Attack on 'Local Nationalism.'" *Sources and Methods* (blog). *Wilson Center*, December 11, 2017. https://www.wilsoncenter.org/blog-post/the-1957-58-xinjiang-committee-plenum-and-the-attack-local-nationalism.

Césaire, Aimé. *Discourse on Colonialism*. New York: Monthly Review Press, 2000.

Césaire, Aimé. Letter to Maurice Thorez, General Secretary of the French Communist Party. Paris, October 24, 1956. https://libcom.org/library/letter-maurice-thorez.

Combahee River Collective. "Combahee River Collective Statement." 1977. https://americanstudies.yale.edu/sites/default/files/files/Keyword%20Coalition_Readings.pdf.

CounterPower. *Organizing for Autonomy: History, Theory, and Strategy for Collective Liberation*. Brooklyn, NY: Common Notions Press, 2020.

Cox, Judy. *The Women's Revolution: Russia 1905–1917*. Chicago: Haymarket Books, 2017.

Davidson, Neil. "Class, Oppression, and the Actuality of Revolution." *Spectre* 1, 2 (Fall 2020).

Draper, Hal. "Anatomy of the Micro-Sect." Unpublished document circulated privately in 1973. Marxists' Internet Archive. https://www.marxists.org/archive/draper/1973/xx/microsect.htm.

Du Bois, W. E. B. *Black Reconstruction in America: An Essay Toward a History of the Part Which Black Folk Played in the Attempt to Reconstruct Democracy in America, 1860–1880*. New York: Harcourt, Brace and Company, 1935.

Duggan, Lisa. *Twilight of Equality: Neoliberalism, Cultural Politics, and the Attack on Democracy*. Boston: Beacon Press, 2003.

Ehrenreich, Barbara, and John Ehrenreich. "The Professional-Managerial Class." In *Between Labor and Capital*, edited by Pat Walker. Boston: South End Press, 1979.

Ely, Robin J., and Irene Padavic. "What's Really Holding Women Back? It's Not What Most People Think." *Harvard Business Review* 98, 2 (March–April 2020): 58–67.

Endnotes. "Onwards Barbarians." *Endnotes*, December 2020.

Engels, Friedrich, and Eleanor Burke Leacock. *The Origin of the Family, Private Property, and the State, in the Light of the Researches of Lewis H. Morgan*. New York: International Publishers, 1972.

Fanon, Frantz. *The Wretched of the Earth*. New York: Grove Press, 1991.

Federici, Silvia. "Wages Against Housework." In *Revolution at Point Zero: Housework, Reproduction, and Feminist Struggle*. Oakland: PM Press, 2012.

Feinberg, Leslie. *Trans Liberation: Beyond Pink or Blue*. Boston: Beacon Press, 1999.

Gimenez, Martha E. "Capitalism and the Oppression of Women: Marx Revisited." *Science & Society* 69, 1 (January 2005): 11–32.

Gramsci, Antonio. *Subaltern Social Groups: A Critical Edition of Prison Notebook 25*. New York: Columbia University Press, 2021.

Gramsci, Antonio. *Selections From Political Writings, 1910–1920*. New York: International Publishers, 1978.

Gramsci, Antonio. *Selections From Political Writings, 1921–1926*. New York: International Publishers, 1978.

Gramsci, Antonio. Vols. 1–3 of *Prison Notebooks*. Edited and translated by Joseph A. Buttigieg. New York: Columbia University Press, 2010.

Haider, Asad. *Mistaken Identity: Race and Class in the Age of Trump*. New York: Verso, 2018.

Harvey, David. "The 'New' Imperialism: Accumulation by Dispossession." *Socialist Register* 40 (2004): 63–87.

Harvey, David. "The Significance of China in the Global Economy." *Anti-Capitalist Chronicles*, Jan 17, 2019.

Ignatin, Noel ( Ignatiev). "Black Worker / White Worker (1972)." In *Workplace Papers*, 22–29. Chicago: Sojourner Truth Organization, 1980.

James, C. L. R. *A New Notion: Two Works by C. L. R. James*. Oakland: PM Press, 2010.

James, C. L. R. *State Capitalism and World Revolution*. Chicago: Charles H. Kerr Publishing, 1986.

James, C. L. R., with Grace Lee Boggs and Cornelius Castoriadis. *Facing Reality: The New Society: Where to Look for it and How to Bring it Closer*. Detroit: Bewick Editions, 1974.

King, LaKeyma. "Inversion and Invisibility: Black Women Black Masculinity, and Anti-Blackness." *Lies: A Journal of Materialist Feminism* 2 (August 2015): 31–48.

Kollontai, Alexandra. "Communism and the Family." First published in *Komunistka*, 2 (1920). Marxists' Internet Archive. https://www.marxists.org/archive/kollonta/1920/communism-family.htm.

Kun, Li, Huang Li, Li Xiang. "An Investigative Report into the Social and Economic Causes of the 3.14 Incident in Tibetan Areas." Translated by the International Campaign for Tibet, Gongmeng Law Research Center, 2009. https://savetibet.org/bold-report-by-beijing-scholars-reveals-breakdown-of-chinas-tibet-policy/.

Lenin, Vladimir. "Imperialism and the Split in Socialism." In Vol. 23 of *Collected Works of Lenin*. October 1916. Moscow: Progress Publishers, 1964.

Lenin, Vladimir. "State and Revolution." In *Selected Works in One Volume*. Moscow: Progress Publishers, 1977.

Ley, David. *The New Middle Class and the Remaking of the Central City*. New York: Oxford University Press, 1996.

Marx, Karl. *Capital, Volumes 1–3*. In *Marx and Engels Collected Works, Volumes 35–37*. London: Lawrence and Wishart, 2010.

Marx, Karl. *Economic and Philosophic Manuscripts of 1844*. New York: International Publishers, 1964.

Marx, Karl. *The German Ideology*. New York: Prometheus Books, 1998.

Marx, Karl. *The Grundrisse: Economic Works, 1857–1861*. In *Marx and Engels Collected Works, Volumes 28–29*. London: Lawrence and Wishart, 2010.

Marx, Karl. "Preface to the Critique of Political Economy." In *Karl Marx and Friedrich Engels, Selected Works, Volumes 1–3*. Moscow: Progress Publishers, 1976.

Marx, Karl. *Theories of Surplus Value: Economic Manuscript of 1861–63* In *Marx and Engels Collected Works, Volumes 30–33*. London: Lawrence and Wishart, 2010.

Marx, Karl, and Friedrich Engels. *The Communist Manifesto*. London: Penguin Books, 2011.

Mies, Maria. *Patriarchy and Accumulation on a World Scale: Women in the International Division of Labour*. London: Zed Books, 1986.

Mitchell, Eve. "I am a Woman and a Human: A Marxist-Feminist Critique of Intersectionality Theory." *Unity and Struggle*, September 12, 2013.

Mitchell, Katharyne. "Multiculturalism, or the United Colours of Capitalism?" *Antipode* 25, 4, (1993): 263–294.

Norbu, Dawa. "Chinese Communist Views on National Self-Determination, 1922–1956: Origins of China's National Minorities Policy." *International Studies* 25, 4 (1988): 317–342.

The Red Nation. *The Red Deal: Indigenous Action to Save the Earth.* Brooklyn NY: Common Notions Press, 2021.

Riddell, John, ed. *Lenin's Struggle for a Revolutionary International: Documents: 1907–1916, the Preparatory Years.* New York: Monad Press, 1984.

Riddell, John, ed. *To See the Dawn: Baku 1920, First Congress of the Peoples of the East.* New York: Pathfinder Press, 1993.

Sekyi-out, Ato. *Fanon's Dialectic of Experience.* Cambridge: Harvard University Press, 1996.

Skeggs, Beverly. *Class, Self, Culture.* London: Routledge, 2004.

Spillers, Hortense J. "Mama's Baby, Papa's Maybe: An American Grammar Book." *Diacritics* 17, 2 (Summer, 1987): 65–81.

Stacey, Judith. *Patriarchy and Socialist Revolution in China.* Berkeley: University of California Press, 1983.

Thobani, Sunera. *Exalted Subjects.* Toronto: University of Toronto Press, 2007.

Tomba, Massimiliano. *Insurgent Universality: An Alternative Legacy of Modernity.* New York: Oxford University Press, 2019.

Tronti, Mario. *The Weapon of Organization: Mario Tronti's Revolution in Marxism.* Edited and translated by Andrew Anastasi. Brooklyn NY: Common Notions Press, 2020.

Tronti, Mario. *Workers and Capital.* New York: Verso, 2019.

Trotsky, Leon. *The Revolution Betrayed: What Is the Soviet Union and Where Is It Going?* New York: Pathfinder Press, 1972.

Wittig, Monique. "One is Not Born a Woman." In *The Lesbian and Gay Studies Reader*, edited by Henry Abelove, Michele Aina Barale, and David M. Halperin. New York: Routledge, 1993.

356 A Separate Star

*Worker's Power* (previously *International Socialist*) issues 21–267 (1970–1978). Marxists' Internet Archive. https://www.marxists.org/history/etol/newspape/workerspower/index.htm

Wright, Erik Olin. *Class, Crisis, and the State.* New York: Verso, 1979.

Wright, Erik Olin. "Intellectuals and the Class Structure of Capitalist Society." In *Between Labor and Capital,* edited by Pat Walker. Boston: South End Press, 1979.

Wright, Erik Olin. *How to be an Anticapitalist in the Twenty-First Century.* New York: Verso Books, 2019.

Wu, Yiching. "Rethinking 'Capitalist Restoration' in China." *Monthly Review* 57, 6 (November 2005): 44–63.

Yaffe, Helen. *Che Guevara: The Economics of Revolution.* London: Palgrave MacMillan, 2009.

Zedong, Mao. "Criticize Han Chauvinism." In Vol. 5 of *Selected Works of Mao Zedong.* New York: International Publishers, 1954.

Zedong, Mao. "Report on an Investigation into the Peasant Movement in Hunan." In Vol. 1 of *Selected Works of Mao Zedong.* New York: International Publishers, 1954.

Zedong, Mao. "Statement Supporting the American Negroes in Their Just Struggle Against Racial Discrimination by U.S. Imperialism." *Peking Review* 9, 33 (August 12, 1966): 24–27.

Ziyad, Hari. "My Gender is Black." *Afropunk,* July 12, 2017. https://afropunk.com/2017/07/my-gender-is-black/.

## Red Braid discussion classes

Many of the articles included in this book are investigating and developing ideas that Red Braid developed as an organization through our discussion classes, which we call "Conditions of Struggle" (COS) classes.

Find the lists (and, in most cases, the PDFs) of readings and discussion points on our website at https://www.redbraid.org/political-education/